D1557548

SINGAPORE

WESTVIEW PROFILES
NATIONS OF CONTEMPORARY ASIA
Mervyn Adams Seldon, Series Editor

Singapore: The Legacy of Lee Kuan Yew,
R. S. Milne and Diane K. Mauzy

†*Taiwan: Nation-State or Province?* John F. Copper

*The Republic of Korea: Economic Transformation
and Social Change,* David I. Steinberg

Thailand: Buddhist Kingdom as Modern Nation-State, Charles F. Keyes

Laos: Keystone of Indochina, Arthur J. Dommen

Malaysia: Tradition, Modernity, and Islam,
R. S. Milne and Diane K. Mauzy

Pakistan: A Nation in the Making, Shahid Javed Burki

†*Vietnam: Nation in Revolution,* William J. Duiker

The Philippines: A Singular and a Plural Place, Revised Edition,
David Joel Steinberg

†*Japan: Profile of a Postindustrial Power,* Third Edition,
Ardath W. Burks

†Available in hardcover and paperback.

SINGAPORE

The Legacy of Lee Kuan Yew

R. S. Milne
and
Diane K. Mauzy

Westview Press
BOULDER, SAN FRANCISCO, & OXFORD

To
Betty, Cheng Lian, Eng Hua,
Heng Chee, and Joo San
(remembering good times)

Westview Profiles / Nations of Contemporary Asia

Photo credits: Photo 2 (the Supreme Court building) courtesy of David Hastings. All other interior photos courtesy of the Ministry of Communications and Information, Press Section, Republic of Singapore. Cover photo: a shoreline vista of the Padang (playing field), cricket club, marina, and high rises in the southern part of the city, 1990; courtesy of Wallace H. Campbell.

Published in 1990 in the United States of America by Westview Press, Inc., 5500 Central Avenue, Boulder, Colorado 80301, and in the United Kingdom by Westview Press, Inc., 36 Lonsdale Road, Summertown, Oxford OX2 7EW

Library of Congress Cataloging-in-Publication Data
Milne, R. S. (Robert Stephen), 1919–
Singapore : the legacy of Lee Kuan Yew / R. S. Milne and Diane K. Mauzy.
    p. cm.—(Westview profiles. Nations of contemporary Asia)
    Includes bibliographical references.
    1. Singapore. I. Mauzy, Diane K., 1942–   II. Title.
III. Series.
DS598.S7M53   1990
957.57—dc20   89-24756
                                                                                 CIP

    ISBN 0-8133-0407-5
    ISBN 0-8133-1091-1 (if published in pbk.)

Printed and bound in the United States of America

Contents

List of Illustrations   viii
List of Acronyms   ix
Acknowledgments   xi

1 Introduction   1

2 The Social Setting   10

Population, 10
Ethnicity, 12
Religion, 14
Language, 16
Education, 18
Culture, 23
The Mass Media, 25
Ethnicity: The Balance Sheet, 27
Women in Singapore, 29
Class Differences, 31
Social Services, 32
Physical Planning: Transportation, 34
Housing: Conservation, 35
The Environment, 38
Traditional and Modern Values, 39
Conclusion, 40

3 From Raffles to Self-Rule, 1819–1959   42

Early History to 1945, 42
Political Awakening: The Turbulent Years,
    1946–1959, 45

4 *The Quest for Stability and Prosperity,
   1959–1989*   53

   The PAP Splits and the Barisan Sosialis
     Is Formed, 57
   Malaysia: From Merger to Separation, 59
   The First Years of Independence: Priority
     to Survival, 62
   The Emergence of a Dominant Party: Elections
     in Independent Singapore, 64
   Adding Ballast to the System: The 1988
     General Election, 68
   Nearing the End of an Era: Problems and
     Issues, 75

5 *Politics and Government in a Dominant-
   Party System*   77

   The Constitution: Formal Institutions, 77
   Informal Institutions, 84
   Conclusion, 102

6 *From the Founders to the Successors*   103

   The Founder Generation, 103
   The Elements of Successful Leadership, 105
   PAP Style and Value System, 106
   The Problem of Political Succession, 114
   The Second Generation, 116
   The Transition, 120
   A Post-Lee Government, 123
   Conclusion, 126

7 *A Dependent But Dynamic Economy*   131

   The Singapore Economy, 1959–1989, 132
   Government Management of the Economy, 138
   International Linkages, 145
   Conclusion, 153

8 *Defense and Foreign Policy*   156

   Defense, 156
   Singapore's Foreign Policy: Requirements
     and Strategies, 161

Singapore and ASEAN, 163
Relations with the Great Powers, 169
Relations with Other Countries, 174
Conclusion, 174

9   *Prospects for Stability and Change*   175

Notes   183
Annotated Bibliography   201
Index   205

Illustrations

Maps

Singapore   xii

Asia   2

Photographs

A 1986 view of the city center   3

The Supreme Court building   9

The Sri Mariamman Hindu Temple   15

Luxury condominiums   32

The Ang Mo Kio New Town   36

Singapore in the early 1980s   38

View of the city during the late 1950s   50

Lee Kuan Yew, prime minister since 1959   54

Singapore crowds listen to Lee Kuan Yew   66

Goh Chok Tong   117

Brigadier-General Lee Hsien Loong   118

National Day parade, August 9, 1984   157

Acronyms

ASEAN	Association of Southeast Asian Nations
CCC	Citizens' Consultative Committee
CEC	Central Executive Committee
CPF	Central Provident Fund
EDB	Economic Development Board
EEC	European Economic Community
EIC	(British) East India Company
GDP	gross domestic product
GNP	gross national product
GRC	Group Representation Constituency
HDB	Housing and Development Board
ISA	Internal Security Act
KAH	key appointment holder
LF	Labour Front
MENDAKI	Council of Education for Muslim Children
MCA	Malaysian Chinese Association
MCP	Malayan Communist Party (later CPM)
MINDEF	Ministry of Defence
MNC	multinational corporation
MRT	mass rapid transit
NCMP	nonconstituency Member of Parliament
NEMP	nonelected Member of Parliament
NIC	newly industrializing country
NTUC	National Trades Union Congress
NUS	National University of Singapore

NWC	National Wages Council
PA	People's Association
PAP	People's Action Party
PP	Progressive Party
RC	Residents' Committee
R and D	research and development
SAF	Singapore Armed Forces
SCDF	Singapore Civil Defence Force
SDP	Singapore Democratic Party
SPA	Singapore People's Alliance
UMNO	United Malays National Organization
WP	Workers' Party

Acknowledgments

Our information was derived partly from government and party publications, books, periodicals, articles published and unpublished, and newspapers. We also benefited from hundreds of conversations with politicians and ex-politicians (both government and opposition), civil servants, businesspeople, diplomats, journalists, academics, and friends. Our thanks are due to all of them, to the Ministry of Communications and Information (for providing government publications, transcripts of speeches, and photographs and maps and for arranging interviews), and to the Institute of Southeast Asian Studies and its director, Professor K. S. Sandhu, for research facilities. R. S. Milne is indebted to the Canadian Social Sciences and Humanities Research Council for a research grant, as is Diane K. Mauzy to the University of British Columbia for a grant from the President's Research Fund.

The following deserve our special gratitude for having read and commented on portions of the manuscript: Chan Heng Chee, Geoffrey Hainsworth, Betty Khoo, Linda Lim, Obaid ul Haq, Pang Cheng Lian, Shee Poon Kim, Mary Turnbull, and Aline Wong.

Responsibility for the contents of the book, however, remains our own.

R. S. Milne
Diane K. Mauzy

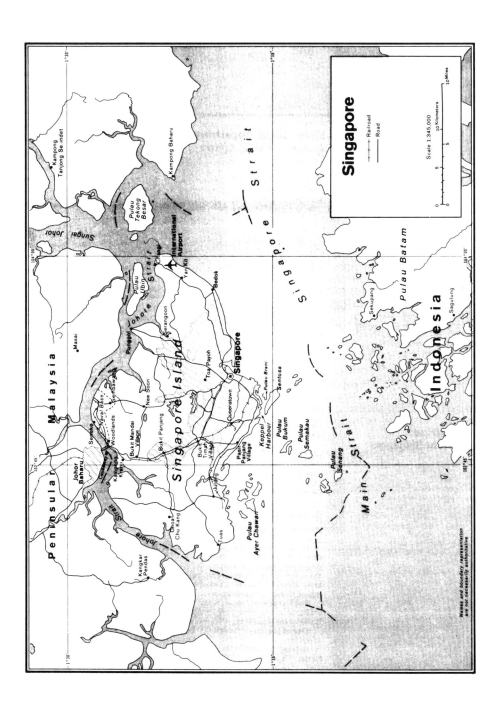

Singapore

‒‒‒‒ Railroad
——— Road

Scale 1:345,000

Names and boundary representation
are not necessarily authoritative

1

Introduction

Singapore is a small tropical island about 100 miles north of the equator, strategically situated at the entrance to the Straits of Malacca, through which passes most of the sea traffic between East Asia (especially Japan) and Europe. Singapore's location determines its climate, which has a maximum daily average of 88°F (31°C) and a minimum of 75°F (24°C). Humidity is high, mean daily relative humidity about 85 percent on the average, but is made tolerable by sea breezes, by fans, and nowadays by air-conditioning. Rainfall is also high—almost 100 inches (255 cm) a year, as might be guessed from the deep storm drains on Singapore's streets. There are two monsoons a year, but the wind speeds are moderate compared with those in some other countries in the area, such as the Philippines.

Singapore's total land area, including its surrounding tiny islands, is only 240 square miles (620 sq km) and about half of it is built up in order to accommodate a population of about 2.7 million. Consequently, Singapore offers few opportunities for seeing local animals, or even birds or plants, in their natural habitat. Nevertheless, the zoo, the Botanic Gardens, the Jurong Bird Park, and a number of nature reserves provide partial substitutes.

Although Singapore was an important trading center as early as the seventh century, it was later conquered by the Javanese, afterward lost much of its population, and for several hundred years was of minimal economic or political significance in the surrounding region. It was a strategic location that had not yet found a role. During the eighteenth century, however, economic and military rivalry among the European powers, particularly Britain, France, and Holland, increased. Stamford Raffles of the British East India Company (EIC) realized Singapore's strategic possibilities and in 1819 established a settlement, convinced that Singapore would become, in his words, "the emporium of the seven seas."

Raffles
EIC

1

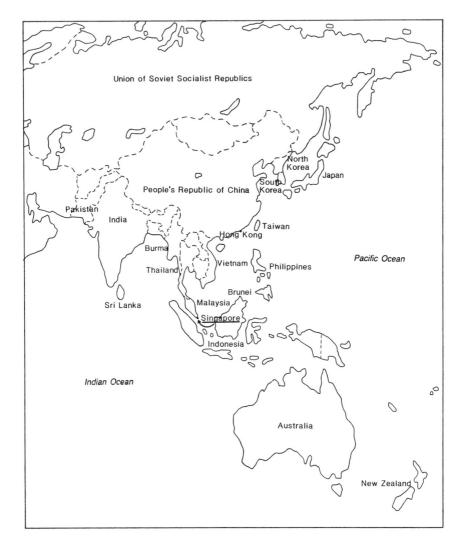

Yet, although Singapore quickly became a trading center, its political future remained undetermined. Along with Penang and Malacca, it became a member of the (British) Straits Settlements in 1826. After World War II (and occupation by the Japanese), Singapore became independent only after an intricate series of events. The British granted independence to Malaya in 1957 but retained ultimate power in Singapore, granting only internal self-government on June 3, 1959, a few days after the People's Action Party (PAP) under the leadership of Lee Kuan Yew came into office. (Britain retained power over foreign policy and defense.)

A 1986 view of the city center. On the left is the Padang (playing field) and the Singapore Cricket Club; in the center foreground are the City Hall and the Supreme Court. High-rise buildings, mainly of financial institutions, provide the background.

In 1963, Malaya and Singapore, together with two British colonies in Borneo—Sarawak and North Borneo—formed a new federation—Malaysia. One of the attractions for Singapore was that its economic links with Malaya would be strengthened. But after two years, differences between the federal government and the Singapore state government proved to be irreconcilable, and Singapore was propelled out of the federation and became a completely independent country. It is extraordinary that what is now one of the most thoroughly and successfully planned nontotalitarian countries on earth had independence thrust upon it in such an unplanned way.

Singapore's expectations of becoming part of a wider trading area were cut short when it broke off from Malaysia (with which it is connected by a 1200-yard causeway). Singapore was a port without a hinterland and with only a small domestic market. In 1967, however, Singapore joined the Association of Southeast Asian Nations (ASEAN), whose other members are Malaysia, Indonesia, Thailand, the Philippines, and, more recently, Brunei. Although economic links among the ASEAN countries are being forged only slowly, Singapore has already gained politically by being part of a wider group that carries more weight internationally than Singapore could hope to exert by itself.

Singapore has three distinguishing features. First, its governing party, the PAP, is probably the only party in the world to have had competing moderate and Communist wings, with the moderates coming out on top. Lee Kuan Yew and his colleagues dismounted from the Communist tiger, so to speak, where they wanted to get off—not where the tiger wanted to take them—and have ruled Singapore continuously since. But their victory was not easily achieved, which may account for the PAP's determination in hunting down Communist opposition (it discovered one "plot" as recently as 1987) and for its tough treatment of suspected Communists and other radicals.

Second, Singapore is the only country in Southeast Asia that has consistently held free elections since independence and also has not resorted to the imposition of military or "emergency" rule. To be sure, the PAP has been victorious in all these elections, although opposition parties are now winning an increasing proportion of the vote, and several features of PAP rule have been criticized as nondemocratic, including detention without trial and restrictions on the freedom of the press.

Third, Singapore has been remarkably successful economically, despite its lack of natural resources (fewer than Switzerland's) and its almost complete dependence on the skills of its population. It has the highest gross national product (GNP) per capita in the region except for Japan and Brunei. Singapore is the busiest port in the world—its Tanjong Pagar container terminal operates every day of the year and handles one container per minute. Its "official" foreign financial reserves are greater than those of Australia and one-third of those of Japan (which has about forty-five times as many people). All of this has been possible only by reason of government's intelligent efforts to expand trade, services (largely financial), and investment, with the cooperation of business and labor.

Singapore's wealth, as well as its orderliness and efficiency, is immediately apparent to the visitor. Arrival at its Changi International Airport (chosen as the best in the world by *Business Traveller* in 1987 and by many other surveys) is almost completely trouble free, and taxis (nearly all air-conditioned) are available and effectively metered. Traffic is disciplined, and the streets are lined with greenery. In Singapore, things work and work cleanly.

Some visitors are disappointed, however. One observer remarked that "tourists found nothing to see or do, only the shops and the skyscrapers, no sense any more of the mysterious east. A sterile place, Utopia gone wrong."[1] More objectively, many have been struck by the immense physical changes that have occurred recently. A town planner who was an adviser in Singapore twenty-five years ago confessed that he could not find anything he recognized on Orchard Road (the city's main shopping center). (On "sterility," however, he commented that "if you've seen some of the other places, other cities, you can stand a lot of sterility."[2]) High-rise apartments and office buildings abound, and on August 8, 1988, the prime minister opened the (then) tallest building in the world outside the United States, the Overseas Union Bank Centre. (It also easily overtopped the highest hill on the island.) Singapore's slums have also been eliminated.

Nevertheless, a 1985 tourist survey (nearly 4 million tourists spent a total of more than $1 billion in Singapore that year) found that one-fifth of those interviewed thought that physical reconstruction should not be too drastic and that old buildings and sites should be preserved. Although they rated the Orchard Road (mainly shopping) area as top, their next favorites were Chinatown, Sentosa, the Botanic Gardens, and "Little India." During the 1980s, and particularly since 1987, there has been a shift in government policy toward the conservation of old buildings and areas. Nevertheless, although the point is perhaps put too strongly, the basic problem is: "How do you lure tourists to an industrial tropical island that has absolutely no natural attractions?"

Singapore is not big enough to offer scenery on the grand scale (except for some ocean views). Nor does it have any really old buildings. It lacks even a small-scale equivalent of Kampuchea's Angkor Wat or Indonesia's Borobudur. Many buildings on the North American continent—the so-called New World—are older. Yet Singapore does have a few buildings that are, or are approaching, one hundred and fifty years old—the Sri Mariamman Temple, the Thian Hock Keng Temple, the Armenian Church, the Ali-Abrar Mosque, and St. Joseph's Church. It also has a combination of less old, but pleasing, buildings around the Padang (a field used for sports and festivities), including the Victoria Theater and Memorial Hall, Parliament House, the Supreme Court, the City Hall, the Singapore Cricket Club, and St. Andrews Cathedral. This area will soon be converted into a major cultural, historical, and retail trade center.

Even some of Singapore's best-known "institutions" lack continuity because they are not (or soon will not be) quite what they were. The notorious Bugis Street, which featured food and drink and a nightly parade of transvestites until the small hours of the morning, was demolished a few years ago but has been rebuilt on an adjacent site. The popular Haw Par Villa, which was constructed more than sixty years ago from the proceeds of the herbal Tiger Balm, featured highly colored statues depicting scenes in Chinese history and myth. However, it is now to be extended and redeveloped with a sponsorship program along Disneyland lines. The renowned Raffles Hotel, founded more than one hundred years ago and associated with such writers as Joseph Conrad, Rudyard Kipling, and Somerset Maugham, has undergone several metamorphoses, including its use as a Japanese operational base from 1942 to 1945. The hotel's existence was threatened by development plans for the area in the late 1970s, and although the hotel was saved and partially restored by the mid-1980s and retained much of its original charm, it was attracting a quite ordinary type of tourist. By that time, the renowned Singapore gin sling, first created in the hotel's Long Bar and now dispensed at the rate of more than one thousand a day, seemed to cater to sweeter and weaker tastes than before. Early in 1989, the hotel was shut down for two years for renovation, which, through the use of period furniture and uniforms, would try to recapture the spirit of the 1920s.

On the positive side, Singapore has attractive features that are not directly dependent on size or history, including gardens and nature reserves. Sentosa Island has, among other attractions, a wax museum containing tableaux of British and Japanese surrenders in 1942 and 1945, respectively. Moreover, Singapore's varied ethnic groups offer a wide range of eating delights as well as a constant succession of cultural festivals. So it is incorrect to say that visitors come to Singapore only because "it is the Orient with plumbing." There are many things to do in Singapore in addition to shopping.

Singapore has to allow for the tourist pull of competing neighboring countries, which can now offer historic buildings, the great outdoors, and (in selected hotels) adequate plumbing. At the same time, Singapore retains an advantage because it offers efficient services and English is widely understood. Too determined a policy of selling Singapore as "instant Asia" could lead to instant fleeting visits, resulting in only small tourist expenditures. It had to work out its own intelligent distinctive approach to increasing tourist revenues.[3]

Modernization in Singapore has gone far beyond constructing high-rise buildings and establishing effective sea, air, and telecommunications links with the rest of the world. Singapore also ranks high in health, welfare, and amenities, surpassing all its Southeast Asian neighbors in the number of doctors, hospital beds, telephones, and autos per capita. It also leads these countries in the proportion of the population with tertiary education—except for the Philippines, where standards vary a great deal. Its leaders are strikingly well educated; the vast majority, not just of the cabinet but of the legislature as a whole, is educated beyond secondary level, and more than one-quarter of the legislators are doctors, medical or otherwise.

Additionally, an increasing number of Singaporeans are becoming English speakers as a result of the government's education policy—a great advantage for a country that depends on trading with countries all over the world. A particular variety of Singapore English (Singlish) has evolved,[4] although this development has been deplored by the government, which has tried to encourage the use of standard English by bringing native English speakers to teach in Singapore. Among the more common examples of Singlish are the use of "isn't it" to ask a question—"You want Carlsberg beer, isn't it?"; the addition of the suffix "la(h)" to indicate solidarity, familiarity, and informality, as in "make it cheaper la!"; and the coining of new words—particularly apposite in view of government campaigns against auto noise is the sign "No horning!"

The spread of English makes communication easier, both internally among citizens of different ethnic origins and with the outside world. But in itself the greater use of English goes only a little way toward promoting national unity. Singapore has three major ethnic groups—the Chinese (76 percent), the Malays (15 percent), and the Indians (7 percent), who are mostly from southern India. Within these, there are further subdivisions. Among the Chinese, for instance, approximately 43 percent are Hokkien, 22 percent are Teochew, 17 percent are Cantonese, and the majority of the remainder are either Hakka or Hainanese. These groups speak different dialects—only recently has there been a big increase in the numbers speaking Mandarin—and Indians speak mainly Tamil, Telegu, Malayalam, Punjabi, or Hindi. Religion is another dividing line between groups. Practically all Malays are Muslims. But Indians may be Hindus, Muslims, Sikhs, or Christians, whereas Chinese may be Taoists, Buddhists, Confucianists (or various combinations of these), or Christians. About 19 percent of the population is Christian, the most rapidly growing religion, which mainly attracts the well educated. Consequently, in view of Singapore's relative "newness" (the word "Singaporean" did not come into existence until Singapore became completely independent in 1965), many Singaporeans are subject to influences from the countries where these ethnic groups originated. In the early 1980s, for example, at a badminton contest in Singapore between Indonesia and China, a large part of the crowd became so enthusiastic in support of the Chinese that they provoked noisy reactions from the other spectators. Singapore's Malays, too, are subject not just to the influence of Malaysia and Indonesia but also to the worldwide rise of fundamentalist versions of Islam. The government has the difficult task of helping to keep the languages and cultures of the various ethnic communities alive as well as fostering the growth of a distinctive Singapore identity.

The values that Singapore's leaders, especially Prime Minister Lee Kuan Yew, wish to instill in the population are "modern" in the sense that they are geared toward promoting success and efficiency in today's world. But they are tougher and stricter than contemporary Western values—indeed, Singapore's leaders regard Western values as soft and decadent. Rather, Singapore's values reflect those of the West in the late nineteenth century and include discipline, hard work, honesty, cleanliness, abstention from drugs, and observance of family obligations, especially taking care of aged parents (which is linked with the teachings of Confucius). Raffles himself is an object of admiration; to be sure, he was an imperialist, but he is regarded as a "modernizing imperialist."

These values are not just advocated in the abstract; they are vigorously promoted and pursued. Prohibitions on smoking in designated places, spitting, littering, and wearing long hair (by males) are strictly enforced. Corruption is relentlessly tracked down and punished. The death sentence is mandatory for first-degree murder and, with only few exceptions, for armed robbery and crimes of violence. (There are about sixty murders each year in Singapore, proportionately about one-twentieth of the rate in Washington, D.C.) The death penalty also applies to trafficking in "hard" drugs, such as heroin or cocaine, and possession of more than a certain quantity of these drugs is taken to be evidence of trafficking. For some offenses criminals can be sentenced to lashing by a cane, which leaves scars on the back for life.

Beyond this, the government aims not just to prohibit undesirable behavior but also, by a mixture of incentives and disincentives, to promote certain long-term goals through a kind of social engineering. For example, it has tried to control the size of the population and even its quality (see Chapter 2). All these measures add up not to totalitarianism but rather to a paternalistic, ordered, and planned approach to society, based on the government's belief that it knows best.

Singapore's undoubted successes have not been easily won and will require constant effort to maintain. There is still a long way to go before an adequate degree of national unity is attained. The country's small size necessitates finely tuned defense and foreign policies (see Chapter 8). Its economic prosperity has to be achieved in a world context, which Singapore cannot significantly affect but can only, with skill, hope to adapt to. During the world recession in 1985, Singapore actually suffered one year of negative growth. Above all, the PAP style of govenment is now undergoing changes. A gradual transfer of power is taking place from the original generation of leaders to a younger generation. A few years ago, Singapore without Lee Kuan Yew was virtually unthinkable, so the transition may be a tricky one. At the same time, many Singaporeans are pressing for less paternalism and for more

The Supreme Court building, an example of colonial architecture. (Photo courtesy of David Hastings)

participation and openness in government. This is particularly true of younger Singaporeans, who are increasingly expressing such views in conversation and through letters to the newspapers. These problems, along with the accompanying stresses and strains, constitute a major theme of this book.

2

The Social Setting

Ethnicity is a pervasive thread in the social fabric of Singaporean society. Ethnic differences divide Singapore and will continue to do so for some time to come. These divisions are reflected in many ways and lie at the heart of numerous government policies designed to reduce their impact on national cohesiveness. A balance sheet on ethnicity suggests that a major factor is the position of the Malays, who in general are likely to be poorer and less well educated than other Singapore citizens. Although they make up only about 15 percent of the population, they are an especially sensitive and strategic component of the population because the two countries closest to Singapore—Indonesia and Malaysia (with combined populations numbering seventy times Singapore's)—have a preponderance of inhabitants ethnically close to Singapore's Malays, who like them, are preponderantly Muslim.

POPULATION

The population of Singapore (1989) is approximately 2.7 million. The density (about 11,000 persons per square mile) is one of the highest in the world. The government, which believes in social engineering and is better able to shape the society than are most other governments, has devoted much attention to three aspects of Singapore's population: its size, quality, and ethnic composition.

In 1959, the annual rate of population growth was high—4.7 percent. The PAP government strengthened the existing family planning program, coined the slogan "Two is enough," and backed it up by, for example, raising hospital delivery fees and imposing tax disincentives for having more than three children. Abortions were cheap and easily obtained—in the late-1980s almost one-third of all pregnancies were terminated by abortion. About three-quarters of the population practiced some form of contraception. Priority for registration (important to parents because it allowed them a choice of schools) at the Primary I entrance level was given to children with at least one sterilized parent.

Until a few years ago, the government was aiming at zero population growth by the year 2030, when the population was expected to stabilize at a figure between 3 and 3.5 million. By the 1980s, however, it seemed that government measures, aided by social and educational factors such as the growing number of women in the work force, had worked too well. One calculation showed that if fertility continued at the current rate, there would indeed be 3 million people in 2030 but that the numbers would then decline to about 2.4 million by 2070.[1] Moreover, by 2030 the proportion of the population aged sixty-five or older would exceed the number aged less than fifteen, which would produce a shortage of industrial workers and military recruits. The government was slow to change its policy, but by 1986 Goh Chok Tong (appropriately enough at a baby show) asked if the policy should not be changed from "two is enough" to "three is better." The government answered this question in the affirmative in March 1987 and announced a bevy of measures, mainly fiscal, to encourage a rise in the birth rate: large tax rebates for third children (in 1989 extended to fourth children) and tax reductions for the wife's earned income, subsidies for child-care centers, provisions for priority registration at Primary I entrance level for children in three-child families, and priority in obtaining larger government flats. For mothers who were civil servants, there were new regulations permitting no-pay leave for child care and facilitating part-time work.

The change in policy led to some dilemmas. Should women who had been sterilized to limit their families still enjoy preference in registering their children for school? Brigadier General (B. G.) Lee Hsien Loong indicated that the answer was "yes." Would abortions now become illegal? They would not, apparently, but doctors could use "social persuasion" to discourage women from having abortions. Would unmarried women who produced a third child benefit? No, they would not.

The 1980 census indicated that groups with the lowest incomes and education levels tended to have the highest birthrates. Lee Kuan Yew had strong views on the need for an elite "talent pool" and on the importance of heredity in producing talent (see Chapter 6), and his views led to the introduction of incentives for the better educated and disincentives for the less well educated. In 1988, by age thirty, only about 22 percent of female college graduates (and 18 percent of those with secondary education) were married, compared with less educated groups; even those women graduates who were married had only 1.7 children, compared with 2.7 for women with a primary education and 3.5 for those with no education. One incentive gave graduate mothers and some other educationally qualified women priority in registering their children for school at certain stages. This scheme aroused opposition, which was forcefully expressed during the 1984 election campaign, and the policy was abandoned in 1985. Another scheme that provoked comment—and some laughter—set up a social development unit (based on a Japanese model) and other organizations to enable well-educated single persons of both sexes to meet, for example, on cruises (the "love boat" scheme), at beach resorts, or at tea dances, with a view to marriage. By 1988, the scheme was showing results, especially among those with tertiary education.

The disincentives consisted of cash benefits for mothers who accepted sterilization, provided that the parents had both low incomes and low levels of education. One idea behind this scheme was that the payment would enable parents living in one-room flats to buy larger flats. Hospital delivery fees in wards used by the poorest patients were raised appreciably, whereas only minor increases were made for the more expensive wards. Beginning in October 1987, married women with some secondary education and fewer than three children had to receive counseling from a doctor before undergoing abortions. Even the changes made in March 1987 to raise the numbers of the population had a bias in favor of quality, at least insofar as they were linked with higher incomes. The new Goh Chok Tong slogan was, "Have three, and more if you can afford it,"[2] and the new tax rebates benefited the rich rather than the poor.

In regard to ethnic groups, the three main ethnic classifications, Chinese, Malay, and Indian (each of which includes many subdivisions), differ widely in numbers, the Chinese being predominant (in 1988, Chinese, 76 percent; Malay, 15 percent; Indians, 7 percent; others, 2 percent). These groups also differ in their fertility rates (to some extent reflecting differences in comparative income and education levels). In 1986, the Malays were producing children at a rate slightly above replacement level, the Indian rate was a little below that level, and the Chinese rate was almost 40 percent below it (which would in time reduce the preponderance of Chinese). Consequently, any government targets for population stimulation or restraint must take account of these differential rates. Lee Kuan Yew's eugenic objectives have to be assessed in the context of the higher Malay birthrate and lower-than-average Malay incomes and educational attainments as well in view of such factors as Islamic leaders' opposition to irreversible sterilization. Fertility rates, especially for the Chinese, rose in 1987 and 1988, but it is too early to say whether this trend will continue.

ETHNICITY

Differences of fertility among ethnic groups are not of merely academic interest. Ethnic conflict and violence are spreading in many parts of the world, and there is a growing awareness that ethnicity and the size of ethnic groups really matter. Only a quarter century ago, many people in the United States assumed that different ethnic groups would gradually come to resemble each other more because they were all subject to the influence of the "melting pot." Similarly, it was thought that modernization would gradually erode the differences among African tribes, between Chinese and non-Chinese in Southeast Asia, and so on. Furthermore, some believed that class differences would become deeper and would eventually override ethnic differences. Nevertheless, these predictions have not been borne out.[3] In most parts of the world ethnic consciousness has increased, partly because modernization has brought growing competition for jobs and status. The competition has been expressed in ethnic terms—for instance, in governments' setting quotas for employment and for places in educational institutions for ethnic minorities.

Singapore is no exception to this trend. Wide divisions in religion, language, and culture separate Chinese, Malays, and Indians. To be sure, important differences exist within each of the three categories—for example, language, how many generations a family has been in Singapore (or Malaya/Malaysia), or, for the Chinese, whether they were educated principally in Chinese or English. In the past, ethnicity often determined where people lived and the occupations they pursued. Nowadays, occupation is less closely linked with ethnicity, but the relationship still exists—for example, there are more Chinese than Malays in commerce.

Concern about "racial imbalance" was shown by non-Chinese in 1989 when some of them expressed unhappiness about the forthcoming influx of Chinese from Hong Kong. Goh Chok Tong reassured them that if as a consequence of this the Chinese percentage of the population rose, the government would increase correspondingly the number of permanent Singapore residents from non-Chinese in Malaysia and Indonesia.[4]

Linguistic, cultural, and religious divisions often reinforce one another. Hardly any Chinese are Muslims, whereas practically all Malays are Muslims. Until very recently, ethnicity has largely determined language, although elites have had a lingua franca in the form of English. Also, very few in each of the three groups habitually eat the staple foods of another group. Indeed, ethnic groups suffer from "their own" particular forms of cancer, which are linked to their dietary patterns.

Why should such ethnic differences constitute "divisions" instead of just providing colorful variety? Should governments try to minimize ethnicity and persuade the groups to adopt common norms? If so, *which* norms? As a minimum requirement, ethnicity should not be allowed to lead to violence. This also implies that loyalties matter. For example, there would be an increased *potential* for violence if a substantial proportion of Chinese were loyal to China rather than to Singapore or if the principal allegiance of Malays in Singapore were to Malaysia or Indonesia.

The Singapore government had an unusually difficult problem because in 1965 it found itself suddenly in control of a new state. It not only had to prevent ethnic tensions and violence but also had to create loyalties and a sense of identity almost from scratch. Its options were limited. No government, even if it had wanted to, could have established a "Chinese" or a "Malay" Singapore without causing grave unrest. The government's approach, therefore, has been multiracial and multicultural and has taken into account religion, language, education, and culture. These should provide a basis for assessing the degree of national unity achieved in Singapore.

RELIGION

Religious differences are particularly easily aroused, often leading to violence, as has been shown throughout the world during the last few decades. The government has exercised great care in dealing with religion. Few serious clashes between religious beliefs and government policies have occurred in the case of religions other than Islam. The most serious contentious exception was probably the Abortion Bill of 1969 (see Chapter 5, note 3). Demolition of Hindu temples and conversion of Chinese graveyards to other uses provoked tensions, but not serious ones. Nevertheless, from 1986 onward, Christians became more strident. Catholic organizations were more active on social issues and laid themselves open to penetration by Marxists (see Chapter 5). Some Protestant groups attempted to convert Muslims to Christianity, which provoked severe backlash. Government relations with Muslims have been more sensitive because of the possibility of Islamic extremism in Singapore, and some leaders of small clandestine Islamic extremist groups were arrested in 1978 and 1982 before they could effectively exploit Islam. To reduce tensions, the government has worked with, and through, the Muslim Religious Council of Singapore, an advisory body, which tends to back policies that many "extremists" would denounce. In May 1986, for example, the council came out for the first time in favor of Muslims donating their kidneys for transplants after their death. The president's speech at the opening of Parliament in January 1989 mentioned that the government would give top priority to preserving racial and religious harmony and would lay down ground rules to prevent the mixing of religion and politics.[5]

The Sri Mariamman Hindu Temple on South Bridge Road, Singapore.

LANGUAGE

To some extent, language differences coincide with religious differences. Malays speak Malay (and usually also English) and are almost invariably Muslims. Chinese and Indians, however, may belong to a variety of religions and also speak a wide range of languages and dialects. Also, Chinese who have been educated in Chinese have less "Western" attitudes than those educated in English, although the numbers of the former are gradually decreasing.

The government's original multicultural approach to language was later skillfully modified. When Singapore became internally self-governing in 1959, the PAP government decided to have four official languages: English, Chinese, Malay, and Tamil. Formally, special prominence was given to Malay as the "national language" because Singapore was surrounded by a "Malay" world and because it believed that gestures such as this would facilitate the merger with Malaya. (For similar reasons, the Singapore flag was based on Malay traditions, and the first head of state was a Malay.) Paradoxically, the designation of four official languages tended to create some loyalty to the state because none of the major ethnic groups' languages was an object of discrimination. Yet, if each group concentrated on its own language and there was no common language in which the groups could effectively communicate with one another, how could there ever be a *national* culture?

The medium adopted for such communication was English. It already had an advantage, from colonial times, in being the language of administration. It fulfilled the requirement of being a main medium for the spread of science and technology and a means of communication with other countries all over the world, particularly in business transactions.[6] Consequently, English was attractive to parents who wished their children to succeed (or at least not fall behind), and the government's education policy took advantage of this preference. The promotion of English was closely coordinated with educational policy and was speeded by the tide of economic advantage. Resistance was most likely to come from those who supported Chinese education and who, a few years previously, had literally fought to defend it. But they were disarmed by the government's obvious concern for Chinese culture, which contrasted with the previous unsympathetic attitudes of the colonialists.

The growing ascendancy of English—by the year 2000 at least 90 percent of those aged thirty or less will be English educated—does not indicate that the government has been unmindful of Chinese language and culture. It believes that the switch to English will not be damaging to Chinese culture, providing that Chinese families continue to transmit their culture to the young, particularly through mothers spending sufficient time with their children and through the maintenance of the extended (three-generation) family. The government demonstrated its concern through its campaign, begun in the late 1970s, to promote the use of Mandarin. To be sure, Mandarin was the dialect taught in schools, and dialect speakers could read it because the characters were the same. In addition, the power of Chinese dialect associations (with their own schools, temples, cemeteries) was on the wane. But after leaving school, many children lapsed into dialect and forgot Mandarin. Consequently, Mandarin was spoken by only about 10 percent of the Chinese population, whereas the most commonly used dialect, Hokkien, was spoken by more than three times as many people. (One estimate claimed, however, that nearly all Chinese *understood* Hokkien, and about three-quarters understood Mandarin.) Some dialects were not intelligible to speakers of other dialects, which produced the strange situation that some Chinese could communicate with each other only in Hokkien or in English. Some recruits, at the start of their national service, could understand commands only if they were delivered in Hokkien, thus earning the title, "the Hokkien Brigade." The prime minister, in urging the use of Mandarin so that Chinese children would be literate in it as well as in English, was thinking not just of *communication* between people; he was also concerned about Mandarin's cultural value. "They must be Mandarin-speakers, able to read the books, the proverbs, the parables, the stories of heroes and villains."[7] Additionally, Mandarin was more useful than dialects in trade and other contacts with China.

The campaign to increase the use of Mandarin required or encouraged those who came into frequent contact with the public to use it, and it was employed more frequently in armed forces camps, in government offices, and on radio and television. Obviously, some older Chinese were unable to adapt. In a novel published in the early 1980s, a Chinese woman showing visitors her Cantonese-speaking mother's television set, exclaims, "I really don't know what will happen when the television dubs all dialect series in Mandarin. . . . I suppose she won't want to watch television any more then, and then this set will be redundant."[8] The campaign has had considerable success and is being vigorously continued. In 1988, 87 percent of the population could speak Mandarin, compared with 76 percent in 1981, and the numbers using it have increased even in the home—the main center of resistance to change.

Language interacts with education. Language groups are concerned to promote the use of their languages in educational institutions. Conversely, children who master a language, particularly English, in school acquire an interest in supporting that language later in life.

EDUCATION

The locally elected governments of Singapore inherited from the British an education system characterized by noninvolvement, if not neglect. Many schools (Islamic, Chinese, Christian mission, Tamil, and English) were "independent," meaning that they were privately financed and controlled. There was little government supervision and no standardization of curricula or required level of achievement for graduating. Chinese-medium schools in particular remained outside government supervision, a situation more or less encouraged by the Chinese.

Under the PAP, which accorded education a high priority, the government became more involved. Official PAP education policy called for equal status and equal financial treatment for the four main education language streams, the use of Mandarin instead of dialect in Chinese schools, and a policy of bilingualism (which was not, however, implemented as an examination requirement until 1966). The PAP also introduced the concept of "integrated schools," two or more monolingual sections housed in one school, as a nation-building strategy. Further, the education system, curricula, textbooks, and examinations were standardized, with an emphasis on language, mathematics, science, and technology, and the PAP initiated an intensive school-construction and teacher-training program. In the early 1960s, technical education was introduced, and by 1969 students were streamed into academic, technical, and vocational schools after Primary VI.

The Decline of Chinese Education

Beginning in the mid-1950s, enrollments in Chinese schools began an inexorable decline. Singapore's Chinese had left the tradition of the Confucian scholar behind when they migrated from South China. In its place, wealth became the measure of social esteem—the upper class was mercantile—and the Chinese community became increasingly pragmatic in its approach to the achievement of wealth and status. Chinese education best prepared a person to work in China, not desirable for most after 1949, or to be a Chinese-medium school teacher, a relatively low-status occupation. English education, however, prepared children to move into government service and the professions and offered business advantages as well. The expected lifetime income of those educated in English schools was far greater than that of those educated in Chinese schools. While the Chinese as a community were willing to struggle fiercely for the survival of the Chinese school system, as individuals they increasingly tended to send their children to English schools.[9]

By the mid-1950s, the ideological radicalization of the Chinese middle-school youth, coupled with growing Chinese chauvinism as a reaction to poor job prospects and perceived isolation, contributed to student protests in 1954 and riots in 1955 and 1956 (see Chapter 3). Subsequent efforts by the locally elected Singapore government to "clean up" Chinese middle schools led to an emotional Chinese voter backlash that helped to propel the PAP into power in 1959. Nevertheless, the numerical decline of Chinese education continued unabated.

Chinese-medium Nanyang University (Nantah) was founded in 1956 and became a symbol of Chinese education. Throughout the 1960s and 1970s, the PAP government urged officials at Nantah to reform the institution, change its radical image, and use more English to secure its survival. Nantah officials agreed to a reorganization but failed to carry one out. In 1978, the prime minister told Nantah officials that they had made a "fatal error" in lowering standards to attract students, and soon after he offered them three options to consider. In April 1980, the Nantah council agreed to one of the options—merger with the University of Singapore to form the English-medium National University of Singapore (NUS). Unlike the emotional outpouring of the 1950s–1960s over "attacks" on Chinese education, the demise of Nantah through merger was accomplished with much public discussion but little fuss over the verdict.

Despite continuing political problems associated with the Chinese schools, which were turning out linguistic militants and increasingly unemployable graduates in the 1960s, the PAP still sought to preserve mother-tongue (especially Chinese) primary education and avoid de-culturation through a policy of bilingualism. Lee said, "I am convinced that if the price for knowing enough Chinese is a lower standard of English . . . it is still worth it."[10] By the late 1970s, however, it was becoming obvious that bilingualism was lowering English standards without creating any kind of *effective* bilingualism and that failure and dropout rates were unacceptably high (mostly because of poor second language exam results). Consequently, Lee commissioned a high-powered task force, led by Deputy Prime Minister Goh Keng Swee, to overhaul the education system. The "Report of the Ministry of Education, 1978," known as the "Goh Report," led to the implementation of a new education system in 1980 under Goh's direction as minister of education.

The "Goh Report" and the New Education System

The "Goh Report" pinpointed the major problem—there was an unacceptably high level of "educational wastage" from dropouts and failures (the primary school attrition rate was about 29 percent), who were unemployable. This had occurred because the goal of full bilin-gualism was beyond the capabilities of many students. Therefore, the "Goh Report" called for increased streaming—at the end of Primary

III and again at the end of Primary VI—and plotted several paths at the secondary level based on exam performance. Streaming had two primary objectives: to identify the most gifted students and put them through a demanding and challenging curriculum at the best schools with the best facilities, and to locate the weakest students and shift them into an extended monolingual stream and then into vocational training, thus reducing failure, dropout rates, and injured self-esteem. In between these poles, students were streamed into "normal" and "extended" bilingual streams (of three- and five-year duration, respectively). Lateral transfers across streams were allowable, in recognition of the possibility of mistakes and the existence of slow developers. The "Goh Report" also called for English and mother-tongue bilingualism, the latter being the choice of the students or parents rather than dictated by ethnic derivation (for example, many Tamils opt for Malay as their mother tongue), and for a concentration on language learning in Primary I–III. As Lee noted, although English was the most useful language for Singapore, he did not want the use of English to lead to deculturalized Singaporeans. Consequently, he said, mother-tongue instruction (and the teaching of Eastern value systems) should be incorporated into the education system to avoid rootlessness.[11]

Identified with the report, although not actually emphasized in it, was the idea of incorporating moral education into the curriculum to introduce the value systems, ethics, and religions of the East as a counter to the penetration of less desirable features of Western culture. While many agreed in principle and recognized that as a society becomes more affluent the need for moral education grows rather than diminishes, there was less consensus on form and content. The government stated in 1982 that the purpose was not to establish a Confucianist state but to ensure that succeeding generations would continue to know right from wrong and would have the intellectual tools with which to judge Western values. The debate was not over the six years of secular moral education but over the two additional years (in Secondary III–IV) of religious knowledge instruction, with six options for the students among the great religions. The Reverend Dr. Robert Balhetchet wondered about the assumption that morals could be taught by teaching the tenets and history of various religions (others wondered whether morals could be taught in the classroom at all) and said that what was wrong with Singapore youths was that they were selfish, willing to exploit friendships for personal gain, and reluctant to cooperate with classmates[12] (attitudes that were perhaps the product of a highly competitive and materialistic society). Beyond this, the debate on the syllabi, especially the Confucian ethics course, was contentious, and as a result implementation was temporarily delayed.

In late 1983, the government announced that beginning in 1987 there would be one "national stream" with English as the only first language and with all mother tongues taught as a second language except in the Special Assistance Plan superschools where two first languages would be taught. This move represented the end, for the time being, of an attempt at full bilingualism for all but the very top students.

In late 1986, as part of a major education initiative, "Towards Excellence in Schools," the government announced a plan to reintroduce some independent schools, applicable to a few institutions with outstanding academic records and sound financial status as a result of endowments. The plan was in accordance with the thinking behind the government's "privatization" drive (see Chapter 7); it was also aimed at incorporating some educational features of good private schools in the United States and Britain. These schools will have more autonomy and greater curriculum freedom, a better student-teacher ratio, and control over the hiring of teachers. In January 1990, Raffles Institution became the sixth government school to become independent.

There have been several other major government initiatives to promote excellence: All schools will eventually be converted to a single-session system (instead of half days for two sets of students)—a move that will require that the government build about one new school a month until 1994; class sizes will be reduced to a maximum of thirty, thus requiring the training of additional teachers; and principals and teachers have been empowered to transfer students to higher streams any time deemed suitable.

In 1989, the government announced plans to strengthen mother-tongue instruction for purposes of value transmission by more than doubling for 1990 the number of primary schools teaching both English and Chinese as first languages (EL1 and CL1, as they are known). Further, the government announced in October 1989 that it was phasing out the teaching of religious knowledge as a compulsory subject and replacing it with an expanded civics/moral education program in secondary schools in 1992. This was motivated by concern that religious knowledge courses were contributing to a growth of religious revivalism in Singapore (especially among evangelical Christian groups). Finally, the government has indicated that it may switch to a German/Swiss model of education (away from the British/American model) with more emphasis on technical and vocational education and with no university possibilities for the vast majority.[13]

The PAP government has always been acutely aware of the multidimensional importance of education to the state and has consistently given the matter of education close scrutiny. Education is viewed as a nation-building tool that can orient and direct political socialization and promote a multiracial Singaporean national identity. It is also viewed as a reservoir from which the best and the brightest of Singapore's youth can rise to the top—a very important consideration for a city-state that must live by the wits of its human resources. Based on the notion that individuals are born with different intellectual capacities and should be appropriately educated and trained to achieve their maximum potential, streaming is the most prominent feature of education in Singapore. The best students are streamed into demanding superschools that give priority to full bilingualism, mathematics, science, and technology; the weakest are streamed into monolingual, vocationally oriented schools geared to providing Singapore with a skilled and competent work force. Lee Kuan Yew has stated that without high standards of personal conduct, "a literate generation could be even more dangerous than a completely uneducated one."[14] Consequently, the PAP government also believes that instruction in moral character, values, and social norms (and physical fitness) is an important component of formal education.

With the New Education System, the school dropout rate has been halved (1976–1985), and the secondary education completion rate has risen from less than 40 percent to 75 percent. The stated purpose of education in Singapore is utilitarian: to produce "a good man and useful citizen." Beyond this, the government clearly desires, and has largely attained, a literate society with an intellectual elite and a skilled labor force. (Perhaps the Confucian scholar has found his way to Singapore.)

Despite the successes of education policy, some problems remain. First, very young schoolchildren and their parents are put under a tremendous strain by the highly competitive nature of the school system. Most children attend kindergarten to get a "head start" and to improve their chances of getting into a "good" primary school, and many students are tutored privately before or after school. The exams are everything—nothing else about the school experience matters much. Students, especially Chinese students, give every impression of being young "workaholics." In March 1987, Minister of Education Tony Tan warned against overloading students and turning them into bookworms and said that too much pressure was robbing them of the joys of childhood.[15] Second, the heavy emphasis given to language, mathematics, science, and technology leaves little time for the social sciences and humanities. This lack of balance in the content of education has been questioned by some.

There have also been many complaints and much unhappiness expressed over streaming, especially at the Primary III level. Parents whose children do not qualify for the gifted stream often believe that a grievous mistake has been made. The government, however, has stood firm on its streaming policy. It has not been receptive to suggestions for a milder form of streaming called "setting" (grouping by ability for each subject).

By far the most important problem sociopolitically is the educational performance gap separating Singapore's minority communities. In 1988 it was reported that although Indians were doing better in school than they had ten years before, they were still slipping behind, with 20 percent drifting into the slower streams (the national average was 12 percent).[16] The Malays, however, constitute the biggest problem. They make up a large proportion of the monolingual stream and suffer disproportionately high exam failure rates. With 15 percent of the population, only 1.5 percent were university graduates, despite provisions allowing qualified Malays a free university education. In 1989 the government proposed changes to the universality of this provision. There was a rough correlation, the data showed, between educational performance and income and family size. The data also showed that Malays performed better in ethnically mixed schools and when English was spoken somewhat at home. In response to these data, in June 1987 the Ministry of Education instructed schools to limit their enrollment of Malay children to no more than 25 percent of their Primary I intake to avoid excessive "clustering." Statistics released in November 1988 showed that the school performance of Malays has improved since 1980; however, the performance gap between Malays and other ethnic groups was closing only marginally.

In the early 1980s, the Council of Education for Muslim Children (MENDAKI) was formed to help Malay students with extra tutoring and exam preparation. Malay university enrollments have increased 50 percent in fourteen years, but there is little other evidence to show that Malays are acculturating to Singapore's competitive meritocracy. MENDAKI's constant complaint of high absenteeism from its tutoring sessions points to a cultural dilemma that will take years to overcome. Given Singapore's geographic location and given the slowly changing ethnic configuration of Singapore (the Chinese population is declining, whereas the Malays are the most rapidly growing community), the political ramifications of a nonacculturated Malay community are significant.

CULTURE

Singaporean culture—a more elusive aspect of ethnicity than religion, language, or education—is in a transitional state. Folk cultures of the various ethnic groups are alive, if not flourishing, and are actively encouraged; there is, for example a Central Council of Malay Cultural Organizations, a revival of traditional Malay music on the *hadrah* and the *kompang* (hand-held drums), and a small group that fosters Javanese culture through dances and a gamelan orchestra. Traditional forms of culture, such as Chinese opera, persist (in spite of difficulty in recruiting new singers willing to work long hours for low pay), but in a modern setting they, and some other outdoor shows, are now required to have noise control devices fitted to their sound equipment. Moreover, many young people are just not interested, despite efforts to attract them by punctuating traditional performances with music by pop bands. Official programs of folk culture try to break through cultural barriers by including music, dances, and other art from all the major cultures.

There are numerous cultural events and performances in Singapore. In the last few years, there has been a traveling exhibition of paintings and photography, a sculpture workshop, a photography exhibition, a young artists' exhibition, and a series of national music competitions that have shown a shift in interest toward learning Chinese instruments. There is also a drama center, a symphony orchestra, and a national museum, which includes a splendid jade collection. To make up for the shortage of biographies, memoirs, and documents about life in Singapore, an oral history unit has recorded numerous interviews to assist in reconstructing and understanding the past. Its projects include "Political Developments in Singapore, 1945–1965," "Japanese Occupation of Singapore, 1942–1945," "Communities of Singapore," and "Chinese Dialect Groups."

Nevertheless, some people are pessimistic about the condition of culture in Singapore—as indeed they are in many other countries. A 1987 survey showed that only 5 percent of Singaporeans habitually attended or took part in arts or cultural activities, whereas 92 percent watched television or videos, 38 percent "lazed around," and 15 percent went to the movies. A 1988 survey indicated that the typical Singaporean culture buff was likely to be a young graduate professional woman with some formal training in the arts. One view, expressed in the mid-1970s, was that there was a general ignorance of Asian cultures and that philistinism prevailed in the form of what Foreign Minister S. Rajaratnam called "moneytheism." On another occasion Rajaratnam observed that Singaporeans had come to the point where they had demonstrated their ability to make money but had not learned how to use it. In the late 1970s, the Ministry of Culture launched a drive to turn Singapore from a "cultural wasteland" into a "haven of culture." But, as yet, government efforts and financing have not been supplemented by sufficient donations from the private sector for the encouragement of culture.

Two observations may be offered about culture in Singapore. First, from the experience of other countries (such as the Tang dynasty in China, A.D. 618–908, and France in the second half of the nineteenth century), an increase in wealth can lay the foundation for a flowering of culture. Second, there have been efforts to produce art and literature that are "authentically Singaporean," possibly reflecting the style and spirit of a modern industrial society rather than the values of traditional cultures. There are bound to be disputes about the meaning of the phrase, however, because of disagreements about what is authentic and what is not.

One dramatic production, staged in Singapore in August 1988, was undeniably Singaporean. *Mama* [Grandma] *Looking for her Cat*, devised by a multilingual cast and directed by Kuo Peo Kun, explicitly treated the theme of obstacles to understanding that derive from language barriers as well as from generational differences. Indeed, the play was so local that some members of the audience believed that its message would not come across in other Chinese-speaking countries with different patterns of dialects.

THE MASS MEDIA

The ethnic composition of Singapore and the government's language and education policies are reflected in the use of the four official languages, particularly English and Mandarin, in the mass media. The mass media reflect differences in language and culture and are also instruments through which the government can promote its policies on language and culture. They are of crucial importance in a country where the government is committed to instilling certain basic values in the population, and the government does not hesitate to use them for that purpose.

Radio and television are both managed by a government corporation, the Singapore Broadcasting Corporation, except for a private company (licensed by the government) that runs a radio rediffusion service. There are five radio channels and five television channels, operating in all four official languages, but with an emphasis on English and Mandarin. Compared with North America, there is less "entertainment," although some U.S. "soaps" are shown. Forty percent of the television programs are locally produced, most being informational and educational. As in many other countries, government politicians receive more exposure than opposition politicians, partly because what they do is more newsworthy. Since 1985, a program, "Today in Parliament," has included excerpts from parliamentary proceedings in both English and Mandarin. This is very popular, especially when it showed verbal duels between J. B. Jeyaretnam, a former opposition member, and PAP ministers. There are differing views, however, about the effects on the viewers. The government has used these media to encourage the switch from Chinese dialects to Mandarin. Also, a local soap opera, "The Awakening," was intended partly to acquaint the young with "the sweat and toil their forefathers went through to build the nation."

Currently, there are three Chinese-language daily papers and three English-language papers (one a business paper with a limited circulation) as well as a Malay and a Tamil paper. In 1984, the total circulation of English-language papers exceeded for the first time that of the Chinese papers, reflecting the consequences of the government's language and education policies.

Control of the press is effected in various ways—through the government's licensing powers, through informal advice (or the anticipation of informal advice), through use of the criminal law (three Chinese newspaper employees were detained in 1971), and through the government's ability to restructure newspaper ownership. The government has shown particular concern over the effects of press reports or statements on ethnic harmony, possible foreign influence on the press, and press items that might call into question the values it deems indispensable for Singaporeans or that might threaten the country's stability. On a less exalted level, the government has temporarily suspended newspapers that have carried sensational crime stories intended to boost circulation.

According to Lee, "We want the mass media to reinforce, not to undermine, the cultural values and social attitudes inculcated in our schools and universities."[17] Applying these standards, the government forced the closure of three newspapers in 1971: the *Nanyang Siang Pau* (for promoting Chinese "chauvinism"), the *Eastern Sun* (for receiving a loan from Communist sources), and the *Singapore Herald* (for accepting finance from foreign capital and eroding people's attitudes on such issues as national service).

In 1982 and 1984, the government carried out a restructuring of newspaper ownership by means of mergers. Practically every newspaper in the country (as well as many other publications) is now controlled by one company, which is the largest industrial group in Singapore. In explaining the move, the government cited the need to secure economies of scale, the advantages of mobilizing ample financial and human resources, and so on. Critics thought, however, that the merger would

reduce the variety of the opinions that appeared in the press.[18] Since then, governmental relations with the local press have apparently been smooth. But in 1986, the government, disturbed by reports about Singapore in foreign journals that it regarded as interfering in its internal politics (and as discouraging to foreign investors), amended the law on the control of the press. Among other measures, the *Asian Wall Street Journal*, the *Far Eastern Economic Review*, *Asiaweek* (and formerly *Time*) have had limits placed on their Singapore circulation. The idea was to hit back at the journals by reducing their advertising revenues. In 1988, the government decided that photocopies of these journals could be circulated provided that advertisements were omitted. Foreign journals had no "right" to circulate in Singapore. Furthermore, on the issue of fairness, newspapers did not have a right to decline to publish replies from the government, or—as the government claimed in the case of *Asiaweek*—the right to make changes in such replies. These events made clear the government's determination that the country's need for stability and ethnic harmony must override any abstract devotion to "the freedom of the press."

ETHNICITY: THE BALANCE SHEET

Government policy on ethnicity has indeed been multiracial in the sense that no ethnic group, language, or culture has been repressed or deliberately discriminated against. Its most potentially explosive policy was its promotion of English. In 1959, it would have seemed incredible that such a policy could have been undertaken without alienating, even to the point of violence, large numbers of Chinese-educated Chinese. As Lee observed in conversation, if "Chinese chauvinists" ever perceived Chinese culture as being threatened, they "would crawl out of the woodwork." Yet, the resentment was contained, and the spread of English automatically created a vested interest on the part of those who learned it, thus helping to ensure that the policy was not reversed. The key to the successful implementation of the policy was gradualness. As Lee Kuan Yew noted, "We are a society relaxed about our diverse communal origins, and we feel no compulsion to make ourselves uniform through forcing the pace of integration or assimilation."[19]

A common language, usually English or Mandarin, that is shared by members of different ethnic groups makes it easier for them to communicate with each other. By itself, however, a common language will not produce homogeneity. As Lee has observed, "One language is a social glue that helps to keep a society together, but it's not stronger than religion or ethnic pulls. [We must] never deceive ourselves that we can become like Hong Kong, Taiwan or Korea—tight, cohesive, with one social response."[20] Clearly, Singapore is not a melting pot. A cabinet minister has likened it to a can of vegetable soup. There is some blending of flavors, but there are also sizable chunks that still contain their own distinctive juices. At the same time, surveys have shown that most Singaporeans have friends belonging to other ethnic groups and that most feel a sense of national identity—as shown, for example, by self-identification as a Singaporean and by positive feelings toward symbols of nationhood such as the flag. Moreover, efficient government and an expanding economy have helped to strengthen loyalty to the state.

The major challenge to the creation of a sense of national unity in Singapore is posed by the Malay community, as may be gathered from the preceding sections in this chapter. Although the Malays are in a minority in Singapore, in the wider context of the surrounding area (Malaysia and Indonesia), they constitute part of a vast majority. The government of Singapore cannot afford to ignore this fact; alternative loyalties for Malays are just too readily available, as was shown in the ethnic riots of 1964. The situation is made more difficult by the growing proportion of Malays in the population.

Goh has remarked that the government has to keep five aspects of the Malay question constantly in mind: the concept of multiracialism, the Malay language, Malay customs and culture, the Muslim religion, and the degree of Malay tolerance regarding the ways and beliefs of other Singaporeans.[21] Government policy is to intervene only minimally in the second, third, and fourth aspects. The first aspect is more difficult to deal with because multiracialism could mean treating the various ethnic groups in a similar fashion. Yet the Malays *are* different from Singapore's other ethnic groups because they are poorer, and special measures are needed to break the vicious circle of low incomes, large families, crowded accommodations, greater use of drugs, and low educational attainments that is conducive to continued poverty. The government does give the Malays special financial help for education but does not maintain any quota system for jobs; thus, for example, Malays are still underrepresented in the top ranks of the civil service. Nevertheless, improving the lot of the Malays is a main concern of the Malay Affairs Committee, the Singapore Malay National Association, and the Central Council of Malay Cultural Organizations. The government also hopes that with the breakdown of ethnic segregation, at least some Malays will learn—by a kind of osmosis—new roles appropriate for modern life and their tolerance of the ways of life of other Singaporeans will increase. Unfortunately, the organizations that the government sets up to help the Malays are viewed by many of them as "government" or "PAP" organizations, thus losing credibility as truly "Malay" organizations.

A number of widely publicized incidents suggest that Malays have quite often found themselves at odds with the government and are not yet well integrated into the system. One was Malay opposition (along with other Muslims in Malaysia and Indonesia) to the visit of the president of Israel to Singapore in 1986 (see Chapter 8). Another was the role of the Malays in the Singapore Armed Forces (SAF) (see Chapter 8), which was hotly debated early in 1987. Minister B. G. Lee stated that although Malays were now being called up for national service, the positions assigned to them would be those in which they could "contribute most effectively" to Singapore's defense. But this led to questions of possible conflict between loyalties to Singapore and to race and religion, to discussion of why Malays did not hold higher ranks in the armed forces, and to sharp comments from Malay leaders in Malaysia that produced rejoinders from Singapore.

A further controversy concerned the extension of MENDAKI to MENDAKI II in order to create an institution to help Malays with economic and social programs. At the time of the 1988 election a Malay minister stated that the government would provide such help, but Goh Chok Tong said that the matter was still under consideration. The issue became entangled with the question of whether Malays had failed to give the government as much electoral support as other ethnic groups. In October 1988, Goh made two main points. First, government support of MENDAKI II was important, but the main factor in improving the Malays' economic and social condition was Malay commitment to self-help. Second, although Malay leaders had called on their followers "to be in the mainstream of national life,"[22] Malays were not enthusiastic about participating in grass-roots bodies (although in late 1988 strong efforts were made to get them more involved in community center activities).

During 1989, the MENDAKI II scheme took shape, and a body was set up, which included Malay leaders elected at the grass roots, to promote Malay educational, social, and cultural interests. Later, the government proposed that MENDAKI II should administer the subsidy for Malay tertiary education, on the basis that better-off Malays should pay their children's costs.[23]

WOMEN IN SINGAPORE

The rest of this chapter discusses some aspects of society in Singapore that are indeed affected by the all-perversive factor of ethnicity but are best viewed in the context of economic development and modernization. A prominent aspect of modernization has been improvements in the status of and opportunities for women. The PAP Women's Charter of 1961 laid down the principle of equal pay for equal work and outlawed polygamy. Other changes took place informally. For example, it is claimed that because women now have more earning power, there was a decline in the traditional practice of preferring children who were grandchildren through the father to those who were grandchildren through the mother. The notion of sex equality was also conveyed through some of the government's policies and slogans, such as its previous advocacy of smaller families through the phrase, "Girl or boy, two is enough."

Women have also made advances in literacy and education. Although a 1984 estimate put the literacy rate at 92 percent for males but only 79 percent for females, in the younger age groups the percentages for the sexes were about the same, women having caught up in the previous two decades or so. By 1980, women constituted nearly half of the kindergarten and primary school enrollments. Since 1982, more women than men have entered university studies, although men still outnumber women in technical and vocational institutes.

Nevertheless, educational advances have not been accompanied by corresponding progress in the labor force. To be sure, by the mid-1980s, 45 percent of women were in the labor force, compared with only 20 percent in 1957. But they tended to be in low-paying jobs, with few real prospects for advancement; their average wage was only three-quarters of the male average, although the gap was closing. Women work mainly in the low-skilled sectors of the manufacturing, commerce, and service industries. Their renumeration tends to peak between the ages of twenty and twenty-four, unlike the pattern for Singaporean males (or for females in many Western countries where some women with older children return to work in relatively well-paid positions). Women are quite well represented among professional people, but very few are in the higher executive or managerial ranks. There has never been a woman in the Singapore cabinet, although a noncabinet female minister was appointed in 1988, and only four members of the Singapore Parliament are women, compared with seventy-seven men. (In 1980, there were no women.) The first woman ambassador, Dr. Chan Heng Chee, was appointed in 1989 to the United Nations.

The government policy of encouraging graduate women to marry and have children also has some implications for the position of women. In many cases, the single status of women graduates may be an indicator of male chauvinism. As Lee Kuan Yew has remarked, too many male graduates look for a marriage partner lower in the social scale. "With their mother's milk they learn that they must be the boss in the family—and if they marry another graduate they won't be the boss."[24] Also, if the government does succeed in increasing the number of women graduates who become mothers, the conflicting pulls of home and job may tend to reduce even further the number of women in professional and executive positions. Another consequence of male marriage preferences is that men at the lower end of the social scale find that few women are available for marriage. By 1988, the efforts of the Social Development Unit and other organizations had resulted in a higher proportion of well-educated males marrying women with equal or superior education.

The most dramatic changes in the role of women have taken place among the Malays. Compared with two or three decades ago, Malay women have made greater advances than Malay men in educational achievements—there are now more female than male graduates among Malays—and their participation in the labor force has greatly increased in the last thirty years.

CLASS DIFFERENCES

Although ethnicity is the most important potentially divisive factor in Singapore, it is not the only one. In many countries, social class differences divide sections of the population and may lead to changes in government or even to authoritarian rule. There are various ways of defining social class. Two often used criteria are income and occupation.

Income differences are considerable. Average income per capita is $8,000 (including resident foreigners, whose incomes are higher than average). In 1989, top salaries for bankers reached $51,000 and for sharebrokers reached $63,000, while newly announced salaries for the highest paid civil servants brought their income to about $86,000.[25] Although the distribution of income is unequal, it is less unequal than in most Third World countries. Moreover, some reduction in the degree of inequality occurred between 1966 and 1983, with the exception of the Malay community where average income fell from about 80 percent of the Chinese average to about 70 percent. Since 1983, the general trend toward equality may have been halted, or even reversed, although Singapore has fewer very poor people today than it did ten or twenty years ago. The government does not object to big differences in incomes (although it would like to improve the position of the Malays) provided that those who are most well off are contributing to the increase in the size of the pie, thus raising the *absolute* incomes of lower paid Singaporeans.

The government has stressed the importance of home ownership as an indicator of social class, and on that basis about 80 percent of the population is middle class. More important than these indices in themselves are people's own perceptions of their social class. A 1988 survey conducted by the *Straits Times* found that Singaporeans mentioned other factors affecting social class in addition to income, occupation, and home ownership, such as education, car ownership, and possession of various household appliances. When all of these were taken into account, 75 percent of the 500 people in the sample identified themselves as middle class.[26]

It is really extraordinary that whereas the PAP's main opponent, the Communist-infiltrated Barisan Sosialis, won more than one-third of

Luxury condominiums for Singapore's "yuppies."

the vote at the 1963 election, the most recent opposition parties' successes at elections do not seem to have arisen from class grievances. The PAP has been remarkably adroit at defusing class issues, as well as ethnic issues. Its concern for the provision of some basic social services has played a role in muting class divisions.

SOCIAL SERVICES

At the center of the web of social services in Singapore is the Central Provident Fund (CPF), founded in 1955. Its primary objective is to enable Singaporeans to save for their lives after retirement, and it is financed by contributions of a percentage of each worker's earnings and a percentage paid by the employer (see Chapter 7). The money collected amounts to a huge sum and is available to the government for investment. Originally, contributors had no access to their savings, unless they were fifty-five (the usual retirement age) or had retired earlier. Later, they were permitted to draw upon their accounts before that age for some specified purposes, such as buying homes or investing in certain shares. Employers were also permitted to use a percentage of their contributions to set up trust funds to provide additional welfare benefits for their employees. (The system now has provisions for Medisave.) In general, the CPF has been popular because it has been the basis of comprehensive welfare benefits. Until recently, the main complaint was that the annual rate of interest on contributions was low compared with alternatives, even though while in the CPF funds were compounded without being taxed.

Nevertheless, when a government-appointed committee on the problems of aging proposed in 1984 that the minimum age for withdrawal of savings should be raised from fifty-five to sixty or even to sixty-five, there was a storm of protests in the press by trade unionists and even by some members of Parliament. An opposition cartoon showing a coffin and a line of aged people waiting to make their CPF withdrawals was captioned "too late." The committee's proposal was not unreasonable, given that people were living longer and therefore needed more money for the additional years of retirement. Nevertheless, this was probably the biggest single issue that swayed votes away from the government at the 1984 election, and it was forced to shelve the proposal. In 1986, the government announced that all CPF savings could still be withdrawn at age fifty-five except for funds deposited in Medisave accounts or needed to provide for old age. Curiously, when employers' CPF contributions were cut in 1986 as an antirecession measure (see Chapter 7), which reduced employees' total savings in the fund, there were fewer complaints. Just before the 1988 elections, the government announced that it would allow withdrawal of CPF savings to finance up to 100 percent of the value of the purchase price of a private house (the previous figure was 80 percent) and that CPF savings could be used to pay for children's tertiary education—but only in Singapore.

Despite CPF coverage, two problem areas exist in welfare services: health (in particular, hospitals) and the care of the aged. The impressive standards of health services in Singapore, as compared with the rest of Asia, may be judged by a life expectancy of seventy-four years and one of the lowest infant mortality rates in the world—7.0 per 1,000 live births.[27] Some health services, such as visits to a doctor or the provision of medicine, are cheap because they are heavily subsidized. But the costs of hospital care, particularly in light of expensive medical technology and an aging population, are high. To combat these costs, the government proposed in 1983 a "medisave" scheme for hospitalization that would also be heavily subsidized but would be partially financed by individuals' CPF contributions. Costs of hospital care had jumped during the previous decade and were likely to rise even more because of improved, and dearer, medical technology and the increasing burden of an aging population. The government rejected the idea of a national health insurance scheme, similar to those in some European countries, because it feared possible abuses by doctors and patients. The government's Medisave scheme was attacked by some PAP backbenchers, who claimed that hospital care ought to be a social responsibility and that coverage under the scheme would be inadequate for the average Singaporean, being sufficient only for a few weeks of hospitalization during his or her working life.

The problem of caring for the elderly has arisen partly because of the decline in the extended family system, but it has been exacerbated by the rising numbers of older persons. Twelve percent of the population will be older than sixty by the year 2000, and by 2030 there will be only three economically active people to support each person older than sixty, as compared with nine in 1980. Various ways of solving this problem have been put forward, such as combinations of fiscal incentives and disincentives to encourage children to look after their old parents and proposals to raise the retirement age. In 1987, a new scheme enabled CPF members to transfer CPF funds (or cash) to top up their parents' savings. Ultimately, however, an important part of the solution may be the establishment of more old people's homes, either by the Ministry of Community Development or by voluntary bodies—although the space available for homes is extremely limited, except at great cost.

PHYSICAL PLANNING: TRANSPORTATION

The government has also provided appropriate physical infrastructures in conditions in which space is at a premium. In order to construct housing, industrial estates, and roads, the government had to acquire land. In the initial stages, the government was so determined to provide these services that the compensation it paid was below market value. Between 1950 and 1980, built-up areas grew by 80 percent (and now constitute about half of Singapore's total area), while farm, forest, and other open areas declined. The supply of available land increased by 6 percent through reclamation during these years, although reclamation is now becoming increasingly costly.

Consequently, Singapore's physical appearance has been transformed. The current plan is based on a "ring" concept, with fifteen "new towns" surrounding the city, each divided into neighborhoods containing between 25,000 and 50,000 dwelling units, mostly in the form of high-rise flats. The central business district also has high-rise buildings, but its resident population fell sharply from 410,000 in 1960 to 150,000 in 1980. To repopulate this district, the government has encouraged developers to build residential units above offices and shops. The waterfront along the Singapore River has also been rebuilt to make it a center for entertainment and cultural activities.

Dispersal of the population has led to increasing pressure on the means of transportation, which before the 1980s consisted of a not very efficient bus system supplemented by relatively cheap taxis, a majority of which were operated by COMFORT, a trade union cooperative. To alleviate this pressure, the government began constructing a mass rapid transit (MRT) system in 1983, part of which came into operation in 1987. When completed (by 1990), the MRT will have several lines, 42 stations, and a capacity of 1 million passengers a day. There will be 66 trains comprising 398 cars (each seating 62 passengers) with a maximum speed of 60 miles an hour traveling over 40 miles of track. Buses will remain but will concentrate on short distances and on routes not covered by the MRT. Most of the "new towns" are also accessible by approximately 85 miles of expressways.

One casualty of Singapore's traffic congestion (although traffic control and discipline are better than in most comparable Southeast Asian cities) has been private cars. In 1971, the government introduced a number of disincentives to slow down the increase in cars—very heavy registration fees for new cars, higher annual road taxes, and an area licensing scheme that imposed charges for entering the central business district at certain times. By 1986, the number of private cars was practically static, but as the country recovered from the recession, the number rose again by about 10 percent a year. The government introduced further restrictions by extending the hours when the area licensing scheme was in force, increasing parking fees, and raising the price of gas. In late 1989 preparations were made for introducing "Electronic Road Pricing," which would monitor traffic flow by computer and bill motorists who drove in congested areas.

HOUSING: CONSERVATION

Government housing has been a main element in converting Singapore from a low-rise to a high-rise society in less than a quarter century. Singapore, once "among the most primitive in the urban areas of the world," is now "the public housing laboratory of the world," according to a persistent critic of the PAP.[28]

Since 1960, the Housing and Development Board (HDB), has built 640,000 flats (apartments) and other residences as well as shops and industrial premises, and by 1988, 86 percent of the population lived in government flats, two-thirds of whom owned equity in their homes. Rentals for flats are subsidized and are therefore below market price; those with low incomes receive further price reductions. Ownership is encouraged because owners become more committed than tenants to taking care of the properties and making them pleasant to live in. Ownership is also subsidized through low mortgage rates and by concessions for some low-income families. In future, however, pricing

The Ang Mo Kio New Town, built by the HDB, houses about 250,000 people.

of flats will depend on their desirability, and government subsidies will probably decrease. In accordance with this policy, the level of family income needed to qualify for obtaining a flat was raised in 1989. The government's aim is to have all its flats owned by the end of the century. These figures compare favorably with those for Hong Kong, where less than half the population is in government housing, and very few of these are owners.

This program was hampered by limited space and by the steep price of land, which contributed to the choice of high-rise buildings. The task was made easier, however, by the rarity of typhoons and earthquakes (which increase building costs) and by Singapore's policy of restricting population growth (now reversed), which slowed the demand for housing.

Because of the need for quick results, initially the quality of the flats was only adequate. Later, standards and variety improved, and in the new towns residents were serviced by town centers, schools, sports and swimming complexes, playgrounds and jogging paths, and hawkers, transplanted from downtown and placed under one roof. Other adjustments and improvements followed. For example, in the early 1980s, in accordance with the government's campaign to maintain the extended family, married couples were encouraged to apply for flats in the same blocks as their parents' flats, and early in 1987 financial incentives were offered and about three hundred flats with an attached "studio" flat for parents or grandparents were made available. The demand for these was less than expected.

The housing program has been successful in achieving its physical targets and in contributing to social and political stability by giving shelter and often a sense of ownership to the poor, thereby lessening a potential source of discontent. The housing program has been a symbol of PAP effectiveness. But it has also raised expectations about performance, and so the government cannot afford to relax. It is widely believed that the PAP defeat at the Anson by-election in 1981 was due partly to the existence of a large waiting list for HDB flats in the area and the government's failure to perceive the political implications of this until after the election. The government was more cautious in the fall of 1986, when during a recessionary period it decided not to go ahead with a proposed increase in the price of flats.

The success of the housing program in psychological terms is harder to gauge. Some studies of life in flats stress the lack of a sense of neighborhood; feelings of isolation, worry, and stress; difficulties in rearing children; and so on. Other accounts paint a more complex and less dismal picture—even for Malays, for whom the move entailed a really drastic change in lifestyle. People living in estates that have Residents' Committees (RCs) (see Chapter 5) are likely to know a higher number of their neighbors than do those living without access to RCs. The same is true in small clusters of flats known as precincts. In addition to making up for the absence of well-established voluntary associations, RCs also help flat dwellers to regulate the common nuisances of high-rise living—noise from the pounding of chilies on the floor, from hammers or electric drills to install fixtures, and from car horns.

One original aim of the housing program was to reduce the ethnic segregation[29] instituted by Raffles, who allocated areas to various ethnic groups. Subdivisions of the major ethnic groups settled in these areas and even specialized in various trades and occupations. For instance, South Indian chettiars clustered in the central business district, whereas Telegu and Malayalee groups were concentrated near the dockyards and the railroad station. A main center for the Tamils—"Little India" or "a second Madras"—was located in the Serangoon Road area, which supplied South Indian cultural, dietary, and community needs. Its survival depended on a number of factors—low wages, long apprenticeships, controlled rents, and the existence of "shophouses" that combined living, working, and selling space.[30] But in the 1980s there were plans to demolish it, as well as Chinatown in the core of the city, despite opposition from local dwellers and conservationists. Even the Malays, who had their own often picturesque settlements, have been largely uprooted, and more than 70 percent of them now live in flats. These

A view of Singapore that could still be seen in the early 1980s. This area is known as Singapore's Chinatown.

changes can be traumatic, and some of those affected may be unwilling to go into business anywhere else. One Chinatown stallkeeper explained, "We were born here and this is home for us. . . . We don't want to do business in the basement of a market complex. It would be like going to hell. We like doing business on road level."[31]

Dissatisfaction on the part of Singaporeans was accompanied by tourists' unhappiness that Singapore did not offer much that distinguished it from any other modern city. In response, the government shifted its policy early in 1987 and began to focus on the preservation of historic and picturesque buildings and areas in order to draw in more tourists. Accordingly, about one-eighth of the central area, including parts of Little India and Chinatown, will be conserved and rehabilitated.

THE ENVIRONMENT

Given Singapore's high population density and growing industrialization, the government has been vigilant about the prevention of pollution. It has gone beyond such routine measures as testing the air for emissions, monitoring drinking water and sewage, encouraging the use of antipollution devices, and carrying out a massive cleanup of Singapore's rivers (1987). It has promoted pollution-free industries in the new towns, has protected existing trees, has planted more trees in urban areas (there are more than 1 million trees in Singapore, two-thirds of them identified on computers), has instituted tough fines for littering and for not flushing public toilets, and has extensively prohibited smoking. New recreational parks have been created, and to supplement the famous Botanic Gardens (whose calm is enlivened by the chatter of mischievous monkeys), the government has constructed the Jurong Bird Park as well as a Chinese and a Japanese garden. The government has waged an unremitting campaign against vandalism in government flats. Recently, "killer litter," thrown from the higher storeys, has been a specific target. The number of dangerous objects thrown out was not all that large, but the diversity was impressive, including chairs, iron pipes, cupboards, dumbbells, and bicycle wheels. The government even passed a law to enable it to turn out families from flats from which litter had been thrown, even if the offender was only a visitor. An official assurance was given, however, that eviction would be only a last resort.

TRADITIONAL AND MODERN VALUES

The government's whole range of social policies is conditioned by the particular "mix" of traditional and modern values that it has adopted. Lee Kuan Yew said that the leadership of each new country must make up its mind just how much of the old to keep and how much to jettison, how to reconcile making progress with keeping enough of its own distinctive self.[32] But, as he was aware, the effects of modernization, and Westernization, are a mixed blessing. In Singapore, Western technology and the English language have accompanied the relocation of hawkers in more structured but less convenient locations; the spread of chains such as MacDonald's and A&W and the replacement of old-style coffee shops by restaurants modeled on the fast-food pattern; and the appearance of modern recreations that include amusement parlors where youngsters play space-age electronic games and break dance, roller skate, and skate board. The government has recently restricted the areas in which these latter pursuits can be practiced. In the 1970s, it started a campaign against imitators of American hippies who wore dirty jeans and long hair. Orders were given that males with long hair were to be served last in government offices. Males entering the country were not allowed in unless they had their long hair cut. In general, however, tourists' tastes were catered to, and they helped to spread Western habits and ideas.

Some commentators claim that modernization—in Singapore's crowded and controlled setting—has been responsible for all kinds of deplorable trends, such as mental and emotional disturbances; ulcers and strokes; conspicuous consumption, especially in the form of expensive cars; complacency; failure to mix with neighbors; and "softening" of the younger generation, which causes it to become addicted to passive amusements and leaves it with no clear sense of distinction between right and wrong. Yet many of these trends might be attributed not to modernization in general but to the disturbance of culture patterns that resulted from the government's program of social transformation, particularly the extensive urban resettlement. Another theory is that the social discipline imposed by the government—while a necessary requirement for Singapore's impressive social and economic achievements—has produced a "dependency mentality" of undue reliance on the government.

Leading politicians have expressed considerable concern that the respect of Chinese for their parents has so diminished that some children have not been prepared to take care of their parents in old age.[33] (In the early 1980s, about 75 percent of the old people who had children did live with them, but the proportion in this category declined about 7 percent between 1970 and 1980.) In 1982, Lee announced that tax changes would be made to help support the elderly and encourage three generations to live under one roof. One change took the form of tax relief for those who made contributions to their parents' accounts in the CPF. The government, believing that this issue was symptomatic of a general decline in traditional Chinese values—which the PAP was determined to preserve—also, for a time, introduced a course on Confucian ethics in the schools in order to minimize this decline.

CONCLUSION

Singapore—a society of only 2.7 million people—is carrying out a rapid social transformation in population control, language, education, physical planning and resettlement, industrialization, and other policies. The physical changes, as well as changes in the standard of living, are easier to bring about than changes in attitudes to produce a desired "mix." Westernization and the spread of the English language may inhibit attempts to invoke Confucian values. Yet at the same time, most people want to be Singaporeans, with some local, Asian components. But the exact nature of what a future Singaporean should and will be like is still not clear. All these changes are being achieved in the face of stringent physical and cultural constraints, as well as external pressures. The process can be be successful only if the government exercises intelligent but not heavy-handed control (Chapters 5 and 6) and if the economic results and benefits are rewarding to most Singaporeans (Chapter 7). Given the immensity of the task, and the activities of a hard-driving government, anxieties and tensions during the process of social change can hardly be avoided.

3

From Raffles to Self-Rule, 1819–1959

Singapore is a "new" state in two senses. In the modern era, Singapore dates as an important settlement only from 1819, when it was established by the British East India Company. Also, although it was in many ways quite well developed sociopolitically and economically, Singapore did not gain complete independence until 1965—later than most of its neighbors in the region.

EARLY HISTORY TO 1945

Singapore's early history has been well documented;[1] consequently, the first part of this chapter provides only a basic sketch of the island's early history as a background to postwar developments. Singapore's existence was noted in ancient Chinese texts and in the Malay Annals, in which it was referred to as "Tumasik." One legend has it that in the eleventh century, a member of the royal family of Palembang named Sri Tri Buana became the island's first king and changed the name to Singapura, City of the Lion (some believe, however, less romantically, that the name is derived from *singgah*, meaning stopover, and *pura*, meaning city).[2]

In the early nineteenth century, the EIC was looking for a sheltered port along its India-China trade route in which it could station its warships in order to protect the route (particularly from the Dutch after the Napoleonic Wars) and keep the Straits of Malacca open, as well as transship goods. An Englishman serving as the lieutenant governor of Bencoolen (off West Sumatra) for the EIC, Thomas Stamford Raffles, was instructed to find a suitable station somewhere south of Malacca. In early 1819, he spotted Singapore island and determined that it commanded the southern approach to the Straits of Malacca, that it possessed suitable harbors, and that there were no Dutch on the island.

By exploiting a succession crisis in Johor, in January and February 1819, Raffles was able to conclude treaties with the *temenggong* (a powerful official of a sultan's government) of Riau-Johor, who was the territorial chief of Singapore, and Sultan Hussein Syah of Johor that allowed the EIC to establish a trading post at the mouth of the Singapore River. The Anglo-Dutch Treaty of 1824 settled conflicting territorial claims over spheres of influence in the region (and was intended to keep French expansion out of the archipelago), leaving Singapore in the British sphere, and in an 1824 treaty the sultan of Johor ceded the entire island and all islands within 10 miles of its shores to the EIC. In 1826, Singapore was joined administratively with Penang and Malacca as the Straits Settlements.[3]

When Raffles arrived in Singapore in 1819, it was only sparsely inhabited by tiny settlements of Orang Laut (similar to Malays) who were fishermen, petty traders, and pirates and by some Chinese who grew pepper and gambier for export to China. The first official census in 1824 showed that the population had grown to nearly 11,000. The Malays were still the largest community, but the Chinese population was rapidly catching up, and the Bugis (sailors, mercenaries, and pirates from South Sulawesi in Indonesia) were declining proportionately. By 1860, the population exceeded 80,000, of whom about 50,000 were Chinese, 13,000 were Indians, and 11,000 were Malays.[4] The European community was growing but remained a small minority consisting primarily of senior administrators and merchants.

Raffles was more of a planner than an administrator or implementer, functions he left to others. His decisions made Singapore a free port and determined that a laissez-faire policy best suited the EIC's limited financial commitment to the island. He also worked out the first town plan (including loosely segregated ethnic areas). Given a healthy modicum of law and order (financed largely by a government opium monopoly), accompanied by few administrative restrictions, Singapore grew on the back of trade as a transshipment and collecting post. Trade and prospects of economic advancement attracted (mostly indentured) immigrants, especially Chinese from the maritime provinces of South China.

After the establishment of Hong Kong in 1842, Singapore became less important for purposes of transshipment, and Singapore merchants consequently began to demand more trading opportunities in Southeast Asia—endeavors the EIC did nothing to promote. This led to growing local pressures for the transfer of the Straits Settlements to the British Crown in order to escape from, among other things, the EIC's neglect and restrictive fiscal policy. (The reasons for the transfer petition were complex and involved feelings among the European community that the Indian link was no longer relevant and that the British connection would allow more local input into affairs of the Settlements and would generate more positive action.[5]) In 1867, the Straits Settlements became a Crown colony. Local merchants also sought British involvement in the anarchic affairs of the Malay Peninsula to protect the investments and commerce, mostly in tin, of Singapore merchants. Although British government policy specifically forbade Britain's intervention in the Malay states, in fact in the 1870s it became increasingly dragged in (known as the British "forward movement" in the Malay Peninsula). These moves, the opening of the Suez Canal in 1869, and the advent of the steamship secured Singapore's continued growth and prosperity for a number of decades.

British colonial policy continued the tradition of basic noninterference in the everyday affairs of the local communities. But law-and-order problems created by "wars" between the rival Chinese secret society gangs (actually neither secret nor illegal before 1889–1890) led to various ordinances in the latter part of the nineteenth century that tried to register, and later to ban, the societies (neither policy was very successful in undermining them). A Chinese protectorate was established in 1877 to give the British administrators direct control over coolie immigration—and later over the secret societies—but it functioned with only limited success. Although secret societies continued to exist and to engage in various criminal activities (along with some residual benevolent functions), by the turn of the century open gang warfare no longer threatened the safety of the general public.

The rise of Chinese nationalism in the early twentieth century and—later in the late 1920s and 1930s—the rivalry between the Guomindang and Communists (in China, but with repercussions in Singapore) led to increased British involvement in Chinese affairs, and increased surveillance and suppression of Chinese political organizations and activities. In 1928, the first Straits Settlements enabling legislation to restrict immigration of Chinese males was passed, but it was not enforced until 1930. While the political attention of most Chinese was centered on activities in China, some locally born and English-speaking Chinese were concerned about local affairs, and a few of them were represented on the Singapore Legislative Council (which also contained representatives from the other ethnic communities). Nevertheless, at this time there was little demand for more representation, elections, or political rights among the local population.

Singapore became strategically significant again after World War I with Western awareness of Japanese armed power in Asia, and especially after the Washington Naval Treaties of 1922 when, as part of a major power agreement to restrict construction of battleships, Britain concurrently agreed not to construct a naval base anywhere east of 110 degrees longitude, thus ruling out Hong Kong and making Singapore the logical site. Construction of the Fortress Singapore naval base, with its big guns designed to fire armor-piercing shells against battleships as the key to its sea defense, began shortly thereafter and was completed just before the beginning of World War II.

In early December 1941, the Japanese landed troops near the Thai-Malayan border and marched and bicycled down the peninsula and accomplished the "impossible"—simultaneously knocking out U.S. sea-power at Pearl Harbor and U.S. airpower in the Philippines and then sinking the two British capital warships off Kuantan on the east coast of the peninsula. The siege of Fortress Singapore lasted only about two weeks. With the big guns useless against a land army, the water supply cut down to a trickle, no ships or airpower to call upon, a civilian population in panic, and troops in semidisarray, General Arthur Percival surrendered Singapore to the Japanese on February 15, 1942.

Syonan (light of the South)—the Japanese name for Singapore—was occupied by the Japanese for three-and-a-half years until British forces landed in September 1945 to accept the Japanese surrender. The occupation was a period of terrible hardship for the civilian population (and, of course, for the prisoners of war in Changi jail and elsewhere). The Chinese were singled out for atrocities because of historical enmities, Japanese frustrations over the continuing war in China, and Chinese involvement in and leadership of the anti-Japanese resistance in Malaya (mainly by Communists). With trade and commerce stifled, the currency worthless, food scarce, health care abysmal, and public services in a state of collapse, the British, under the direction of the British military administration, were welcomed back to Singapore as liberators. As with the rest of colonized Southeast Asia, however, the situation was not the same as before the war—the myth of "white supremacy" had been irrevocably shattered, and Singaporeans began demanding more political say in policies that affected their lives.

POLITICAL AWAKENING: THE TURBULENT YEARS, 1946–1959

When British civilian rule was reestablished in April 1946, the Straits Settlements was disbanded. Malacca and Penang were joined with the Federated and Unfederated Malay States to form the Malayan Union, and Singapore was made a separate Crown colony. Although in 1948 the Malayan Union was replaced by the Federation of Malaya, the 1946 geopolitical division was maintained, primarily because Singapore's large Chinese population would have upset the ethnic balance in Malaya but also because Britain wanted to ensure its continued control of Singapore for strategic purposes.

Although the Labour government in Britain was encouraging the goal of eventual self-government throughout its colonial empire, the British were concerned about the growing influence of the Communists inside Singapore's trade unions and Chinese middle schools.[6] The unions were already flexing their considerable muscle in a series of highly disruptive strikes, first in October 1945 and then regularly throughout 1946 and 1947. Further, the first indigenous Singaporean political party, the multiethnic Malayan Democratic Union, formed in December 1945 to protest the Malayan Union, was thought by many to be a Malayan Communist Party (MCP, later CMP) front organization (the party dissolved itself in June 1948 to avoid being proscribed). British concern for internal security in Singapore was heightened when "the Emergency" was proclaimed in Malaya in 1948 as a consequence of the MCP's guerrilla violence.[7]

Because of internal security problems posed by the Communist challenge, and fear that the Communists would ride the wave of postwar nationalist emotions unless progress was recorded in the direction of political liberalization, the policy of the British was to transfer gradually some power to the non-Communist English-educated Straits-born subjects of Singapore. The critical political division that was emerging in Singapore was between the English educated of all races and the Chinese-educated Chinese. The former were stereotyped as privileged, politically apathetic, exam oriented, competitive, individualistic, and not culturally "solid." The latter were identified as cultural chauvinists and either Communist or pro-Communist. Their attachment to Chinese culture was viewed as a political and emotional attachment to China and, after October 1949, as pride in the strong "New China" under Mao Zedong (the Communist victory in China undermined the traditional leadership of the conservative Chinese business leaders, many of whom were Guomindang supporters).

The political divisions between the local population took on more salience when the British agreed to hold elections, although the franchise initially was very restricted. At the first elections for the Legislative Council in March 1948, for six elected seats, only a fraction of the populace was eligible to vote, and only a fraction of those bothered to register and vote (interestingly, because of literacy qualifications, Indians made up 45 percent of the registered voters). The Progressive Party (PP), which had been formed less than a year before, enjoyed significant electoral support and won three of the seats (the other three were won by Independents). The elected members were all English-speaking lawyers and political moderates.[8] The PP also won most of the contested seats on the Municipal Commission in 1949. In the 1951 Legislative Council elections for nine seats, about 50,000 electors registered, more than double the number in 1948. The PP won six of the seats, and the dominance of the moderates continued, but the party was extensively pro-British and was badly out of touch with the masses.

It was clear to the British that with constitutional progress, as pledged, increasing numbers of Chinese-educated people would invariably get the vote and that these were the people to whom the MCP was devoting its energies, with some success. Singapore was still simmering with discontent: There was widespread unemployment, housing was critically short, wages were low and working conditions poor, and union agitation and ethnic animosity kept political tempers hot. In 1950, there were riots over the future of a Dutch girl brought up as a Muslim by a Malay family (the Maria Hertogh riots), and in 1954 police and Chinese students clashed violently over the British attempt to get Singapore males to register for national service (the scheme was then dropped).

Despite security reservations, in 1953 the Rendel Commission (under Sir George Rendel) was appointed to provide a new progressive constitution for Singapore. It issued its report in 1954, and the "Rendel Constitution," which came into force in 1955, provided for the automatic registration of voters and a legislative assembly with an elected majority. The leader of the majority party would become the chief minister and would select a cabinet. There would be some degree of self-rule, but several important subjects would be reserved as British prerogatives. Also, the British governor would not be required to accept the advice of the chief minister. Elections were set for April 1955 and provided the stimulus for the formation of several new parties. In late 1954, the Labour Front (LF) was formed, under David Marshall and Lim Yew Hock, as a liberal but moderate left-wing party, and in November 1954 the People's Action Party held its inaugural meeting at Victoria Memorial Hall. Under the leadership of some English-educated professionals led by Lee Kuan Yew (see Chapter 5), the PAP was backed by pro-Communist trade unionists and Chinese students who could generate the support of the Chinese-educated Chinese and the lower classes. The PAP was viewed as a radical, socialist, anticolonial party, and its clenched fist salutes and singing of international Communist songs did little to alter this view. The PAP demanded immediate independence through merger with Malaya, although this position was not to the liking of the Communists (see Chapter 4). In February 1955, the Democratic Party was formed as a conservative and communal party dedicated to preserving and enhancing Chinese culture. Also contesting was the PP, which remained confident that it would repeat its earlier successes, and the Alliance (a coalition of separate ethnic organizations, like its parent and namesake in Malaya).

The electorate was now more than 300,000 and included a much higher proportion of Chinese-educated voters. The Labour Front won the most seats, ten out of twenty-five, and with the support of the Alliance (three seats) and two nominated members, it formed the government with Marshall, a lawyer of Iraqi-Jewish extraction, as chief minister. The PP and the Democrats performed poorly (they later joined forces as the Liberal Socialist Party). The PAP contested only four seats and won three, with the strong support of pro-Communist organizations. The PAP could probably have formed the government if it had contested more seats, but Lee and his English-educated colleagues believed it would be politically fatal to form a government under the Rendel Constitution. As Lee said, "History has shown that those who take office before independence never take office after it."[9]

The political career of David Marshall has become a subject of some interest because judgments on his motives, political stands, and performance differ. Some are critical of Marshall as a headstrong, hot-tempered, flamboyant, and egotistic individual who never really seemed to anticipate or appreciate fully the consequences of his political words and deeds. Others view Marshall as a charming, principled idealist who, despite some honest blunders, believed himself to be a populist moving to the same rhythm as the people.[10] He may, in fact, have been all of these things. What is beyond doubt is that his tenure as chief minister was stormy and that later in his career he was badly used and misused by the pro-Communists.[11]

Marshall's fourteen months as chief minister were punctuated by riots (the bloody May 13, 1955, Hock Lee Riots and the 1956 rioting in Kallang Park), a Chinese school sit-in, and strikes (in 1955 there were seven times as many strikes as in 1954). The mob in the streets was in a combustible mood, and the government was viewed as having capitulated to unionists and Chinese students and as being incapable of controlling leftist provocations.

The British were exasperated by Marshall's unwillingness to take firm action and had little confidence in his ability to govern effectively. Nonetheless, after Marshall provoked a constitutional crisis over the governor's discretionary powers, the British acquiesced in his demand for talks on constitutional reform. Marshall then swore that he would resign unless the talks resulted in complete self-rule for Singapore. The first All-Party Constitutional Mission to London (First Merdeka Talks) occurred in April–May 1956. After tough negotiations, the British offered almost everything the delegates had sought, including the enfranchisement of 200,000 China-born aliens, but would not yield control over emergency internal security powers. Lee and a majority of the other delegates urged Marshall to accept the package, but he refused.[12] In June 1956, Marshall resigned, fully expecting that his cabinet would follow suit, but it did not.

Lim Yew Hock, the former deputy leader of the LF, became the new chief minister. He has been described as the "antithesis" of Marshall— a tough, action-oriented, hard-drinking, white-collar trade unionist, allegedly with some Triad associations; bold and resolute but also relaxed and pragmatic, he could communicate with most local people in their native language.[13] Faced immediately by a wave of union strikes and Chinese student protests and sit-ins, Lim hit back with an extensive anti-Communist security crackdown involving liberal use of the legal weapons of detention, banishment, deregistration of organizations and societies, and closure of two troublesome Chinese middle schools. Unlike Marshall, Lim was willing to use a whole arsenal of measures against disturbances and to call in the British Army when deemed necessary. He was, in fact, committing political suicide by using strong-arm tactics, which led to his being viewed by the people as a tool of British imperialism and a colonial stooge. He compounded this by using as much force against the students as he applied against rowdy unionists (and thus was perceived as attacking Chinese culture) and by claiming all credit himself (rather than pointing at the British) for the security drive. The worst violence occurred during the October 25–30, 1956, riots that followed a student sit-in, a government ultimatum, and the arrest of most of the pro-Communist Middle Road[14] (or Open United Front) trade unionists (thus inadvertently relieving considerable pressure on PAP moderates). The riots left 13 dead, 127 injured, more than 1,000 arrested, and extensive property damaged.

Historically, however, the most important arrests occurred on August 22, 1957, when thirty-five pro-Communists, including five on the PAP Executive Committee (later called the Central Executive Committee) were detained. These arrests were particularly significant because at the PAP party conference elections on August 4, the pro-Communists had contrived to seize control of the party from the moderates through manipulated elections. The arrests gave the moderates the opportunity to regain control and alter the party constitution to prevent any further "coups" (see Chapter 5). Thus, for the second time, the Lim Yew Hock government greatly aided the PAP moderates. Was this coincidental? John Drysdale wrote that there is no evidence of any collusion, and Dennis Bloodworth reported a conversation with Sir William Goode (the chief secretary at the time and later the governor) in which Goode denied there was any idea or plan to rescue Lee and the PAP moderates.[15]

Lim Yew Hock was politically committed to seeking constitutional reform, and although the prospect of giving the vote to most Chinese residing in Singapore must have been chilling (if indeed he appreciated his political predicament), he might have thought delivering a new constitution would afford some political payoff. The second All-Party

View of the city along the waterfront during the late 1950s.

Constitutional Conference was held in London in March 1957, and substantial agreement was reached. The third conference, to settle details of the new constitution, was held in April and May 1958. The new constitution gave Singapore nearly complete internal self-rule (Britain retained control of defense and foreign affairs). The thorny issue of internal security was resolved by the novel approach of an internal security council comprising equal numbers of Singaporeans and British but with the deciding vote in the hands of a representative from the Federation of Malaya. The Singapore (Constitution) Order in Council came into operation on November 28, 1958.

A citizenship act was passed that created a new Singapore citizenship for those born on the island or who had resided there for eight years, and the process of registering voters began. Meanwhile, however, the LF had fallen apart. Marshall had objected to the constitutional agreements in 1957 and had quit the party. As the new darling of the Left, he formed the Workers' Party (WP) in November 1957. A year later, Lim Yew Hock grouped his followers into the new Singapore People's Alliance (SPA). In December 1957, the first elections for City Council were held. The PAP obtained the most seats (thirteen of fourteen contested), and PAP populist Ong Eng Guan became the mayor. The pro-Communists had worked for both the PAP and the WP (which won four out of the five seats it contested). Soon after, however, the MCP issued a directive to support the PAP and not split the progressive vote (the Communist bosses still believed that Lee could be handled, or discarded, once the PAP came to power), and consequently the WP lost overwhelmingly at a by-election in July 1958.

For the May 1959 Legislative Assembly election, registration had been automatic and voting compulsory. More than half of the nearly 590,000 electors would be voting for the first time. Lim Yew Hock's government was clearly in trouble—it was tainted by its use of security measures and by allegations of corruption, and, strangely, it was not given much enthusiastic political credit for the new constitution. Further, its performance record was suspect, even given the excuse of colonial interference: The economy was in shambles with trade declining; unemployment was rising; severe shortages existed in housing, schools, and health clinics; and the local birthrate was unmanageably high. During the campaign, the Liberal Socialists and the WP (after it was dumped by the pro-Communists) were left wondering what had happened to their audiences and party workers.

The PAP looked a winner. The PAP announced its continuing commitment to complete independence through merger with Malaya and its promise not to take office, if elected, until eight detainees (basically the Middle Road group) were released from Changi jail (action on other detainees would depend on the merits of each case). Nevertheless, the focus of the campaign was on bread-and-butter issues, with merger as the ultimate cure for economic woes. By this time, the British had full confidence in Lee Kuan Yew,[16] although not all in Singapore shared this view. Civil servants feared purges and cutbacks, and businesses feared nationalization (approximately thirty-six firms were planning to move to Kuala Lumpur if the PAP won),[17] but the latters' fears were soothed immediately after the election.

The election swept the PAP to power with forty-three of fifty-one seats and more than 53 percent of the popular vote. Lim Yew Hock's SPA won four seats, the Alliance won three, and an Independent captured the remaining seat. Marshall's WP and the Liberal Socialists were humiliatingly shut out (Marshall himself lost to Lim Yew Hock). Huge celebrations were held on the evening of June 3, when Singapore was proclaimed a state.

On June 4, after the British had granted permission for the release of the eight prisoners and after the detainees had signed documents proclaiming their conversion to democratic socialism and to the PAP's non-Communist aims, they were released. The detainees were photographed as a group joyfully releasing a white pigeon (some say it was a dove) from a cage. Bloodworth noted that Western innocents might regard this as a symbol and gesture of peace. The Chinese, however, have another allusion: "Freeing the white pigeon" is Cantonese slang for a successful and profitable caper."[18] Lee was not laboring under any misapprehensions. During the campaign, he had said that the "real fight" between the PAP and the MCP (many of whose members were in the PAP) would begin *after* the election. None of the detainees was given an important job in the government or position in the party, and all were denied access to secret files.

4

The Quest for Stability and Prosperity, 1959–1989

On 5 June 1959, we formed the government. Few men took over with less euphoria. We knew we were in for a grim and gruelling battle.

—Lee Kuan Yew[1]

Yet there were no publicly visible doubts or discernible fears in the PAP government that assumed power on June 5, 1959. Under Prime Minister Lee Kuan Yew, it was a young, action-oriented government, with tendencies toward zeal and puritanism and a relentless impatience to achieve results. The average age of the members of the first PAP cabinet was thirty-seven years. Eight of the nine were English-educated university graduates; the ninth was Chinese-educated but bilingual. They were bright, energetic, restless, eager, and determined.

Lee and his "moderate" associates had already decided that the survival of their government was probably going to depend on effective performance.[2] The PAP had not made vast and unrealistic campaign promises (on the contrary, it had stressed the need for economic sacrifices) or inordinately raised expectations. But because the PAP Communists and pro-Communists[3] were potentially capable of toppling the moderates since they controlled most grass-roots associations and much of the trade union movement and could whip up the support of the Chinese educated, the moderates believed that they had to gain the confidence and allegiance of the people before the next review of Singapore's constitution (due in 1963).

The first act of the government was, as promised in the campaign, to abolish the City Council as cumbersome, expensive, and unnecessary for such a small place. The move also eliminated the position of Ong Eng Guan, the PAP's populist and rabble-rousing mayor and chief rival to Lee for leadership of the PAP. In the first few days of the new administration, after finding the government treasury depleted and a

53

Lee Kuan Yew, prime minister of
Singapore since 1959.

substantial public debt, ministers volunteered for salary reductions,
teachers had their salaries cut, and civil servants earning more than
$270 per month (mostly English educated and mostly not pro-PAP) had
their supplementary allowances cut off. Budgets were frozen, expenditures
pared, and taxes raised on gasoline, land, and cigarettes. Weekly "Meet
the People" sessions between PAP legislative assemblymen and constituents were initiated; a massive cleanup of Singapore by squads of
volunteers, including ministers, was launched (the Keep Singapore Clean
Campaign); and the Corrupt Practices (in Chinese, Foul Greed) Investigation Bureau was established. Additionally, strip shows and cabarets
were banned, and newspapers and periodicals, which were subject to
license renewals and permits, were warned to be objective in their
reporting and not to assume automatically an adversarial posture (several
permits were immediately withdrawn).

The government targeted two areas for reform: the bureaucracy
and the trade unions. The civil service had worked for the colonial

regime and was viewed by the new leaders as not having wanted the PAP to form the government. The PAP therefore took a number of measures to bring the civil service into line (see Chapter 5). Morale dipped at first but recovered as policies brought in positive results.

Dealing with the trade unions and the unruly labor situation, and consequently undermining Communist influence, was a more delicate political matter. The government position was set out in a memorandum by Minister of Finance Goh Keng Swee in October 1960: Singapore needed industrialization, and to achieve that it needed industrial peace. The government intended to begin securing that peace by curbing splinter unions (the Trade Unions [Admendment] Act of 1959) but did so by couching its actions in terms that implied that unionism would be strengthened as a result. In fact, unions were not really "tamed" until legislation in 1967 and 1968 stripped them of most powers. By then, the National Trades Union Congress (see Chapter 5) had been built up as the premier "umbrella" body over unions and was openly the partner of the government.

The main thrust of the PAP's social policies was directed toward building more schools and health clinics and, above all, toward providing government housing through the Housing and Development Board (see Chapter 2). Because of limited resources, the government aimed initially only at achieving a "minimal standard" of education, health care, and housing for all. Economically, industrialization was seen as an important, although partial, answer to Singapore's chronically high unemployment. Merger with Malaya (and a common market) was held out as the panacea to Singapore's economic problems. To pave the way toward merger, Malay was made the national language.

The PAP governing style emerged quickly: its leaders wore white short-sleeve cotton shirts open at the collar as befitting busy government servants intent on turning ideas into action. There was no pomp, no junkets abroad, no graft or scandal—only examples of hard work, thrift, and dedication.[4]

Lee and his moderate associates in the government, realizing that most party branches and secondary organizations were under Communist or pro-Communist control, used the government machinery to establish grass-roots organizations, such as the People's Association (PA) and Citizens' Consultative Committees (CCCs) and community centers (see Chapter 5), to build support for their policies and counter the influence of the radical wing of the PAP. Further, to undercut the radicals, the government stopped using the party or legislature as forums for discussing policies. A style of no discussion and little consultation developed out of this background. Similarly, the pattern, which persists, of largely ignoring the party machinery and ordinary membership between elections was a result of the internal PAP struggle between the moderates and the radicals (see Chapter 5).

In 1961, the PAP faced two important by-elections. By this time, there was considerable dissatisfaction with the party, and its popularity was slipping. Some of the reforms had seemed overhasty to observers; the belt-tightening economic policies, especially the taxes, at a time of recession and inflation had hit the poorer classes; and many resented what they perceived to be an unfeeling and arrogant government unwilling to listen to any criticisms. Furthermore by 1961 there had not been enough time for PAP measures to take effect (for example, the numbers in public housing rose only 2 percent between 1959 and 1961) and thereby lend credibility to the government. Nevertheless, the PAP felt confident going into each of the by-elections.

In December 1960, a disgruntled Ong Eng Guan, having been sacked as minister of national development for incompetence and expelled from the PAP in July and then suspended from the Assembly in December after unsupported charges of nepotism against Lee and another minister, resigned his seat. Ong, a Hokkien, stood in the April 1961 by-election against the PAP candidate—Jek Yeun Thong, a Cantonese—in Hong Lim, a poor, mainly Hokkien-speaking constituency in the heart of Chinatown with a high percentage of illiteracy. Jek and Lee were frustrated in the campaign by their inability to speak much Hokkien (later, Lee learned the dialect); the issues put forth by the PAP were rational and logical but complex for the electorate; and the personal attacks against Ong (for bigamy) backfired and generated support for the underdog among an electorate that admired a man who had two wives. In addition, Ong was a charismatic figure with wide popular appeal that extended beyond his own dialect group, and he won 72 percent of the votes cast (despite the fact that the Communists had backed the PAP candidate). As one PAP old guard summed it up, Ong's victory taught the PAP that if "the ground is not with you, no amount of organization can turn the tide."[5]

The second by-election, in July 1961 in Anson, was a contest between the PAP and David Marshall of the WP. The rift within the PAP had now reached a crisis, and the Communists were prepared to humble the government and show the moderates that they could not survive without Communist backing. Halfway through the campaign most of the party workers walked away, and just before the balloting the PAP head of the Harbour Board Workers' Union, whose members and families constituted more than 20 percent of the electorate, advised his union members to vote for Marshall. Marshall won by 546 votes— another crushing blow to the PAP.

The crisis that led to Marshall's July victory had its origins in a May 27, 1961, luncheon speech in Singapore by the prime minister of the Federation of Malaya, Tunku Abdul Rahman, who had suggested, to the surprise of many, that perhaps Malaya, Singapore, the British colonies in Borneo, and the British protectorate Brunei (which ultimately declined) might be united as "Malaysia." Tunku Abdul Rahman later said that he did not think his speech was anything more than a tentative suggestion, but Lee and the PAP moderates, who (like the two preceding chief ministers) had long sought merger and who needed a solid issue to use in the inevitable showdown with the radical wing, proceeded as if the Tunku's speech constituted a formal invitation. A vote of confidence on merger was held in the Assembly on July 21, 1961, and the PAP scraped by with a bare majority (twenty-seven votes in a house of fifty-one members). Thirteen PAP assemblymen defected to the opposition. The Communists were completely opposed to Malaysia—they did not want to become subject to the federation's tough internal security regulations—and they were prepared to split from the PAP over this issue.[6]

THE PAP SPLITS AND THE BARISAN SOSIALIS IS FORMED

On July 26, the thirteen parliamentary defectors, along with twenty-two branch officials, were expelled from the PAP. They then announced that they were forming a new political party, the Barisan Sosialis. Within hours of the split, thirty-five of fifty-one branch committees, nineteen of the twenty-three paid organizing secretaries, and about 70 percent of the PAP's rank and file defected to the Barisan. They seized premises, furniture, bank accounts, stationery, and even sewing machines. Furthermore, some government grass-roots organizations had been infiltrated, and the split left them in a state of disarray. Goh Keng Swee later commented; "What shook us was not that we had lost the fight to the communists, but that it was done with such contemptuous ease: just one flick of the hand, and we were down on the floor."[7]

The task of the PAP, with its precarious Assembly majority, was to prevent any further defections while it regrouped, reorganized, and began the task of selling merger to the people. In November 1961, a white paper was released stating the PAP position on the conditions for merger, and a referendum on merger was scheduled for 1962. The PAP conducted a relentless campaign based on intensive political communication: radio talks and debates, speeches in constituencies, and a newspaper barrage aimed at explaining merger and convincing the people of its merits.

The Barisan, which inherited most secondary organizations down to music and sewing clubs and which could mobilize mass support, lacked the critical element of astute leadership. A series of tactical blunders gave the PAP a chance. First, the Barisan came out in favor of its version of merger instead of demanding independence (because the colonialists had artificially separated Singapore from Malaya), thus giving up what might have been the winning position.[8] Second, the Barisan called the PAP proposal a "phoney merger" that would deprive Singaporeans of full political rights, a position considerably weakened by the Tunku's agreement shortly thereafter to give all Singapore citizens automatic Malaysian citizenship. Third, the Barisan demanded "complete merger" as a constituent state—unaware that such terms would disenfranchise nearly half of Singapore's citizens (those who were foreign born) because strict federation citizenship laws would apply. Fourth, the Barisan insulted the Tunku. This had the effect of alarming him and removing his lingering doubts about unification. He threatened he would close the causeway (the bridge joining Singapore to the peninsula) if Singapore rejected Malaysia. Fifth, the Barisan took its battle back to the streets, with strikes and mass protests, but this type of political agitation had more appeal against a colonial regime than against an elected self-governing administration.

The September 1, 1962, referendum on merger offered three different sets of terms of merger. An ordinance stipulated that blank ballots would be interpreted to mean that the voter was leaving his or her choice to the Assembly (the Barisan, later in the campaign, had called for a blank ballot vote as a protest). The referendum did not offer the choice of no merger—the PAP rationale was that it had been elected on a promerger platform. The results gave a stunning victory to the PAP. Its favored terms—a merger giving Singapore autonomy in labor, education, and other agreed matters and automatically making citizens of Singapore also citizens of Malaysia—obtained 71 percent of the votes (there were also 25 percent blank ballots).

The next challenge for the PAP was to win reelection in 1963. Despite the referendum success, it was not a forgone conclusion that the Barisan could be defeated again. This was clearly Singapore's most crucial election. The PAP was prepared to "play for keeps" and willing to use the entire legal arsenal of government. The Barisan blundered again. During the abortive Brunei revolt in December 1962 in which a group of radical leftists tried to seize power from the sultan, some of the Barisan's leaders agreed to recruit volunteers for rebel leader Sheikh Mahmud Azahari and thus left themselves open to charges of subverting Malaysia and abetting an illegal insurrection. In Operation Cold Store (a police operation to arrest subversives) in February 1963, 107 pro-

Communists alleged to be subversives were arrested, including 24 Barisan members (most of its executive committee) and 21 union leaders. This deprived the Barisan of its most effective mass mobilizers and left the leadership largely in the hands of its rather inept legislative wing (as Bloodworth wrote, the Barisan continued to frog-march to the cliff edge of political oblivion[9]). Soon after, seven Barisan assemblymen were detained when a demonstration turned violent, and they spent most of the campaign period in court. The Barisan was further crippled when the PAP froze the funds of three of the largest unions under Barisan control and dissolved five mass organizations.

When the election was called for September 23, 1963, the minimal legal notice (five days) was given, and the minimal legal campaign length (nine days) was specified (the campaign was interrupted by the birth of Malaysia celebrations on September 16). The PAP made full use of the mass media and ran a well-organized poster and banner campaign. The Barisan, by contrast, was unprepared and had trouble locating printers for its posters (local printers were fully booked with Malaysia Day orders; the PAP had lined up printers in Hong Kong), and the PAP had been first in booking assembly halls and securing advantageous spots for its posters. Government effectiveness was also evident by now: Unemployment was less than 3 percent (as compared with 13.6 percent in 1959); the low-cost housing scheme was making an impact; schools, clinics, and hospitals were steadily being built; and the Jurong industrial complex was a showcase. Finally, the PAP's success in achieving merger and ending colonial rule was a crucial factor operating in the government's favor. The election results gave the PAP thirty-seven of fifty-one seats (47 percent of the vote). The Barisan won only thirteen seats, although it collected 33 percent of the vote (the final seat went to Ong Eng Guan, now heading the United People's Party, while the old right-wing parties won no seats).

MALAYSIA: FROM MERGER TO SEPARATION

After all the efforts involved to achieve Malaysia, the results for Singapore were traumatic and unhappy: Twenty-three months of a turbulent relationship were terminated by Singapore's quick expulsion from the federation on August 9, 1965. The period of Singapore's incorporation in Malaysia and the separation have been extensively studied;[10] only the highlights of the events leading to the breakdown will be discussed here.

The problems derived from ambiguities in the terms of merger and in Singapore's proper role in the Federation and from profound incompatibilities between the styles and personalities of the Alliance (the ruling coalition government in Kuala Lumpur) and those of the PAP leadership, especially between the Tunku and Lee Kuan Yew: "The Alliance was conservative, the PAP socialist; the Alliance was bent upon defending Malay privilege, the PAP demanded a "Malaysian Malaysia" in which all races would have a seat in the sun; in Malaya the Alliance governed and the PAP was in the opposition, in Singapore the PAP governed and the Alliance was in opposition."[11] These problems were exacerbated by Indonesia's aggressive policy of armed confrontation against Malaysia as a "neo-colonial" creation.[12]

There were early disputes over the division of revenues (which were magnified in December 1964 when Kuala Lumpur wanted to increase Singapore's financial contribution to the federal government), over the terms of Singapore's development loan to Borneo, and over budgets. Furthermore, the promised progress toward a common market, which was very important to Singapore, did not materialize, reputedly because Malaysian finance minister Tun Tan Siew Sin, president of the Malaysian Chinese Association (MCA), did not want to increase Singapore's economic advantages at the expense of MCA members engaged in business. The PAP's entry into Malaysia was greeted with hostility by the MCA, which recognized it as a dangerous rival for the support of the Chinese, and the "ultras" of the United Malays National Organization (UMNO)—the dominant party in the Alliance—who were appalled by the implications of the victory of three PAP Malay candidates over UMNO candidates in the 1963 Singapore election and to whom the PAP's support of multiracialism was anathema.

The PAP for its part seemed devoid of ethnic and political sensitivity and barged into politics in Malaysia without appearing to recognize the delicate fabric of the new federation. With cold logic and fiery public pronouncements, Lee and the PAP sought in turn to replace the MCA in the Alliance, establish a straight coalition with the Alliance, and then, rebuffed and determined to forge a realignment, challenge the Alliance with an alternative coalition based on the concept of a "Malaysian Malaysia" (which called for ethnic equality and the end of Malay political dominance).

An exasperated Tunku noted, "Instead of doing what they want in a quiet and practical way, they tread on everybody's toes, knock everybody's head and bring about chaos, suspicion, misunderstanding, hatred and trouble," and at the time of separation, "as soon as one issue was resolved, another cropped up, where a patch was made here a tear appeared somewhere else and where one hole was plugged other leaks appeared."[13] The ambiguities and the contrasting styles and personalities of the leaders made the union very difficult to manage, the sabotage by the MCA and Malay ultras was corrosive, and the PAP's determination to become a significant Malaysia-wide political actor rapidly doomed the merger.

Several events led directly to the Tunku's decision to expel Singapore. First, the PAP's intrusion into the Malayan peninsular elections in 1964, albeit minimal, angered the Tunku, who believed that it was contrary to his agreement with Lee (also contrary to the understanding were the activities of peninsular UMNO and MCA workers in Singapore). The PAP's electoral participation soured its relations with the Tunku and raised ethnic tensions in the process. Second, on July 12, 1964, UMNO ultra Syed Jaafar Albar organized a Muslim convention in Singapore, headed by a Malay national action committee, against the "victimization" of Malays by the PAP, thus escalating ethnic emotions and hatred. Nine days later, a procession of 25,000 Muslims convened to honor the Prophet's birthday degenerated into race riots in which 21 were killed and 460 injured during eleven days. In September, following the death of a trishaw driver, more race riots broke out and more deaths resulted.

On May 9, 1965, the Malaysian Solidarity Convention, which comprised five opposition parties from various parts of Malaysia, led by the PAP, was formed as an alternative to the Alliance. To Malays, this represented provocation. At the UMNO General Assembly one week later, there were persistent and angry demands for the Tunku to arrest Lee Kuan Yew. The Malay ultras had wide and vocal support and successfully pressured the UMNO moderate leadership to take action about Singapore. They tried first to create a split in the PAP leadership by encouraging Goh Keng Swee and Lim Kim San to replace Lee at the helm and second, it is alleged, to undermine the PAP, preparatory to arresting Lee, by persuading Ong Eng Guan to quit his Hong Lim seat (which the PAP had lost twice) in the hope that the Barisan candidate would defeat the PAP in the ensuing by-election in July 1965.[14] But the PAP won the by-election. To some observers, at this point the death knell sounded for Singapore's incorporation in Malaysia.

While convalescing abroad after a painful attack of shingles, the Tunku decided that Singapore had to be expelled because of the danger of further race riots and because of the pressure on him to arrest Lee and administer Singapore under emergency regulations. Last-minute talks in Kuala Lumpur proved futile. A genuinely sorrowful Lee went on television to announce the separation, lamenting that "all my life, my whole adult life, I have believed in merger." Now he had to offer to Singaporeans, and had to govern, what he had previously called a "political joke"—an independent Singapore.

THE FIRST YEARS OF INDEPENDENCE:
PRIORITY TO SURVIVAL

Independence for the island of Singapore was a sudden, shocking, and sobering fact. In the end, it brought out the extensive talents of the PAP leadership, and it tapped successfully the abilities and energies of the Singaporean people. But at first even survival seemed a daunting task. Economically, Singapore had no natural resources, not even enough of its own water for its needs, and its domestic market was too small to give much support to its economy. In terms of security, Singapore had no defense forces at the time of separation other than two battalions of an infantry regiment, and many of their personnel were stationed in Sabah. Relations with Malaysia were barely civil, the result of economic barriers, retaliatory measures, and Malaysia's refusal to order its troops to vacate their barracks in Singapore (see Chapter 8) until British financial pressure was applied in 1966. (Malaysia's recalcitrance reflected, in part, security concerns that grew out of Indonesia's confrontation policy.)

The Singapore Constitution, adapted rather hurriedly from the existing state constitution inside Malaysia, established some of the basic parameters for government. Singapore would be a republic and a parliamentary democracy with a figurehead president as head of state. There would be one legislative tier only (Parliament), as previously. Multiracialism would be a guiding principle, but cognizant of geopolitical and historical factors, Singapore's leaders made Malay one of the four official languages and continued its status as the national language. Furthermore, the flag would be based on Malay symbols, and the Constitution would recognize the special position of the Malays as the indigenous people, although this would apply more to certain special opportunities, such as free university education for qualified Malays, than to rights. (See Chapter 2.)

The initial tasks of the PAP leadership were to identify sociopolitical, economic, and security priorities; study small-state models (Switzerland, Israel, Finland, and, later, Sweden); develop appropriate strategies and programs for these priorities; and then rigorously implement them. The overall goals were political stability, economic prosperity, and security, and the political lexicon stressed survival, the "rugged society," mobilization and modernization, guts and stamina, and the development of economic skills and self-reliance. Much of the onus for survival was put on the citizenry, which had to be dedicated, willing, committed, and able to comprehend that the government's goals required loyalty, order, discipline, public-spiritedness, and a "tightly knit society" (structurally integrated, cohesive, and possessing the spirit of teamwork). These were attitudes and traits the PAP leaders believed helped to explain how some small states survived. "At the leadership level it demanded unified purposefulness; at the administrative level, efficiency; and at the popular level, obedience."[15] Having decided that Singapore should not act or be perceived as a "third China," the PAP leaders set out the guidelines for the long process of inculcating a genuinely multiethnic Singaporean national identity. Steps were taken to promote this identity through integrated housing, integrated armed forces, an emphasis on bilingualism, constant political reminders in the media, and national holidays complete with parades, rallies, and political symbols.

The PAP government wanted a compliant citizenry so that it could get on with building the new state and nation. Because the PAP had extensive legitimacy at independence, especially given the prevailing sense of crisis, and because the PAP enjoyed extensive voluntary compliance from the citizenry, the government did not indulge in many liberal sentiments over sectors of society it deemed troublesome. Although it did not ban the Barisan (no party has been proscribed in Singapore except the Communist Party of Malaya), the government undermined the Barisan's support bases among students and unionists. Students seeking entrance to university were required to obtain "suitability certificates," and university instruction, especially in the departments of political science and philosophy, was scrutinized. In October and November 1966, student protest sit-ins and examination boycotts resulted in a number of arrests and expulsions (many of the students were Malaysians). The press also came under close government scrutiny and control (see Chapter 2).

Economically, the PAP leaders decided that to industrialize and modernize quickly and successfully, Singapore needed (1) the capital and technology of multinational corporations (MNCs), which were invited to share in Singapore's economic growth; (2) policies to promote and develop their concept of the world as Singapore's market place (or extended "hinterland"); and (3) proper domestic conditions to attract MNCs and trade. By conditions, the government meant political stability, an educated and skilled work force (preferably English speaking), a recognized set of rules for foreign firms and freedom from excessive red tape, no graft or corruption, appropriate support industries and institutions, and, most of all, industrial peace and established wage norms, that is, tame unions (see Chapter 7). In August 1966, a trade union act made strikes illegal unless the majority gave its consent by a secret ballot; the act also banned noncitizens and those with criminal records from being union officeholders. A series of further acts in 1967 and 1968 severely pared down the unions' areas of legitimate concern.

Singapore also had to survive the shock, announced in 1967 and implemented in December 1971, of the British withdrawal from its military bases on the island (and nearly everywhere east of Suez). At one blow, Singapore lost 20 percent of its GNP and 30,000 jobs directly (civilians working at the base and domestic help). The shock was cushioned, however, by the free transfer to Singapore of British military real estate and fixed assets and British financial assistance, and fortunately by late 1971 industrialization had progressed sufficiently to pick up the slack.

One of the highest priorities of the governors of Singapore at independence (and to this day) was defense and security. Relations with Malaysia were uneasy, and each government was suspicious of the intentions of the other (the Malaysian government had difficulties adjusting to Singapore's new status as an independent and sovereign state, which was compounded by UMNO ultra opposition to the "solution" of separation and by Indonesia's attempts to play up to Singapore while still fighting Malaysia through confrontation). As an adjunct to the existing two regular battalions constituting the SAF, a voluntary people's defense force was created (including several ministers and members of Parliament [MPs]). A group of Israeli military advisers was brought in to assist, and in March 1967 compulsory military national service for males was introduced (see Chapter 8).

By 1967, Singapore's fears about its neighbors had subsided considerably, and relations were on the mend with Malaysia as matters such as double taxation, import quotas, duties, and licenses were regularized and their currencies were separated (in June 1967, after sixty years). Singapore's citizenry was responding to the government's various pushes, and the economy was taking off. After two years and an enormous amount of energy, resolve, courage, clear thinking, and astute planning, Singapore's leaders had built a new nation-state and Singapore had survived and begun to prosper.

THE EMERGENCE OF A DOMINANT PARTY: ELECTIONS IN INDEPENDENT SINGAPORE

At the time of separation, the Barisan Sosialis should have been in a position to reap political rewards from the failure of merger. After all, it had condemned the terms of merger with Malaysia as "phoney" and late in the day had in effect opposed merger itself. But incredibly, the Barisan called Singapore's new status a "phoney independence" resulting from a neocolonial plot perpetrated by British and U.S. imperialists.[16] This demonstrated a complete misreading of the mood of the people. The Barisan compounded this denigration of independence by calling for the removal of British bases—the source of employment for thousands of Singaporeans.

In November 1965, the Barisan announced that it would boycott Parliament. The party's legislative agenda had never had high priority, and now the party chose to avoid facing the vote in Parliament on the legislative changes needed to take account of Singapore's independence. In 1966, the Barisan announced that it was quitting parliamentary politics and adopting a "back to the streets" strategy of mass political agitation. (Reminiscent of the turbulent 1950s, there were big street protest marches between March and June 1967 and riots after May Day political demonstrations; politically, however, the strategy failed to elicit a favorable mass response.) In October and November 1966, the remaining Barisan MPs resigned their seats. This was not a ploy to spark a series of by-elections to test the PAP—the Barisan did not contest elections again until 1972.

In 1968, with the Barisan boycotting, the PAP won all fifty-eight of the parliamentary seats in the general election (fifty-one were uncontested). No PAP candidate received less than 82 percent of the popular vote. The PAP, campaigning on its social and economic record,[17] also won every seat in the general elections of 1972, 1976, and 1980 (and all by-elections between those years), gaining between 69 and 75 percent of the popular vote against a handful of opposition parties, including the Barisan. (There are about twenty registered parties in Singapore, of which between six and eight contest regularly.) With no opposition in Parliament (1966–1981), the PAP clearly fitted the mold of a dominant party (as opposed to a one-party system, in which opposition parties are either illegal or nonexistent). Nevertheless, Lee Kuan Yew warned against complacency, saying that the opposition would inevitably return if there was a severe economic downturn or a desire for change on the part of younger voters.[18]

The PAP's parliamentary monopoly ended on October 31, 1981, when in a by-election Anson voters rejected the PAP candidate and returned J. B. Jeyaretnam (after several failed efforts to win a seat) of the Workers' Party. Many view this opposition victory as a watershed of sorts because it punctured the myth of PAP invincibility and stimulated not only renewed opposition efforts but the interest of Singaporeans in the *idea* of an opposition (many of the voters, by this time, were too young to remember the economic dislocation, deaths, and destruction resulting from violent political activity in the 1950s). The PAP contributed to its own defeat in Anson through a number of political decisions that angered the electorate: the Port of Singapore Authority decision to demolish blocks of flats in Anson to make way for a new container complex (and the fact that the PAP candidate was related to the head of the Port Authority); the long waiting list for housing and the availability of only noncentral resettlement locations; and the Speak Mandarin

Singapore crowds listen to Prime Minister Lee Kuan Yew during a campaign rally, December 1984.

campaign, which was unpopular with many of the 78 percent Chinese in Anson (see Chapter 2). The campaign was the first run by the "successor generation" (see Chapter 6), and some mistakes were made. For example, the threat by a second-generation minister that the government might curtail certain government benefits if the PAP candidate was not elected was not well received (and, in fact, no benefits were curtailed).

The December 1984 general election introduced 215,000 new young voters into a total electorate of 1.7 million. The PAP went into the election in a fighting mood—determined that Anson should prove to be an aberration, not a precedent. But the PAP also went into the election fast on the heels of pushing a series of unpopular policies, thus violating its previous standard procedure of a one-year moratorium on such policies prior to an election. This departure from procedure was the direct result of the PAP's urgent preparations for the transition from the old guard to the successor generation. PAP leaders felt that this might be Lee Kuan Yew's last election and that he would be able to carry the burden of these harsh and somewhat unpalatable "medicinal" social remedies better than his successors.

The most contentious policies were the raising of the CPF withdrawal age (which especially angered the forty-five to fifty-five age group that would have to wait longer before being able to cash in savings) and the introduction of Medisave, a compulsory health insurance scheme (see Chapter 2). The other unpopular policies were the introduction of "streaming" of students at the Primary 3 level (see Chapter 2) and the "graduate mother" scheme of incentives to try offsetting an undeniably "lopsided pattern of procreation" (see Chapter 2).

The speed, and unavoidably cruel nature, of leadership transition further weakened the PAP and thereby undermined morale and organizational efforts as the experienced old guard was shoved into retirement. In 1984, two more senior ministers and fourteen MPs did not seek reelection. The ministers, especially Dr. Toh Chin Chye, were somewhat resentful (and, in fact, Toh was prudently given his seat to contest, although he did not regain his ministry and has since become an outspoken critic of certain government policies).

For the seventy-nine seats in the election, the PAP put up twenty-six new, young, highly qualified university graduates (including four Ph.D.s, eight M.A.s or equivalent, and fourteen B.A.s, of which six were professional degrees). Against the PAP were forty-eight candidates from eight opposition parties, which coordinated their efforts in a loose front, and three independents, contesting forty-nine of the seats (thirty PAP candidates were returned unopposed). The opposition parties offered little by way of alternative programs or policies, except promises of more welfare spending. But they hit upon a responsive chord with the simple complaint that the government was elitist, arrogant, "meddling," and unfeeling.

The election results left the PAP hurt and surprised and the opposition jubilant: The PAP won only seventy-seven of the seventy-nine seats. Jeyaretnam retained his Anson seat with an increased majority, and Chiam See Tong, leader of the Singapore Democratic Party (SDP), captured Potong Pasir, a constituency that he had cultivated since 1979. A handful of other PAP candidates won by very narrow margins. The PAP was shocked not so much by the loss of two seats in troublesome constituencies as by the general voting pattern, which saw the PAP popular vote decline by 12.6 percent (to 62.9 percent) across the board. It was clear that the electorate was registering a loud protest. As one local academic put it: "Poorly educated candidates with only rabble-rousing arguments, whose commitment to Singapore and its political life were questionable, managed to score impressively."[19] In one constituency, an unknown opposition candidate who did not campaign because of ill-health received one-third of the votes against a senior cabinet minister.

ADDING BALLAST TO THE SYSTEM:
THE 1988 GENERAL ELECTION

The PAP in the 1980s was aware of the problem of a changing electorate—better educated, economically secure, less compliant (possibly the result of being educated in English), with no personal memories of the political turmoil of the 1950s and early 1960s, interested in political rights and freedoms, and enamored of the *idea* of political opposition. Lee Kuan Yew noted ruefully in respect to the absence of strong political competition that the young voters "think they are missing something." To satisfy the desire for some opposition in Parliament and to discourage electors from voting for the opposition solely on this ground, in July 1984 Parliament passed an act providing for the appointment of up to three nonconstituency MPs (NCMPs) allocated to the opposition candidates with the highest losing percentage of votes. But this act did not seem to diminish the protest vote in 1984; the nonconstituency seat offered after the election was rejected by the opposition as a "second class" seat and remained unfilled for the life of that Parliament.

On January 1, 1985, the new cabinet, which comprised the successor generation, Lee, and two other old guards, was announced (political succession is discussed more fully in Chapter 6). Goh Chok Tong, the first deputy prime minister, stated that Lee Kuan Yew would not be involved in the daily administration of the country and that unless the issues were so fundamental that they involved Singapore's national security, the new team did not expect to be overruled by the prime minister.[20]

The new team declared that it intended to be more open and to consult the people on major issues, it also admitted that some mistakes had been made in not explaining policies more fully and in not listening to criticisms. At the same time, the new team did not want to be perceived as caving in to pressure or as seeking short-term popularity at the expense of long-term effectiveness. Beginning in mid-1986, a series of tough and controversial actions were taken. Legislation was passed restricting the circulation of certain foreign publications (see Chapter 2) and curtailing the political activities of the Law Society, a number of youth were arrested under the Internal Security Act (ISA) for involvement in an alleged Marxist conspiracy, and a diplomatic wrangle occurred with the United States as the result of the activities of a U.S. diplomat (the "Hendrickson affair") in allegedly encouraging Francis Seow (who was detained under the ISA) to organize an opposition group of English-educated professionals (see Chapter 5).

With two opposition members elected to Parliament, the government began televising parliamentary debates to educate the citizenry and to expose the opposition for what the PAP believed it was—incompetent, poorly informed, and impractical. The debates were widely viewed (better than the soap operas, some said). The audience was able to see that Chiam was polite, deferential, and totally without guile (and almost seemed to cringe when the prime minister entered the chamber)—he was a "good man" who was "afraid of the PM." Jeyaretnam won respect as a dogged and persistent performer who "[stood] up to the PM" and was perceived as not being as bad as the PAP had proclaimed, even though he often got his facts wrong or was not able to substantiate his allegations.[21] Surprisingly, a newspaper survey in April 1985 showed that 63 percent of the viewers who watched the parliamentary debates were left with negative feelings about the PAP, and another 20 percent were neutral or uncertain. Viewers clearly felt sympathy for the intellectually outmatched and numerically outnumbered opposition—as underdogs and martyrs.[22] Parliamentary debate lost some of its spark after November 1986 when Jeyaretnam was disqualified from holding his seat as a result of his conviction and sentence for false declarations about party accounts, although Chiam bravely carried on alone.

Because of the leadership transition, the decline of nearly 13 percent in the PAP's popular vote, and Lee's instinctive distrust of some aspects of democracy and majoritarian rule (sentiments apparently shared by the successor team), the government began to look at ways of altering the political system to add "ballast" so as to provide protection against the worst vagaries of the one-person, one-vote system. PAP leaders talked constantly about how everything could be dismantled overnight by a "freak election result"—an anti-PAP protest vote that inadvertently pushed the PAP from power; an outcome, widely recognized, that many of the protest voters would not desire. In November 1985, Goh Chok Tong said that the one-person, one-vote system would be left intact but that minimal qualifications for candidates might be imposed and that elected MPs might jointly serve as local town councillors so that voters would benefit directly by electing competent representatives at the local level.[23]

The idea of minimal qualifications was subsequently dropped, but in early 1987 Goh Chok Tong proposed the establishment of a "team MP system," later called Group Representation Constituences (GRCs), for about half of the constituencies. Under this system, three constituencies would be collapsed into a single voting bloc (like a super constituency) and each elector would cast a vote for a three-person team (a party would have to offer three candidates as a team in the enlarged GRC, all of whom would become MPs if they polled the most votes). Linked directly with the GRC concept was a plan to introduce MPs as town councillors in charge of managing the massive complexes of government flats in the new town areas. Thus, stated various PAP leaders, the voters would have to "live with their choice of MPs," not only as national representatives but more intimately as town councillors making local decisions directly affecting the lives of constituents.[24] The rationale appeared straightforward: Electors would think twice about voting for unqualified or potentially untrustworthy candidates if these people might become their own town councillors.

The PAP contended that the change would be "politically neutral." The opposition and a good number of Singaporeans, however, complained before and during the Parliamentary Select Committee hearings in January 1988[25] that the strategy was designed to "fix" the opposition by subterfuge and by changing the electoral rules. Certainly the scheme appeared to disadvantage the opposition parties, which had been largely "parties of personality" coalescing around one leader. With the team voting system, the leader, if he contested in a GRC, would have to run collectively with two party members against the PAP team, thus diluting the force of his personality. Further, the opposition had always had trouble finding good, qualified candidates, and the need to put up a solid team compounded this problem. Finally, many suspected that some "troublesome" constituencies, such as Anson, might be combined in a GRC with two strongly PAP constituencies.

To counter these widespread charges, the government published its cabinet papers on the subject, including letters and memos, which showed that Lee Kuan Yew had proposed such a system as early as 1982 as a way of ensuring continued minority and especially Malay representation in Parliament. The GRC teams, the government pointed out, would be required to include minorities. Lee, who said that he had allowed himself to be overruled on the way the scheme was presented to the public, blamed public cynicism on the second-generation leaders who had decided to avoid explaining the ethnic basis of the plan, choosing instead to present the proposal as a management scheme for town councils.[26]

The opposition responded that Lee was trying to fix what was not broken because no PAP Malay candidates had lost for years (to which Lee replied that he was looking ahead, over the horizon). Some Malays were unhappy about their ethnic group being singled out as needing Chinese team members in order to win electorally, and some Indians were unhappy about *not* being singled out as a special minority. But by openness and astute management, the issue was successfully defused, and by the time the GRCs legislation was passed in Parliament in May 1988, the PAP motives no longer seemed to be a major issue.

With the constitutional changes, the electoral system has been altered so that no fewer than one-fourth and no more than one-half of the total parliamentary seats can be combined as GRCs. Further, each team contesting a GRC must contain at least one member of a minority (with committees established to certify minority candidates as genuine). At least three-fifths of the GRCs must be set aside for Malay minority representation; the rest comprise Indians and other minorities. All remaining seats continue as single-member constituencies. Goh Chok Tong called the GRCs a necessary modification of the British model of democracy and an unprecedented institutional mechanism to ensure multiethnic parliamentary representation.

Under the legislation for electoral boundary changes enacted in June 1988, the number of parliamentary seats was increased to eighty-one (from seventy-nine), with thirteen GRCs (containing thirty-nine seats) and forty-two single-member constituencies. Seven constituencies were eliminated as a result of population shifts out of the center, and nine new constituencies in the new town areas were created. Most of the "troublesome" and potentially difficult constituencies were eliminated by being split into other constituencies,[27] although Chiam's constituency of Potong Pasir was left intact and remained a single-member constituency (Chiam reported that he had been given a choice).

The town councils legislation passed in Parliament in late June 1988 called for MPs to run the housing estates (in which a majority of Singaporeans lived) by chairing the town councils. The program was to be introduced gradually so that by February 1991 all constituencies would have town councils led by MPs. The legislation met with little determined opposition because it represented some decentralization and was viewed as a step toward the exercise of local government and grass-roots democracy. Nevertheless, the government made it clear that the legislation was intended as an agent of political stabilization against "temporary voter mood swings." Because the MPs would now have a greater direct impact on local affairs, the people would need and want to vote for competent, trustworthy, and dedicated candidates. Given the PAP's ceaseless scouting and cooptation of talent, the implication was that such qualities were virtually a PAP monopoly. Furthermore, the government asserted, badly run councils would not be bailed out; the voters would have to take the consequences if they elected corrupt or incompetent MPs.

Another major constitutional initiative to be raised in 1988 was the proposal for an elected president. It was first suggested publicly by Lee Kuan Yew in a National Day speech in 1984 (and apparently had been discussed in cabinet as early as 1982), and it was widely assumed that the position was being created for Lee when he resigned as prime minister. After considerable public discussion and excitement, the issue disappeared from public view until mid-1988 when the government put the proposal before Parliament for debate and issued a government white paper on the subject. Once again, the government expressed concern that the system needed ballast and safeguards, that if the opposition gained power because of a freak election result, it could raid the painstakingly built-up national reserves and dismantle overnight the attributes of an honest, meritocratic public service. Consequently, the government proposed to have an elected president with some blocking powers playing a "custodial role" (see Chapter 5 for details and Chapter 6 for its implications vis-à-vis the political succession process). The elected president proposal, still widely viewed as an institution especially designed for Lee Kuan Yew, elicited immediate and strong negative reaction, even by a number of PAP backbenchers during the parliamentary debate. The government had to promise that it would not rush the legislation through Parliament but would send it to a parliamentary select committee and expose it to full public discussion and scrutiny.

On the evening of August 17, 1988, Parliament was dissolved, and a general election was called for September 3, 1988 (making this the first election since 1972 not held in December). On nomination day, the PAP found itself challenged for seventy of the eight-one seats, including a contest in the prime minister's constituency.[28] The WP put up thirty-two candidates, campaigned under the slogan of "It's Time," and clearly pinned its brightest hopes on winning the GRC of Eunos, with the team of Francis Seow, who had been released from detention, Lee Siew Choh, the former leader of the Barisan Sosialis, and a TV star, Mohd. Khalit bin Mohd. Baboo, as its minority member. The SDP, with eighteen candidates, concentrated its campaign on appealing to electors to deny the PAP a two-thirds majority necessary to alter the constitution. The WP and SDP arranged an electoral agreement to avoid splitting the opposition vote. Five other minor parties contested twenty-one seats, and there were four Independents.

The PAP campaigned on its record under the slogan "More Good Years" and focused on the issues of the town councils and elected president. In an election that saw the departure of the final remaining old guard apart from Lee Kuan Yew, the PAP put up fourteen new candidates as part of its rigorous self-renewal program. Unlike the situation in 1984, the PAP did not go into the election on the heels of a series of unpopular decisions and actions. The economy was buoyant, the government had dropped a plan to cut the size of the public sector by 13,000 places (emphasizing zero growth instead), and the government promised public service bonuses if economic growth was maintained. Further, the PAP approved in principle the use of CPF savings for tertiary education costs, had effectively defused the GRC issue, and the town council scheme was not only generally popular but also an immensely persuasive factor in the PAP's favor. As one letter in the *Straits Times* put it, while many would be prepared to vote for an oppositon candidate and would enjoy watching him criticize the government in Parliament, they would be less prepared to entrust the quality of their lives and comfort of their homes to an opposition MP.[29]

Some PAP problem areas did exist, however. There was considerable unhappiness over increasing government restrictions and repression, especially the arrests under the ISA in 1987 and 1988 (see Chapter 5). Nevertheless, these issues appeared to be of major vote-determining concern only to a segment of the young, English-educated middle class, whereas the majority remained more concerned with traditional bread-and-butter issues.[30] Although the opposition centered its campaign around broad themes of alleged PAP abuse of power and the need to check perceived authoritarian trends in Singapore politics, the most controversial issue to emerge was the proposal for an elected president. Not only were there numerous questions asked about particular details and ambiguities, by PAP backbenchers as well as the opposition and citizens in letters to the newspapers, but the opposition was able to suggest that the legislation might subvert the power of Parliament and change the system in ways unanticipated by the citizens. The opposition also hinted that the post was being tailored for a "towering figure" and raised the specter of future amendments to strengthen further the powers of the president. Prime Minister Lee complained that "if I had taken this through in 1984 when I first raised it, there would not have been all this fuss. But the opposition has stirred up and caught up with a certain mood of querulousness" among Singaporeans.[31]

To recapture the initiative and further explain its intentions and motives, the PAP, in an unprecedented move, agreed to debate the elected president issue on live television against the WP and SDP. There were three debates—one each in English, Mandarin, and Malay—on August 30 and 31. During the debate in English, Goh Chok Tong said that the prime minister had told the cabinet that he was not interested in becoming the elected president. Goh also backed away from an unequivocal "no" on holding a referendum on the issue.[32] Finally, to defuse the issue, in one of the final campaign rallies Prime Minister Lee hinted at the possibility of holding a referendum and stated that he would not seek to become Singapore's first elected president.[33]

There was one other very curious incident during the campaign that left nearly everyone perplexed. This was a speech by Lee Kuan Yew in which he criticized Goh Chok Tong. Some observers felt that the prime minister's comments hurt the PAP because the opposition was able to make good use of them (saying, for example, that Singapore deserved better than "second best"). Others believed that the PAP benefited by a sympathy vote for Goh (see Chapter 6 for implications on the succession issue).

The election results gave the PAP eighty of eighty-one seats, losing only Potong Pasir to incumbent Chiam of the SDP. Lee Kuan Yew was returned with the largest majority (81.6 percent), followed by Lee Hsien Loong (79.1 percent), both against Independents. But the PAP did not regain the nearly 13 percent of the popular vote it lost in 1984, and in fact the party dropped 1 percent (to 61.8 percent) in its percentage of total votes won. Conversely, it could be said that the PAP was successful in virtually halting the decline. Although the opposition won only one seat, it came close in a handful of seats, especially those with a high Malay vote.[34] The PAP narrowly won the GRC of Eunos, which had a sizable Malay community—by 1,279 votes out of about 72,000 cast— against the WP team, despite an announcement that Francis Seow, probably the most popular of the WP team members, would be tried for tax evasion in December. Interestingly, this time the WP agreed to accept two NCMPs, for Francis Seow and Lee Siew Choh of the Eunos team, although Seow was later convicted of tax evasion before Parliament convened in January 1989 and thus was disqualified from being an NCMP.

The opposition was pleased with the popular vote it received, sensing a permanent shift of voter allegiance that put it on the brink of a significant breakthrough against PAP dominance. The leader of the WP felt that the opposition did not win more seats because of the new electoral boundaries, the GRCs, the PAP use of government grass-roots organizations, media bias, the success of the "Swing Singapore" party on Orchard Road (see Chapter 9), and the town council scheme. Chiam of the SDP noted that the task ahead was to dispel voter fears that the opposition could not run the housing estates, and he added that to begin to do so, the opposition needed to recruit better-qualified candidates.[35]

Even before polling day, it was widely recognized that one important feature of the election would be Lee Kuan Yew's reaction to the results. It was thought that Lee was already impatient about the way Goh was running the campaign, with the PAP on the defensive about the elected president issue and with concessions under pressure concerning the possiblity of a referendum. It was believed that if the prime minister was unhappy with the results, he would delay his retirement, and Goh might be maneuvered out as successor[36] (see Chapter 6).

The prime minister's postelection statement seemed positive. He said, "This is the people's verdict on the new guard. . . . Their consultative style has won them support."[37] Lee seemed satisfied that the PAP had more or less maintained its level of support in spite of an 18 percent change in the composition of the electorate (since 1984, 50,000 former voters had died and there were 206,000 new voters—in addition to 215,000 new voters in 1984). On the other hand, there is still some uncertainty about Lee's political intentions. Both Lee and Goh indicated that the prime minister would step down "within two years" of the September 1988 election—by some reckoning a delay in his departure (see Chapter 6).

NEARING THE END OF AN ERA: PROBLEMS AND ISSUES

As retired PAP stalwart S. Rajaratnam once commented, "Success has its contradictions." The PAP today faces the critical tasks of revitalizing the dominant party and completing the political transition from the founders to the successors while avoiding potentially damaging internal factionalism (see Chapters 5 and 6, respectively). The changing nature of the electorate, which is increasingly younger, English educated, and middle class and therefore potentially less compliant and less accepting of authoritarianism, is a further challenge to the governing party. Nearly two decades ago, Lee noted that the English educated do not riot. They may still not riot, but today Lee sees opposition as the product of Western attitudes encouraged by an English education.[38]

There has always been an anti-PAP vote of about 25–30 percent. Many intellectuals and professionals, well-educated "yuppies," and idealistic youth want the PAP to respect and show regard for their political views, and consequently they resent the PAP's "we know best" attitude. The PAP's ability to gain about 75 percent of the popular vote may be a thing of the past: The new benchmark is about 60 percent, below which the opposition begins converting votes into seats. Some of those who vote against the PAP undoubtedly desire a change of government, but a large number are simply making a statement: They want to be consulted on major issues, have their criticisms taken seriously and have a more open and competitive political system (without, of course, sacrificing on government efficiency and effectiveness). "People may think that the PAP are an arrogant lot, but they can rule, and they can deliver the goods—the opposition still has a credibility problem."[39] There is a danger, however, that the "soft" anti-PAP vote could harden and turn cynical if the PAP responds by tightening the system and repressing dissent; tactics that worked in the past when all kinds of dangers to Singapore seemed real and immediate may not work in the future, unless democratic practices are abandoned altogether. The dilemma is that the PAP leaders, old guard and successor generation alike, in fact have little faith in the masses' ability to understand their own best interests and to make rational political choices.

It appears that the change accompanying the new team is one of style (which does not mean that it is merely cosmetic) more than of substance (the successor generation *does* share the values, philosophies, and political ideas of Lee and his original cohorts). Nevertheless, within the PAP hierarchy an ongoing debate of vital consequence to Singapore's future must surely be taking place to define the limits of participation and legal dissent.

Many Singaporeans are nervous at the thought of Singapore without Lee Kuan Yew. He has largely transcended partisan politics—he is the founding father, not a distant historical figure like George Washington but still profoundly a father figure. Thinking Singaporeans are proud of his international renown and what has been accomplished in Singapore, and his wishes for Singapore are given respect and credence despite the growing awareness that he is an elitist (he has never disguised the fact) and that his style can be arrogant and abrasive. It was not a fluke that he received the highest percentage of popular vote in the 1988 election. There is not much gratitude in politics, however, and there is now also a growing yearning to "give Goh Chok Tong a chance" and a fear that Lee may eventually overstay his tenure (hence much of the controversy over the elected president issue).

Beyond this, and in spite of the undoubted stature of Lee Kuan Yew, the PAP and the successor generation have a problem. Most democratically elected dominant parties eventually decline simply because people want a change, regardless of performance or the consequences of such change. As Goh Chok Tong has noted, "Electoral amnesia can set in after a prolonged period of peace and plenty."[40] Consequently, the PAP needs to cut a new image in the post–Lee Kuan Yew era and build up its credibility and legitimacy on a new basis that offers a perception of change but does not lose any governmental dynamism and effectiveness. It is a tall order.

5

Politics and Government in a Dominant-Party System

THE CONSTITUTION: FORMAL INSTITUTIONS

Singapore's Constitution provides the framework for the political system, particularly the executive (the president and the prime minister/cabinet), the legislature (Parliament), and the judiciary. The relative powers of these bodies differ from those in a presidential-congressional system, such as the United States. The executive, although a "product" of Parliament, actually dominates it. The judiciary's powers are fewer than they are in the United States because it is more limited in its ability to strike down laws as contrary to the Constitution; in particular, it is less able to restrict the executive from detaining citizens without trial. The Constitution also provides for institutions that implement the laws, including the armed forces (see Chapter 8) and the civil service.

The Constitution dates from colonial times, so it "is really what the British had given to a municipality."[1] Changes to the Constitution were made when Singapore became part of Malaysia in 1963 and again after Singapore had independence thrust on it two years later. The result is a variation on the British theme of parliamentary government. There is an elected legislature (with elections at least every five years), and the leader of the party that has a majority of the seats is appointed prime minister and governs with the aid of a cabinet, which he chooses from members of the legislature. The cabinet is responsible to the legislature; it ceases to be the government upon losing the legislature's support.

The system differs from Britain's in four main ways. First, Singapore has a constitution, which can be amended by a two-thirds majority of the total members of the legislature (some constitutional changes also need a two-thirds majority in a referendum), while Britain has no formal constitution. Second, Singapore has only one house of Parliament; there

77

is no equivalent to the British House of Lords. Third, Singapore has an appointed advisory presidential council with rather limited powers; the council can draw attention to some types of proposed legislation that it thinks may discriminate against any racial or religious community. Fourth, instead of a monarch, Singapore has a president, elected by Parliament for four years, although reappointment is possible.

Political Institutions: The Executive and the Legislature

The first four presidents were, respectively, Malay, Eurasian, Indian, and Chinese. The third of these, Devan Nair, formerly a successful politician and trade unionist, was forced to resign the presidency on grounds of alcoholism. The president in 1989 was Chinese, Wee Kim Wee, a former journalist and diplomat who performed his duties with dignity and aplomb. The president's duties are not onerous, being mostly routine or ceremonial and acting as a focus for national loyalty and solidarity. If Singapore ever had several parties, however, and it was uncertain which party could put together a majority coalition, the presidency could become important because the president appoints the prime minister. Presidents may become bored; it is said that the second president, Dr. Benjamin Sheares, who was a surgeon, occasionally sought a change of pace by performing a few operations, and Devan Nair, after his appointment, said that he suffered from loneliness.

Just before the 1988 election, the government proposed that the president's powers be extended (see Chapter 4) to include the power to veto any measures by a future government that in response to popular pressures for spending threatened to dissipate the country's carefully amassed reserves. The proposal was spelled out in a government white paper as a basis for legislation (which would require a constitutional amendment but which as of November 1989 had not yet been introduced). The president (and a vice-president) would be elected by the people for a six-year term, but intending candidates would have to be approved by a small, impartial panel that would certify that the candidates possessed ministerial, executive, or administrative experience, preferably in the public sector, and had the ability to discern and take account of the public interest. The president's powers would also include control of other government assets and surpluses and some government loan-raising. Irresponsibility by a future government would also be limited by giving the president a check that would preserve the integrity and ability of the public service. He would be given a veto over certain specified appointments in the judiciary, in commissions making appointments in the public service and the armed forces, and in certain public boards, mainly financial ones. He would be able to attend, address, and send messages to Parliament.

The white paper was widely discussed before the 1988 election, and objections were made both inside Parliament—some government backbenchers spoke out strongly—and outside it. One criticism was that though the president was not "executive" he might still have sufficient power to diminish the role of the prime minister and the cabinet and their responsibility to the people. Another objection was that the proposed list of officials whose appointment would be subject to his veto was too long. Others admitted the desirability of checks on the government but advocated alternative means, such as a second chamber. Perhaps the greatest criticism was directed at the provisions for a vice-president. The white paper proposed that he would be required to have the same qualifications as the president and that he would be approved by the same panel. His job would be to assist the president, act for him if he were ill or absent from Singapore, and succeed him if he were incapacitated by death, illness, or resignation. The vice-president would be nominated by the presidential contestant and would face election at the same time. The chief objection was that—unlike the president—if he were a member of Parliament or the cabinet when chosen vice-president, he could continue in that office. Opponents objected that the vice-president could extend the president's influence in Parliament or in the cabinet and that in the event of a clash between the prime minister and the president, the vice-president could be torn by divided loyalties.[2]

The cabinet usually has between twelve and fourteen members. Although its decisions are made collectively, some members have more influence than others, as is obvious from the designations "prime minister," "first deputy prime minister," and "second deputy prime minister." Even in the days before there were deputy prime ministers, however, there was an inner circle in the cabinet consisting of Lee, Goh Keng Swee, and S. Rajaratnam, and a new version of such a group exists currently. Additionally, because the cabinet is formed on party lines, high rank in one tends to be associated with high rank in the other.

Parliament plays a restricted role in the system, partly because the cabinet is so powerful and believes that its policies—without much alteration—are likely to be the best for Singapore. Additionally, from 1968 to 1981, the PAP government held all the seats in Parliament. Given the strict discipline in the party, parliamentary debate tended to be limited.[3] In 1981, an opposition candidate was elected; in 1984, two; and in 1988, one.

By 1987, the PAP's feeling that government dominance should be tempered with more open dialogue and its desire to have more constructive opposition in Parliament led to the introduction of a new system of government (party) committees in Parliament. Nine committees were set up (the number was later increased to ten), each specializing in the subject matter of one or more ministries. Each committee had a chairperson and a secretary and was empowered to appoint a group of specialists to provide advice. These replaced party committees outside Parliament, which had been appointed after the 1984 election. In 1988, the government announced that soon the committees would be allowed to hold public hearings, as in the U.S. Congress. The committees were not meant to undermine the basic principle of ministerial and party control. It was unlikely that committee members would vote against a government bill; at most, they might express disapproval by abstaining. The new device should help secure more informed and responsible criticism, make better use of the time of backbenchers (now better educated than previously), promote additional feedback through links with the public, and prevent Parliament from degenerating into a rubber stamp. The committees have already contributed to making parliamentary debates better informed and also more lively.[4]

The Judiciary: Detention Without Trial

Singapore's judicial system consists of the Supreme Court (which has three divisions—the High Court, the Court of Appeal, and the Court of Criminal Appeal) and a number of subordinate courts. In some important cases, there may be an appeal to the Judicial Committee of the Privy Council in London[5] (a colonial practice that has been continued in some Commonwealth countries). The judiciary has been criticized for its pro-PAP leanings, although such allegations are difficult to substantiate. Trial by jury was abolished in 1970. There has been frequent criticism (by bodies such as Amnesty International) of the practice of detention without trial, which began in colonial days and which the government has continued to use against suspected Communists, left-wing trade unionists, students, "Chinese chauvinists," gangsters, and drug traffickers. This practice puts the onus on those detained to prove their innocence.[6] The numbers detained have dropped from hundreds to about a dozen during the last twenty-five years. By April 1987, only one left-wing political prisoner remained in detention, but further detentions (mostly for short periods) were made in 1988.

The rationale for detention is rooted in the "moderate" wing of the PAP's struggles against Communist organizations and knowledge of their methods. The government defends the practice, without apologies. Lee has referred to the difficulty of getting witnesses to testify in court because of the fear of reprisals. Additionally, he has asked why Communists who have lost in elections should be permitted to invoke the democratic process in their bid for power, when upon winning office themselves they would cut their opponents off from making use of that same process.[7] Detainees have been released only after providing signed, and often televised, confessions, although in the last few years these requirements have sometimes been relaxed.

In May 1987, sixteen persons were detained, as were a further six in June. The detainees were predominantly English-educated young professionals or Catholic social workers. About a third were released immediately; the rest faced detention of up to two years. The leading figure, Vincent Cheng, admitted that he had been influenced by Tan Wah Pow, a student activist of the mid-1970s who fled to Britain in 1975 to avoid national service. Cheng acknowledged having had Communist contacts, and the government claimed that a Marxist conspiracy had infiltrated Catholic organizations, the Law Society, and a drama group. (Later, four activist priests were banned from preaching.) In September 1989 Cheng repudiated his taped "confession," asserting that it had been made under duress.

By the end of 1987, only Cheng out of this group was still in detention. But in April 1988, eight who had been released after detention asserted their innocence, alleged ill-treatment during detention, were rearrested, and then reaffirmed the truth of their original statements. Patrick Seong, who had acted as a lawyer for some of the detainees was also arrested in April. The government contended that he had gone beyond his responsibilities as legal counsel, having become a propagandist for and instigator of his clients. He was released a month later together with most of the other detainees. A bizarre twist occurred when the government asked for, and obtained, the recall of a U.S. diplomat in Singapore for alleged interference in Singapore's affairs (an event that fortunately had only minimal effects on the good relations between the two countries). The government claimed that he had urged several Singapore lawyers to contest the next election as opposition candidates. One of these, Francis Seow, had been counsel to some of the detainees (including Seong) and was a former president of the Law Society (see Chapter 4). He was arrested in May on grounds similar to those given for Seong's arrest and was detained for two months. His release was timed to allow him to prepare for contesting the forthcoming elections. All these happenings excited considerable interest in Singapore and abroad and raised questions about the nature and the size of the alleged Communist threat involved. In August 1988, Amnesty International urged the Singapore government to investigate complaints of police torture and called for the release of the half dozen or so persons still in detention.

In May 1989, the last of the "old-time" political detainees, Chia Tye Poh, was released. He was not required to make any confession but was forbidden to leave the island of Sentosa without permission or to take part in any kind of political activity. A little more than a month later, however, the two remaining political detainees, Vincent Cheng and Teo Soh Lung, first arrested in May–June 1987, had their periods of detention extended for another two years.

The Civil Service: Statutory Boards

In order to put its policies into effect, the cabinet has to work through the public bureaucracy, which consists of two main elements— the civil service and a number of statutory boards. Singapore's civil service went through a difficult period when the PAP took power in 1959. Previously, the bureaucrats in most of the top posts had been "expatriates" (British and other foreigners) who had been responsible to another set of bureaucrats in Britain. The PAP government had only a few years to achieve its objective of replacing the expatriates with local people. Some of the existing local civil servants owed their positions to seniority rather than merit, many had not yet become accustomed to accepting responsibility, and a few found it hard to get used to the idea that they were now responsible to ministers elected by the people. They had to function as "servants" of a popular democracy, not as a ruling caste. Additionally, from a political angle, the PAP wanted not just to recruit English-educated Chinese, Malays, and Indians but also to harness the talents of bright, young Chinese-educated people, who, if denied power, were wide open to Communist influence.[8] On the other hand, some existing local civil servants feared that the new government had fixed stereotypes of them as servants of colonialism unalterably biased toward the status quo.

The government tackled these problems in a number of ways. It set up a political study center that gave courses on contemporary issues, emphasizing the influence of nationalism and communism and the nature of democracy. It reduced civil servants' allowances, as an "economy measure," although many thought that the main motive was to signal a "get tough" policy. Within a year or two, the allowances were restored, and after the 1963 election civil servants were given an ex gratia payment as a reward for their faithful service.

The government, acting through the Public Service Commission, was ruthless in stressing achievement criteria in the civil service both for hiring and promotion. It encouraged merit, as opposed to seniority, and there was no personal favoritism, although civil servants were expected to work loyally with the PAP. Many top civil servants' ability was recognized early, and they were given government scholarships at universities. Their salaries were (and still are) high as compared with neighboring countries (reducing temptations to be corrupt) and were competitive with those in Singapore's private sector. Nevertheless, many higher-ranking civil servants left to join the private sector, partly because of quicker promotion prospects, and in May 1989 the government announced large salary increases in an effort to arrest the trend. At the same time, corruption was ruthlessly tracked down and suppressed.[9] It is widely acknowledged that Singapore is not just the least corrupt country in Asia; it is also less corrupt than some Western countries. Currently the main anticorruption agency is directly under the Prime Minister's Office (PMO), indicating the high priority attached to it.

Politicians and civil servants work well together. The former feel that they can control the latter,[10] who, for their part, are spared having to put up with "masters" of only mediocre ability. After the PAP's nearly thirty years in power, civil servants expect ministers to produce their own top-level policies; many of these, such as the encouragement of female graduates to become mothers, are the product of the prime minister's far-reaching mind. Singapore is probably one of the few countries in the world where a civil servant can say "Yes, minister"—and, especially, "Yes, prime minister"—and the minister can be sure that his instructions will be carried out. Civil servants, for the most part, are left to evolve policies at lower levels.[11] The civil service is now so accustomed to dealing with a PAP government that it would have to make great adjustments to function with a government run by another party.

Singapore, on one definition, has approximately eighty statutory boards, which are useful for performing social, economic, and developmental functions because they are not covered by the same rigid regulations on budgeting, personnel, and so on, that apply to the ordinary civil service. Furthermore, decentralization, by allowing some autonomy to such bodies, lightens the load on civil service. The appropriate member of the cabinet appoints members of a particular board, usually with the approval of the prime minister. Some of the boards were already in existence when the PAP took office, but their numbers and the range of their functions have multiplied since then (see Chapter 7). To add to the complexity of the system, many of these bodies hold shares in private enterprises, thus indirectly extending the interests and reach of the government.

Singapore's limited talent pool requires that the membership of the statutory boards include some high-level civil servants. For example, in 1986, J. Y. Pillai, permanent secretary to the Ministry of Finance, was managing director of both the Monetary Authority of Singapore and the

Government of Singapore Investment Corporation, as well as chair of Singapore Airlines. In the past, some civil servants have been members of almost a dozen boards. So, paradoxically, while statutory boards decentralize government by allocating some functions outside the civil service, they also add to the duties (and subtract from the time) of some high-level civil servants. Boards also add to the power of these civil servants, which, given the increasing complexity of government and the economy, could become overwhelming if adequate political control were lacking.

In the formal system of government, the locus of power is in the cabinet and, particularly, in the prime minister. Parliament plays a smaller role, and interest groups are of even less account. The politician-civil servant relationship is a peculiar one. Politicians are much too able and the PAP has been too long in power for the civil servants to be "on top." At the same time, the responsibilities of the latter, especially those who are implicated in the operations of the statutory boards, are extensive. Additionally, it has become increasingly usual for civil servants and prominent employees of the boards to be selected as members of Parliament or even as ministers.

Perceptions of the exact roles of the various elements in the political system may differ, but it is undeniable that the system functions most efficiently. This is partly because merit is encouraged and corruption repressed. Also, factors such as smallness and Singapore's social discipline make control easier and obedience to government more probable. In the last analysis, however, Singapore's efficiency is rooted in the PAP's appreciation of the importance of implementation (a rarity in the Third World) and in the PAP's determination to achieve it.

INFORMAL INSTITUTIONS

The remaining institutions of government may conveniently be given the label "informal" because they are not described in detail in the Constitution. They include political parties and the elections in which they participate, a variety of interest groups, and several types of grass-roots organizations. Yet, as mentioned earlier, they do not operate apart from the formal organizations of government. For example, the PAP is often hard to distinguish from the government, and the trade unions and grass-roots organizations are very closely associated with the government and/or the ruling party.

The Party System and the PAP

Stability in a modernizing state depends largely on the strength and institutionalization of its political parties and party system. The parties are the organizations that control and channel participation and, through elections, provide legitimacy for the governing elite. In a modernizing state, dominant- and one-party systems tend to provide more stability than competitive multiparty systems (and the Westminster democracy ideal of alternating winners and losers is rarely found).

In Singapore, the PAP is a dominant party that operates within a framework of democratic procedures. Other parties exist—in October 1986 there were twenty-one registered parties. Since 1959, however, the ideas, policies, methods, and style of the PAP have dominated, although not completely controlled, the political process (the PAP must be somewhat responsive to citizen's demands and opposition complaints).[12] The PAP began as a mass mobilizing nationalist party, but, once in power, the parliamentary wing did not make extensive use of the party apparatus (the party bureaucracy and the branches) to maintain power. Nor did it continue to promote mass political participation. Furthermore, candidates and prospective ministers were recruited overwhelmingly from the civil service and the professions rather than from party workers and activists. Soon there were few party activists, and the party apparatus languished except at elections. The links for MPs at the grass-roots level were provided mainly by government agencies and institutions rather than by party channels. The roots of this unusual approach can be found in the party's internal struggle in the late 1950s and early 1960s.

Not too surprisingly, there has been a blurring of the fine line separating the government and the dominant party. Lee has said, "I make no apologies that the PAP is the Government and the Government is the PAP," and in late 1984 the party redefined itself as a "national movement."[13] To charges of using government organizations to partisan advantage, the PAP leaders have replied that the agencies and organizations set up as government institutions are for the PAP to direct and control because the PAP *is* the government—for example, in 1985 a minister announced that the HDB would give priority to PAP districts in providing maintenance services. The government has also not allowed opposition MPs to take charge of community centers or other government agencies in their constituencies. In the last several years, however, as the successor team has started to influence policy more, there has been an effort to revitalize the party and separate it in the public mind from the government.

The PAP has been able to forge its dominance over the Singapore electoral scene primarily through the exercise of political control and through effective governmental performance, significant economic growth, political stability, and incorruptibility. To do this, the PAP has regimented Singapore into a tightly knit society and meritocracy with strong laws to deter deviants. The PAP has also successfully filled all the available central political space as a "catchall" party that is basically nonideological, responsive, and anxious to recruit and/or coopt the best available political talent.[14] The PAP has done this without mass party membership (it is more interested in support than in card-carrying members) and without a massive party organization. Although never ideological in any formal or dogmatic sense, the PAP in the 1950s and 1960s espoused "democratic socialism" with an emphasis on the state's providing adequate health, educational, and housing services and on the goal of attaining a more just and equitable society. More recently, the party has labeled its ideology "socialism in the final analysis," meaning a mix of state capitalism, company welfarism, and socioeconomic self-reliance (less reliance on government welfare). The PAP leadership has also understood that it had to operate within the context of the prevailing political culture (see Chapter 6), but it has also worked hard to influence cultural values by seeking to preserve those it deems desirable while disparaging those it believes impede modernization and the promotion of an intelligent, informed electorate.

The origins of the PAP can be traced to Britain in 1949–1950, when a group of tertiary-level students from Singapore who had known each other from their days at Singapore's elite Raffles College found themselves caught up in the nationalist fervor sweeping through the community of foreign students from all parts of the empire. Lee Kuan Yew, Goh Keng Swee, Toh Chin Chye, and K. M. Byrne believed that Malaya (and Singapore) would gain independence soon and that, as was the case elsewhere, the British-educated graduates should provide the necessary leadership. By 1952, this group and journalist S. Rajaratnam had decided that there was a political vacuum on the Left and that they should form a political party to fill this space by aiming to attract the lower socioeconomic strata, especially unionists, and the mainstream of the Chinese community.[15]

To forge the bridge between the English educated and the Chinese masses, the English-educated group had to join forces with a number of Communist and pro-Communist political activists, led by Lim Chin Siong, who themselves needed the "cover" that the respectable English educated could provide for a legal party. As a result of this marriage of convenience, the PAP was established and held its inaugural meeting at Victoria Hall in Singapore in November 1954. Lee has described the united front as "an inarticulate, inchoate, indefinable compact" whose only glue was anticolonialism.[16] There was no trust between the two groups, but they understood one another.

During 1955–1956, many of the English educated in the party dropped out because of the growing extremist postures of the party and the violence being provoked in the streets. The moderates at the top of the party, having been captured from "below" were cut off and became incapable of guiding the course of events. Then the Communists decided to take firmer control of the party hierarchy. At a party conference election on August 4, 1957, the radical wing, having stacked the meeting with its own supporters, captured six of the twelve seats on the Executive Committee (later called the Central Executive Committee, or CEC), and the moderates refused to take office. On August 13, however, the Lim Yew Hock government arrested five of the six leftist members of the executive in a roundup of subversives (see Chapter 3). A special party conference was held on October 20, 1957, to elect a new CEC, and the moderates reassumed control.

The English-educated moderates then began to change the party rules to prevent takeovers in the future. In May 1958, all PAP members were reregistered and required to commit themselves to support of the party's non-Communist democratic objectives (one-fourth dropped out). Then in November 1958, the cadre system was introduced, dividing the party into ordinary and cadre members (party membership lists were [and are] secret, but there were approximately three hundred cadre and nine thousand ordinary members). The cadre were elected by a majority vote of the CEC after cautious and laborious scrutiny. Under the new party by-laws, only the cadre could attend party conferences, now to be held biennially, which elected the CEC.

The arrests of the top radicals and the subsequent changes in the party by-laws gave protection to the moderates in the CEC, although the Communists controlled most of the party branches and supporting auxiliary organizations. Despite the fact that the PAP had formed the government in 1959, the question of merger with Malaya led to an inevitable party split in September 1961. About two-thirds of the PAP membership, nearly all of its branches, and most of the party bureaucracy defected to the newly formed Barisan Sosialis (see Chapter 4). The PAP was left with only the shreds of a party organization with which to fight the referendum and the subsequent election, so it had to use government machinery and government organizations for grass-roots links. This marked the decline of the role of the PAP party and its complete subordination to the PAP government and parliamentary wing.

Today most of the roles one would expect a major party to perform are carried out by government agencies and organizations. The party becomes activated only at elections for help in the management of ground-level activities. Raj Vasil described the party as having little influence on government; no officials outside the parliamentary-ministerial wing; no organizational wing with a separate identity and mass base; no strong bureaucracy; no effective institutions for mass mobilization, recruitment functions, or loyalty-building; and no separate organizations for youth, women, or workers.[17] (A youth wing and a women's wing have now been established, however). Furthermore, political communication is transmitted largely from the top down rather than from the ground up.

Power in the party is concentrated in the CEC (twelve members are elected and up to six, but usually two, can be appointed), and this elite overlaps and coincides almost exactly with the top government leaders (hence adding to the difficulty of distinguishing between party and government). There are branches in every parliamentary constituency, but the MPs, who are branch chairs, devote little time to the branches, and constituents generally ignore the branch organization when seeking help or advice. The branches have virtually no say in the choice of candidates (the process of selecting candidates is carried out by the top government leaders/CEC members). There is no residence requirement for candidates, and few choose to relocate in order to reside in their constituency. Party functionaries and career workers are generally not rewarded with a candidacy, so party membership and work are not regarded as an appropriate channel for the ambitious and upwardly mobile. Summing it up, one senior minister commented, "There is not much for the party to do."

The institutional strength of a political party is measured largely by its ability to survive its founders.[18] The view of many or most Singaporeans is that Prime Minister Lee Kuan Yew *is* the party (and the government). Consequently, the problem of succession has been, and remains, a critical concern (see Chapter 6). The replacement of party veterans with years of experience and service and the retirement (at times virtually forced) of the founders, aside from Lee, have been rapid, divisive, and often contentious. Morale problems and the absence of "street-smart" veterans in the campaign undoubtedly contributed to the PAP electoral setbacks in 1981 and 1984 (see Chapter 4). To consolidate further power in the CEC in order to guard against the emergence of any dissident group within the party, a number of changes in the PAP by-laws were enacted in November 1982 (for example, biennial party conferences are no longer mandatory but are held only when the CEC deems necessary).[19]

In the September 1984 party conference election, Secretary-General Lee emerged as the only founding member on the CEC (although two were veterans who were not part of the successor generation). Since 1985, when the new team moved into all the important cabinet positions except that of the prime minister and in large measure became responsible for running the government, there have been efforts to rejuvenate the party, recruit more members, make it distinguishable from the government, and both raise and soften its image.

Throughout 1985, Goh Chok Tong, the first assistant secretary-general and first deputy prime minister, visited branches to discuss what needed to be done in order to reorganize and strengthen the party and to reach the target of recruiting twenty thousand more members by the end of 1988.[20] A number of initiatives have emerged. First, in April 1986, the CEC appointed ninety-six cadre members drawn from its branches and representing all occupational walks of life. Second, workshops, forums, seminars, "walkabouts," and "walkajogs" of leaders have been scheduled on a regular basis. Third, *Petir*, the party journal, has been instructed to devote more space to party and political issues (as opposed to social, educational, and governmental issues). Fourth, a PAP community foundation (to which the party donated $500,000) has been established to increase the party's involvement in grass-roots social, educational, and community projects, such as day-care centers, kindergartens, and scholarships (about two-thirds of all kindergarten children attend PAP education centers). To facilitate the functioning of the community foundation, the PAP planned to establish an additional party branch in each constituency—the already established constituency branches would continue to carry out political work, while new "foundation branches" would take care of the party's social and educational activities.

More significantly, the party also established a youth wing in September 1986 headed by B. G. Lee. The rationale for this move was that the party had been concerned with self-renewal at the top and had not given enough attention to recruitment (particularly of youth), channels of feedback, visibility and party image, and strengthening of the party machinery. The Youth Wing, for those between the ages of seventeen and thirty-five, was a means of mobilizing young activists, some of whom presumably would be MP material, and of getting a new generation of voters not only involved with the grass-roots but also openly identifying with the PAP.[21] Party leaders decided that the Youth Wing's activities would center primarily on political matters involving the mobilization of support for the policies of the PAP government among the young, affluent, and well educated—a segment of society that grew more critical of the PAP in the 1980s (in fact, the Youth Wing has also been involved in such nonpolitical activities as raising money for charities). At its high-profile inaugural convention in September 1987, two-thirds of its members were reported to be new recruits, and by October 1988 its membership had climbed to two thousand. Each of the party's eighty-one branches has established a youth wing headed by an appointed chair. At the top, as a coordinating body, is a central committee. In the 1988 general election, the Youth Wing produced five new MPs, all of whom were members of the central committee, and future candidates will likely be identified from and developed within the youth organization. The Youth

Wing is not intended as a pressure group, however, and there are no seats reserved for the Youth Wing on the party's CEC.

Another initiative has been the launching of a new Women's Wing of the PAP in July 1989 under the chair of MP Aline Wong. Goh Chok Tong first suggested the idea in 1987, but initially some of the leading PAP women had reservations that it would turn into a "tea ladies" organization. Subsequently they were reassured that the wing would not be expected to concentrate on "women's issues." Its goals are to help integrate women into the national decisionmaking process and to identify prospective women parliamentary candidates.[22] Interestingly, the PAP revitalization effort has increased the need for party funds, and in July 1989 the PAP held a first-ever fund-raising dinner.

As part of a general drive to alter the image of the PAP to meet criticisms that it is too authoritarian, arrogant, and paternalistic and in order to facilitate feedback and a sense of consultation, the party has put together a new manifesto called the National Agenda for Action. This is an effort to devise the means for achieving the high goals stated as the party's 1984 election theme, "Vision '99." Intended as a massive consensus-building and consultation effort, the PAP manifesto committee, under the chair of B. G. Lee, presented a detailed list of questions, including some politically sensitive ones, aimed at covering the major challenges and obstacles ahead and then invited people to join in a national debate on the options. As B. G. Lee stated in January 1987, the PAP would canvass the nation for ideas and then incorporate useful ideas from a broad cross-section of society.[23] For example, in 1988 a day-long seminar with a number of preuniversity students was held to solicit student views and discuss pertinent agenda issues. Because the manifesto committee was chaired by B. G. Lee and the first Youth Wing convention conducted five workshops on National Agenda topics, the National Agenda was viewed as having given the new wing an important and highly visible initial task. Since the National Agenda was approved in principle by Parliament, the PAP government has largely taken over the consultation task through submissions (more than one thousand by July 1988) to six advisory councils entrusted to draw up programs for and ways to implement the National Agenda for Action. The advisory councils themselves represent a consultative exercise—each is headed by a cabinet minister who appoints knowledgeable citizens to sit on the council.

It is too early to tell if the exercise has succeeded in its main goals of consensus-building, consultation, and participation. Much depends on whether PAP officials are perceived as having listened seriously and on the extent to which the PAP credits the citizenry with providing ideas. One problem that has been noticeable is that, among the well educated, those who have not been invited to participate on one of the councils or have not had their views specifically solicited feel annoyed at being overlooked. Although practically it is not possible for everyone to be consulted, Singapore is just small enough and the consultation aims are just grandiose enough for consultation to seem feasible. If the exercise eventually elicits a favorable citizen response, however, it could lead the new team to adopt a more open and consultative style.

Opposition Parties

The opposition—tiny, weak, poorly organized, and thin on policy proposals—gets 25–35 percent of the vote in Singapore elections. It gets support less because of its merits than from sympathy for the underdog, the belief that there is a need for *some* opposition, a desire to register displeasure with the PAP, and also from those who are implacable foes of the PAP.

As history has shown, dominant parties often decline, sometimes from rigidity, succession problems, corruption, or internal factionalism and sometimes just because people want a change. Youth, particularly, is attracted, however unreasonably, to the excitement of adversarial and oppositional politics. In dominant-party systems, the opposition usually presents a platform that is basically negative (antigovernment) wrapped in exhortations about the virtues of wider participation in the affairs of state. The opposition generally does not have a full or coherent set of policy proposals; it appeals to the disaffected, the impatient, and the bored. Such parties are often called "parties of pressure" because they can cause the dominant party to adjust its policies and practices and perhaps attempt to absorb or coopt them.[24] One prominent Singaporean (and long-time PAP supporter) commented that "the opposition gets sympathy because they are trying to do a job that more and more Singaporeans think is necessary—that is, articulating grievances."[25] Opposition parties are also quite often dominated by the personalities of their leaders, who can be motivated by a variety of reasons.

Singapore's opposition parties are mainly parties of personality and only marginally parties of pressure. Only a handful contest regularly, and most of those that do put up only a few candidates at each election. Most opposition parties have feeble or nonexistent party organizations, little money, few active party workers, and few policy positions aside from criticisms of PAP policies and pronouncements. In a by-election in 1981, J. B. Jeyaretnam, leader of the WP, won against the PAP and broke the myth of opposition impotency. In the 1984 general election, Jeyaretnam successfully defended his seat, and Chiam See Tong, leader of the SDP, also won. In 1988, the only opposition member elected was Chiam See Tong (see Chapter 4).

The WP was formed in 1957 under David Marshall. After he quit the party in 1963, it languished until 1971 when it was reactivated by Jeyaretnam—mainly because this was easier than registering a new party. The WP has the best machinery and probably the most coherent set of policies of the opposition parties. It has a number of lawyers in its ranks, including Francis Seow, although as a mildly leftist party, it aims at winning support from the working class and underprivileged. The WP's platform calls for the abolition or amendment of a number of socially restrictive and antilabor laws. As a social democratic party, it supports a mixed economy, a more egalitarian distribution of wealth, and extensive welfare measures. But basically the party campaigns on criticisms of the PAP's arrogance and elitism and on its restrictions on individual freedoms and welfare measures. Jeyaretnam, who has a legal background, has often claimed that his role is that of a watchdog for human rights and a voice for the "little man." It has also been said of him that he is simply and solely an advocate for the *idea* of an opposition.

The SDP is a small, moderate party founded in 1980 by lawyer Chiam See Tong. Its political philosophy is based on democratic socialism—equality and justice in a noncommunalist, non-Communist, socialist Singapore. The SDP seeks to enhance the dignity of labor and proposes an economic union with Malaysia and then with ASEAN. The party opposes government oppression and centralism, elitism, educational streaming, and controlled trade unions. By Chiam's own admission, the SDP does not aim to form the government and concentrates instead on exposing what it considers to be bad PAP legislation and government abuses. The SDP's goal is to provide a check on otherwise unfettered PAP power by appealing to the electorate to save the fragile fabric of democracy by denying the PAP the two-thirds it needs to change the Constitution. Even more than the WP, the SDP is a one-person party of personality.

The opposition operates under a number of disadvantages.[26] First, Singapore is a small place with only one tier of elected government, so the opposition cannot penetrate local or municipal government bodies as a stepping stone to power or a base for dispensing patronage (although the new system of having MPs serve as town councillors is a step toward local government). Second, the electoral system, in which the candidate or team with the most votes in each constituency wins, translates the opposition votes into very few seats. Third, the resettlement of Singaporeans into multiracial high-rise flats has largely broken up constituencies containing large ethnic or socioeconomic blocs. Fourth, some of the opposition parties suffer from internal dissension and poor morale, symptoms that afflict long-time losers. Fifth, the opposition is hindered by lack of full access to government information and cannot always get its message across in the mass media. Finally, and perhaps most importantly, the PAP leaders do not easily forgive or forget the opposition contenders or their more visible supporters, and consequently the opposition parties quite often have considerable difficulty in finding candidates to stand for election.

Lee Kuan Yew has stated that it is not his job to build an opposition but that it is his job to make an opposition possible.[27] The PAP leaders occasionally make the point that an opposition in Parliament provides good training for the new team, and they understand that the opposition satisfies a growing demand for greater participation and serves as a necessary safety valve. In 1983, the government even toyed for a while with the idea of putting forth a series of measures (unspecified) to encourage the growth of an intelligent, constructive, and generally worthy opposition that would accept the basic political and socioeconomic parameters guiding the state. Later the PAP decided that it was wasteful to divert a portion of Singapore's small talent pool to the opposition, and the idea was dropped. But the government also passed legislation to provide up to three nonconstituency seats to the opposition (see Chapter 4) to deflate demands for some kind of opposition in Parliament, and in 1989 the government announced that it had decided in principle to create a category of nonelected MPs (NEMPs) to allow more political participation (the NEMPs will be able to contribute to debate, speak on motions, raise questions, but not vote).

Basically, the PAP believes that the kind of opposition it now faces is obstructionist, time wasting, and impractical, with little grasp of the realities of politics in an Asian city-state. The PAP also believes that the opposition fails to offer constructive ideas, being solely concerned with discrediting the government. Consequently, the PAP position has been to make life as difficult as possible for political opponents. It has done this by restricting access to constituency-level government bodies, delaying the provision of HDB constituency offices, withdrawing party services to opposition-held constituencies, initiating civil actions for libel against incautious opposition members, prosecuting transgressions in personal conduct that violate the law (such as through investigating tax returns), and rigorously enforcing the laws or rules of parliamentary procedure.

The government appears to have little patience with the likes of Jeyaretnam, and he has been relentlessly pursued by a series of civil libel suits, criminal charges, and various parliamentary charges and actions brought on by Jeyaretnam's unsupportable accusations and poor party bookkeeping. In 1982, he was forgiven on two charges of abuse of parliamentary privilege after he apologized (the motion was withdrawn). But there has been no forgiveness since then.

In November 1986, Jeyaretnam was deprived of his parliamentary seat and barred from standing for Parliament for five years (unless the president extends permission). This was a result of the fine ($2,500) imposed for his conviction and unsuccessful appeal on charges of making a false declaration of his party's accounts and defrauding creditors of the WP. Then, in January 1987, Parliament accepted the recommendations of its committee of privileges, which found Jeyaretnam guilty of abuse of parliamentary privilege and in contempt of Parliament (in statements in five newsletters) and fined him $13,000. Chiam sat on the committee, although he abstained on the voting, saying that the fine was excessive and that it would have sufficed to admonish Jeyaretnam.[28] Jeyaretnam was also barred from practicing law, but because this was a civil action, he was able to appeal it to the Privy Council in London, which concluded in October 1988 that Jeyaretnam had been wrongfully disbarred. In May 1989, however, Jeyaretnam's petition to the president for a pardon for four criminal convictions was rejected.

In 1988, the rising star in the WP was formerly detained lawyer Francis Seow. A good public speaker and audacious in his attacks on the PAP, Seow attracted some of the largest crowds in the 1988 election campaign and emerged as a minor folk hero. Although his WP team lost in Eunos, it was a close contest, and Seow was named as one of the two nonconstituency MPs (the other being an old-timer, Lee Siew Choh). The PAP had been unhappy about the prospect of Seow as an opposition force for some time, and some Singaporeans believed his detention under the ISA (as part of the Hendrickson affair) was motivated at least in part by a desire to stop him from contesting (he was released early so that he could contest in order to squash this perception). It has also been suggested that the PAP believed that Seow was being used by disgruntled former PAP leaders seeking to undermine the government. At any rate, Seow was a targeted man, and some flaws were found. In December 1988, Seow was tried in absentia and convicted of tax evasion. Because he was fined more than $1,000, he was automatically disqualified from being an MP (he was fined a total of $9,500).

The PAP treats the more timid and guileless, but game and gentlemanly Chiam with more forbearance and apparently views him as a closer approximation to the ideal of a loyal opposition. This forbearance was shown in the government's acquiescence in Chiam's request for a public inquiry into the Teh Cheang Wan affair after Chiam alleged that there had been some kind of cover-up. (Teh, who was the national development minister, committed suicide in December 1986 while under investigation for allegedly receiving $395,000 in bribes.) Chiam was appointed to participate in the deliberations of the commission of inquiry, was granted a three-month extension by the commission, and was given access to files pertaining to his specific allegations. He was unable to substantiate any allegations of wrong-doing in the end.[29] Furthermore, the PAP government did not hold back on establishing a Chiam-led Potong Pasir Town Council in June 1989 and in August included Chiam among the Singapore delegation to a meeting of ASEAN parliamentarians in Manila. Chiam and the PAP seem to have arrived at some kind of modus vivendi. The government is according Chiam more of a legitimate parliamentary role, and he is careful to get his facts correct, acts respectfully (particularly toward the prime minister), acknowledges good PAP actions or aims where he sees them, and generally tries to be constructive in his criticism.

For all the difficulties encountered by Jeyaretnam, Chiam and Dr. Lee, they have had some impact. Parliamentary issues have been aired more fully and discussed in greater depth, and public reaction to the televised broadcasts of Parliament has forced the PAP to modify its behavior so that its members do not appear to the public as vultures waiting to descend the moment the opposition rises to speak (this was at one time the perception despite the fact that PAP speakers fully observed proper parliamentary decorum). In the broader perspective, the opposition as a whole, by winning more than one-third of the popular votes in 1984 and 1988, has influenced the PAP's style and prompted the government to drop (at least temporarily), amend, or postpone for reconsideration some unpopular policy decisions.

The Role of Elections in the Political System

Elections can contribute greatly to a government's legitimacy (so long as they are perceived to be fair and honest). Legitimacy, in turn, is a vital ingredient for political stability. Elections stimulate a sense of political participation, reinforce the notion of governmental accountability, provide feedback for the leaders, enhance political education for the electorate, and so tend to strengthen respect for the institutions of the state.

In the Third World, competitive elections are sometimes destabilizing because of heightened political emotions, violence, and perceptions of a "zero-sum game" in which the winners win everything and the losers lose all. Consequently, in many Third World states political competition is constrained so as to cool political temperatures. An election satisfactorily concluded according to the established "rules of the game" enhances the legitimacy of the political system as well as of the government.

Singapore used to have contentious political elections, but for the last two decades they have been peaceful and orderly. There are regular parliamentary elections (now for eighty-one seats). The party winning the largest number of seats forms the government, and its leader becomes the prime minister. The life of Parliament is five years, but the government may call or be forced to call an election prior to the deadline—the norm in Singapore has been to have elections every fourth year. Candidates are elected on the basis of a "first-past-the-post" electoral system (the candidate or team with the most votes in each single-member constituency or GRC wins). Consequently, the percentage of total votes does not necessarily match the percentage of seats won (as in some types of proportional representation).

In Singapore, registration for voting is automatic and voting is compulsory (nonvoters can be fined or even deprived of their voting rights, although reinstatement is generally easy). Elections in Singapore have the reputation of being scrupulously honest, which enhances legitimacy. There is no ballot-rigging, intimidation of voters, inaccurate or slow counting of ballots, or fiddling with the registration rolls to produce so-called phantom voters or multiple voters. Despite the fact that ballot papers and receipts are numbered, and thereby theoretically traceable, there have been no formal objections on grounds of violations of secrecy (although some people do worry about this). The justification given for numbered ballots and receipts is that they help prevent cheating.

The task for the PAP today is to make selective changes that provide some cushion against sudden voting fluctuations without altering the system in obviously self-serving ways that would undermine government legitimacy. The problem is that despite their longtime dominance at the polls, the PAP leaders have little confidence in the ability of the masses to vote intelligently. This attitude clashes with a growing demand for less government dominance and more citizen participation. Even though the government is attempting to respond to this demand by channeling certain controlled avenues of participation, it may also eventually need to loosen its tight grip over interest group activity.

Interest Groups

In Singapore, as in most Third World countries, the government does not like interest groups, and its policies are not much affected by representations from them. Strong interest groups would frustrate the government's determination that there should be no independent centers of power. This situation is very different from that in the United States, where the government has to make compromises with powerful interest groups. In Singapore, the government pays attention to trends of opinion and sometimes makes adjustments (after the 1984 elections, for instance). It may consult particular interest groups or even put their representatives on advisory bodies, but generally it believes itself capable of looking after "the interests of the majority" without being bothered by particularistic demands. Additionally, some groups are suspect as targets of Communist infiltration.

In 1985, about thirty-five hundred societies in Singapore were registered (that is, approved by the government). Many of these were cultural or sporting groups with few claims on government. Here, there is space to look at only three of the more important types of groups: the trade unions, some business and professional organizations, and some community groups established by the government.

The Trade Unions. Although Lee Kuan Yew owed much of his early political support to the unions for which he acted as legal adviser, when the PAP came into power and the split developed between moderates and pro-Communists, the government took steps to regulate employer-employee relations, to reduce the number of unions (about 230 in 1959), and to wrest control from left-wing leaders. A decisive stage occurred when the former National Trades Union Congress broke up after 1961 and two rival blocs emerged, the government used its power to ensure that the moderate bloc prevailed. The left-wing Singapore Association of Trade Unions ceased to exist when its application for registration was refused (1963), and early in 1964 the moderate National Trades Union Congress (NTUC) was formed, to which the vast majority of Singapore's trade unions now belong.

The government-NTUC relationship is often described as "symbiotic." To be sure, each one does contribute to the health of the other, but the term fails to convey where power lies. The government is able to control the very existence of unions through the process of registration and deregistration. The government's industrialization program requires an absence of strikes and wage rates that will not deter investors. Consequently, a number of acts were passed that restrict strikes (a strike in January 1986 was the first since 1977), define which industrial issues are "negotiable," and set up machinery for establishing wage guidelines.[30] Devan Nair, formerly the NTUC secretary-general, has said that no explicit provision for PAP control over the unions existed, that the interaction was "voluntary not mandatory," and that the NTUC was always consulted about changes in the rules of the industrial game. At the same time, it accepted the government as first among equals.[31] In the past, PAP leaders have pulled no punches in exhorting organized labor. The new generation of leaders is unlikely to use such strong language as Lee did in addressing dockworkers in August 1967:

> Your livelihood is at stake. If you don't try hard enough, Singapore will be in trouble. But you . . . the dockworkers will be in bigger trouble. Whatever we run we want to make it pay. You are not going to fool

around. This is not a government in a mood to fool around. I am trying for you. But please remember you must try for yourselves all the time. I can't do the work for you. I can work for you, sometimes 15 hours a day. I only ask you to work hard and well for yourselves 8 hours of the day.[32]

Recently, government control over wages has become less direct. The National Wages Council (NWC), set up in 1972 and composed of representatives of government, employers, and labor, has issued annual wage guidelines. In 1982, the government announced that it would gradually assume a less active role, and that the other two elements would be left to negotiate, thus putting the onus on employers to accept increases only when justified by performance. For a transitional period, however, the government, partly because employers were less well organized than the unions, would still be represented on the council, would provide data to the negotiators, and would prevent any "runaway wages" by limiting increases to firms making higher profits. The council's recommendation in 1986 that there should be a freeze in average wages for at least two years was accepted by the unions. So was the cut in employers' CPF contributions on behalf of employees that was designed to make Singapore exports more competitive (see Chapter 7). Also, with economic recovery in the late 1980s, there were pressures from unions for higher wage increases (see Chapter 7). Nevertheless, there has been some rank-and-file grumbling among unionists at the spread of house (company) unions during the last few years. The 1980s also saw a drop in the percentage of the work force in unions; a little more than 20 percent of workers were in unions in the mid-1980s. This low figure is attributable partly to the transient nature of part of the labor force, which contains a high proportion of women and foreign workers. But it could also result from some workers' recognition that the kind of participation available has little effect on decisionmaking, which is concentrated at top levels of the union or the NTUC or in the government.

The PAP leaders have placed bright young professional, business, and public service people in top union leadership positions as well as in Parliament and the cabinet. Indeed, some now hold positions both in Parliament and/or the cabinet as well as in, or as advisers to, trade unions. These formal linkages are substitutes for the personal relationships that previously existed between the leaders of the moderates in the PAP and the moderate union leaders and were forged during the struggle against the pro-Communists in the late 1950s and early 1960s. Ong Teng Cheong, a technocrat, is now secretary-general of the NTUC as well as second deputy prime minister. He had previous contacts with labor when he held the labor and communications portfolio in the cabinet.

His predecessor in the NTUC position, Lim Chee Onn, also a technocrat, was at one time a minister. Lim's history shows, however, that there are limits to the adaptability of technocrats. Lim himself perceived the problem. In a seminar, he defended the practice of injecting talented persons with university degrees into the union leadership but added: "Of course, in the final analysis, it is up to these new elements to prove themselves to the rank and file [and show] that they really do have the interests of the workers at heart."[33] Apparently his failure to achieve this was one reason he was forced to resign in April 1983.

The NTUC and the unions enjoy some compensations for their subordination to government. They benefit from the interlocking power structure by having representatives on the statutory boards, such as the Economic Development Board (EDB) and the HDB, just as some top civil servants do. Like these also, one trade unionist may be on a half dozen or more boards. Additionally, the NTUC engages in business through cooperatives on the Scandinavian model—for instance, in life insurance, taxis, and supermarkets. These ventures provide funds to educate and train unionists. They also bolster the image of the unions and provide additional incentives for loyalty to the movement. Finally, although the government is dominant in its relations with the unions, genuine consultation and cooperation exist between them.

Business Groups. These have fewer formal links with government than do trade unions. The various chambers of commerce, the Singapore Manufacturers Association, and the Singapore Association of Bankers, as well as employers' groups make numerous representations to the government and are usually consulted on appropriate issues. The Federation of Chinese Chambers of Commerce and Industry, which speaks on behalf of Chinese businesses, is of particular importance. It speaks, for example, about unfavorable treatment of local firms as compared with multinationals and unfair competition with business by government or quasigovernment bodies. It also speaks on behalf of Chinese culture, language, and education, so the government is more attentive to its wishes than to those of the vast majority of interest groups.

Professional Groups. Organizations such as those representing doctors, engineers, or architects also have some input into decisionmaking. But the government draws strict limits—for example, it condemned the Law Society of Singapore for criticizing 1986 legislation that toughened restrictions on the press and tightened the requirements for holding office in its governing body, which entailed the exclusion of Francis Seow. According to the government, the Law Society had no business getting involved in politics; lawyers who felt strongly about political issues should form a political society with political objectives plainly spelled out in its constitution.

The opinions of intellectuals generally (including faculty and students in the university system) are not highly regarded, unless they are in line with the government's views.[34] Those who offer "independent" criticism have no place in the effective elite. To quote one such person— "The PAP doesn't seem satisfied with anything less than complete support on every issue." In 1987, there were signs that the government was concerned about the situation. Goh Chok Tong and others held dialogues with representatives of professional and social groups, who expressed their fears that government was intolerant of dissenting views and would not be sincere in seeking them; they were also critical of the team MP concept. There was agreement, however, on the need for strong, efficient, and clean government.

Strict lines are also drawn for religious bodies, especially since the detentions of May and June 1987. In his 1987 National Day Rally speech (August 16), the prime minister warned that if religious groups challenged the social and political theory behind the way the government did things, the government would take action.

Grass-Roots Organizations

Singapore's grass-roots organizations—the PA and its community centers, the CCCs, and the RCs—consist of groups harnessed to the needs of the ruling party. They are examples of *controlled* mobilization and participation.[35] The PA was formed by the PAP in 1960 to consolidate existing community centers that promoted social, cultural, educational, and athletic activities. It was used by the PAP in its struggle against the Communists, who had already founded or had taken over similar social organizations. According to one PAP leader, "We had to fill up all the available space." The PA was able to appeal to those who feared involvement in politics and who would have distrusted an organization run by the civil service.

The PA, now a statutory board, has about one hundred and thirty community centers, each run by a management committee. Its social and cultural activities have kept pace with the times. Education and handicrafts have been supplemented by beauty care, squash, and ballet, thus making the centers more attractive to the middle classes. The centers also provide day care and kindergartens, and other age groups are taken care of by a youth organization and nearly fifty senior citizens' clubs. From the start, however, the PAP encouraged participation in public affairs on behalf of the government, and the community centers were used to stimulate support for the campaign in favor of Malaysia.

The CCCs, dating from 1965, are linked to parliamentary constituencies and provide backing for the local member of Parliament, who selects the committees subject to later approval by the PMO. The committees make representations about their welfare needs and about amenities, such as efficient drainage, and in turn are informed about government policies. Apart from strengthening the PAP base, they help to promote social cohesion, which has been weakened by the massive rehousing program.

Most RCs (established from 1978 on and now numbering about three hundred forty) are in areas of high-density flats. They are chosen by committees chaired by the local (PAP) member of Parliament and contain a representative of the PMO. Like the CCCs, but with a tougher assignment, the RCs aim to encourage neighborliness (through sports, culture, forums) among people who have been uprooted and then transplanted into what often seem to be alien and impersonal surroundings. The RCs also fight crime and vandalism in these areas. Politically, they serve similar purposes to the CCCs, and there is some duplication of functions between the two.

The three types of organization differ in some respects. The initial leadership of the community centers and the CCCs consisted of the existing informal leaders of the community, mostly Chinese and often small or medium businesspeople. Later, they were replaced by "new blood"—younger people and a higher proportion of the English educated. Because the RCs were founded later, they started off with this kind of leadership. The CCCs are apparently becoming more social and less political than the other two. Yet all three, while performing useful social functions, are firmly tied to the government. The PAP looks on them as progovernment, and they are still brought into play at election campaigns, even though the Communist threat is now remote. When Jeyaretnam was elected to Parliament in 1981, there was some speculation about how an opposition member could fit in as an adviser to the grass-roots organizations in his constituency. But this question proved beside the point—the government, still determined to insulate these organizations from opposition influence, made its own choice of an adviser.

In 1988, a further development was implemented at the local level. Town councils were established in HDB estates (each covering either one or three parliamentary constituencies), with MPs as council leaders (see Chapter 4) and with appointed councillors. This change is enabling people in the estates to take over planning and management functions previously undertaken by the HDB. (The HDB is scheduled to form a company, probably with private-sector participation, to provide management services to the councils.) The range of management and financial responsibilities being transferred is quite wide—maintaining and improving facilities in the estates, acquiring and holding public property, setting charges for services, penalizing vandals, and so on. These changes, however, do not and will not amount to a system of "local government" unless at some date the councillors are elected, not appointed.

CONCLUSION

Economic hardships, the expectations held by a more educated electorate, and the rise of a "second generation" of leaders contributed to a new government sensitivity to public opinion in the 1980s. A feedback unit was established in 1985 to receive comments on topical issues and thereby supplement the existing channels provided by MPs and grass-roots organizations. (Another previously used method was reports of coffee-shop gossip.) Letters to the unit have been concerned with such matters as medical services, the state of the economy, education, tourism, and taxi fares. Except initially, very few letters have contained purely personal appeals or complaints. The unit has held televised forums on, for instance, the state of the economy. In the mid-1980s, correspondence columns in the newspapers also increasingly expressed more open and sophisticated views on the issues of the day. Neither kind of feedback is a substitute for interest group activities, but both suggest that under the new generation of leaders the role of interest groups in the governing process may be expanding.

6

From the Founders to the Successors

History is replete with examples that demonstrate the prime importance of leaders for the condition of their people. Especially at critical junctions in a nation's history, the question of *who* is making the important decisions is often the vital consideration in determining a nation's course in its "tryst with destiny." Singapore has been unusually fortunate in that from its founding it has been led by an extraordinarily dedicated, competent, and far-sighted group of leaders: Lee Kuan Yew, his inner circle of colleagues—Goh Keng Swee, S. Rajaratnam, and Toh Chin Chye—and other PAP ministers. To a far greater extent than in most states, these leaders have molded and shaped Singapore in their image.

THE FOUNDER GENERATION

The founders, although differing in temperament, ambition, and special abilities, shared a similar intellectual and elite background, compatible visions and goals, and nearly identical political instincts. They were committed to the twin tasks of nation-building and modernization in a small, multiracial, resource-poor island city-state situated in the turbulent Third World. They melded into a cohesive team with an almost obsessive sense of obligation, great energy, a conviction that performance counted for more than civilities, and a firm belief that on the basis of their logical analysis and rational planning, they knew what was best for Singapore.

Lee Kuan Yew, the Architect of Modern Singapore

Of the group, Lee Kuan Yew has clearly been the prime mover. He possesses that rare combination of persuasive political skills, ideas and vision, and talent as an administrator. He has been the dominant political figure of Singapore since coming to power in 1959. Indeed, he is often equated with modern Singapore.

Lee Kuan Yew's personal and leadership qualities and his views have been analyzed and interpreted in countless articles and books, in which he has been both praised and vilified. The personal side of his life, partly because of his efforts to discourage a cult of personality and his instinctive sense of privacy, and partly because no "kiss-and-tell" type books have emerged, remains somewhat mysterious to Singaporeans. In sweeping terms, he is described as a Fabian socialist (perhaps lapsed), nationalist, modernizer, and Confucianist. Few would quarrel with a description of him as an intellectual workaholic who is disciplined, determined, noncorrupt, and fully possessed of the qualities of a ruler. He has also often been said to be arrogant, intolerant, argumentative, sarcastic, and sardonic, with little sympathy for human failings. He is described as a confident thinker and planner who nevertheless worries about the unkind vagaries of fate, an ideas man who determinedly and relentlessly oversees policy implementation. He is at once an impassioned "I'll-fix-you" campaign speaker and a precisely controlled parliamentary debater whose facility with language and use of cold logic and facts intimidate most opponents. He can be polite and gracious; he can laugh and appreciates irony. He is also reputed to have a fiery temper and can be blunt and rude, even in public. He is said to be impervious to flattery and to hate sycophants, although his very dominance encourages such. He is vigilant in "setting the record straight" (sometimes through libel suits) when his official conduct or propriety, or his government's, has been attacked.

Although Lee's political views have undoubtedly evolved and developed with age and experience—for example, he now appears less identifiable as a socialist—more striking is the consistency of his political views and the difficulty the observer has in trying to pin precise labels on these views. As Dennis Bloodworth noted some years ago, "It says much for Lee Kuan Yew that bold and outspoken men have accused him of being a Fascist, a Communist, even a democrat at different times, and at those different times all of them have ostensibly been right."[1]

Lee's Cabinet

Despite the dominance of Lee Kuan Yew, the Singapore record of achievement under the PAP first generation was as much the product of a small, highly intelligent, well-balanced, like-minded, and cohesive cabinet team as the work of a single man. These men contributed not only to the implementation of decided policy but to the formulation of ideas and plans. Longtime minister E. W. Barker explained in a 1983

BBC interview that although Lee was a "strong leader," he was "not a dictator." He listened to his cabinet colleagues and on occasion he was "outvoted." He could be persuaded to change his mind. "When we are against him, in the end he's with us."[2] Lee explained in a 1989 interview that he does not waste time in cabinet seeking opinions before proffering his own ideas about what the government ought to do, and about half the time "everyone more or less agrees with me." But, he continued, the cabinet is not a one-man show and has never been complacent or compliant.[3] Likewise, when Lee paid tribute to Goh Keng Swee upon his retirement in December 1984, he said that Goh's biggest contribution was that "you stood up to me whenever you held the contrary view. You challenged my decisions and forced me to re-examine the premises on which they were made."[4]

The most valuable colleague of Lee's was probably Goh Keng Swee. In the cabinet, Goh, with a London Ph.D. in economics, was a man of ideas, with a fertile, innovative mind and considerable intellectual daring. Considered a mandarin (a technocrat), Goh was reputedly an uninspiring political campaigner and was known to dislike the rough edge of politics (although apparently a supporter of tough government measures to ensure order and stability). As a man who could correct or solve a problem, plug a gap, reform an institution or adjust a policy, buttress or constrain the views of the prime minister, Goh's contribution was extensive. It appears that he never aspired to be prime minister.

Toh Chin Chye, a former academic, was one of the other two men in the inner circle. He played an important role early on as the chief party technician—the man responsible for the party machinery—especially during the period of Ong Eng Guan's challenge to Lee and the PAP split. In recent years, Toh has emerged as a maverick. He is reported to have objected to the fast pace of promotion of second-generation leaders and only reluctantly surrendered his own cabinet portfolio.

S. Rajaratnam was considered to be the PAP's theorizer, the man who explained (along with Lee) the rationale of PAP policies, often in the context of the experience of world history. A former journalist without a graduate degree but widely read in history and political philosophy, Rajaratnam was a counterweight to a team otherwise top-heavy with technocrats. With a flair for words, Rajaratnam could expound philosophy to a diplomatic audience and then readily put on his verbal knuckle-dusters to take on PAP opponents and critics.

THE ELEMENTS OF SUCCESSFUL LEADERSHIP

A key to understanding why the PAP founders were able to work so well together and to create for Singapore a secure and respected place in the world was that they agreed on political fundamentals and a set of guiding values and principles for Singapore. First, they believed that the "best" should lead the nation—those few who in any society constituted the brightest, wisest, most able, and virtuous, that decisionmaking should naturally be from the top down, and that leadership should be by unreproachable moral example. In their minds, they constituted such an elite.

Second, they believed that political stability was the top priority because it was a prerequisite for development and modernization. This belief accompanied a shared apprehension about the transferability of Westminster democracy to an Asian society and an underlying conviction that unfettered "democracy," in the Aristotelian sense of the term, contained within it certain frailties always threatening to degenerate into mob rule. Although sacrifice of certain individual freedoms for the good of the whole (a concept traditionally part of Asian political cultures) and for stability was necessary, at the same time they believed in constitutionalism and the rule of law as the only civilized alternative to arbitrary personal rule, the plague of the Third World. Despite reservations about the ability of the voting public to understand the issues fully, constitutionalism seemed to require, among other things, that the government periodically seek a mandate from the people (after which it was the government's responsibility to lead rather than to be guided by popular demands).

Third, they believed that society needed to be organized and imbued with certain values to enable it to respond to government directions in a nationwide effort to create a modern and well-functioning state. Through persuasion and exhortation, incentives and disincentives, and government intrusion into sociocultural and economic areas, the PAP leaders hoped to mold a tightly knit, racially tolerant society that was rugged, skilled, hardworking, disciplined, forward looking, politically compliant, cooperative, and organized along hierarchical and meritocratic principles.

Fourth, as leaders, they believed in the value of logical calculation, planning, and rationality and in the general superiority of science and technology in overcoming societal problems. Consequently, their decisionmaking and problem-solving approach was to set out goals and priorities, plan strategies, chart and evaluate alternatives, and anticipate problems. They also appreciated the role of fate in sometimes confounding the best-laid plans, and so an important guiding principle of the PAP leaders was political pragmatism and policy flexibility.

PAP STYLE AND VALUE SYSTEM

The style of the PAP has been consistent with the founders' guiding principles and values. This style can be characterized as morally upright, elitist, resolute, tough, truthful, and paternalistic. The PAP leaders have set an example of almost Spartan purity: no-nonsense hard work, incorruptibility (a few have fallen and have not been rescued), thrift with public funds, self-discipline, and virtuous conduct. They have been unabashedly but almost unself-consciously elitist: "We decided what is right. Never mind what the people think—that's another problem."[5] They have had a "don't flinch" resolve in the face of popular demands that they perceive to be associated with the "soft state" (indiscipline, individualism, too much politics, adversarial trade unions, the welfare state). They have been tough, at times ruthless, in suppressing dissent that strays beyond the limits of permissibility and in countering criticism that verges on slander or libel. They have been blunt, truthful, and forthright with the citizens, to a degree rarely seen, in stating what the problem or goal is, what the government proposes to do about it, and what the citizen is expected to do for his part. They have not asked for permission, or often for advice, but they have explained their policies. Sometimes they have floated ideas to test or even sway public opinion (such as with the dissolution through merger of Chinese-medium Nanyang University).

Perhaps the most noticeable characteristic of the style of the PAP has been the role of the leaders as persistent educators. Devan Nair once said of Lee: "He doesn't resort to oratory. He doesn't aim for the solar plexus. He converses, shares his analysis, so that even the least intellectual Singaporean begins to understand."[6] Beyond this, Lee has also, in the style of the stern Confucian father, consistently demanded much from Singaporeans, often accompanied by scant praise. He has "channelled their energies and suppressed their urges, exhorted them, dragooned them, threatened them, led them."[7]

The PAP leaders have believed from the beginning that it was government performance, not words or transient popularity, that counted. The basis of the contract that developed between the people and the government has been that they obeyed and the government delivered the goods. Thus, it is important to look at how values and style have been translated into policies and into a modus operandi for governing.

Leading by Example

The PAP has set forth six basic principles of governing: give clear signals and do not confuse the people; stay clean and dismiss the venal; reject soft options so as to win respect rather than popularity; spread benefits; strive to succeed; and never give up.[8] Raj Vasil[9] has suggested some broad guidelines that cover the political management practices of the PAP government in Singapore. They include control of all possible rival centers of power, including the civil service, the trade unions, business and ethnic organizations; depoliticization; and recruitment of political leaders from among persons of proven abilities. At the same time, PAP practices dictate that nepotism and corruption should be rooted out and that the government should operate scrupulously within the framework of the Constitution and the law.

The belief in elitist principles has led to the establishment in Singapore of an achievement-oriented meritocracy based on competitive educational and job performance. The system is geared to reward achievers from an early age through school streaming and scholarships, and merit is the principle used in recruitment to government service and promotion within it. Salaries paid to MPs and especially to ministers rank among the highest in the world in order to attract the best people and discourage corruption. In a 1980 speech explaining why so many new nations and some old industrial nations were failing, Lee drew a distinction between those states, such as Singapore, that recognized and rewarded the intelligent and the able and those states that in the name of egalitarianism drowned their talented in a sea of mediocrity.

The PAP has attached great importance to its reputation and to the idea of leading by example. Being the "best" carries with it the responsibility for being the most able and virtuous. Those who have not performed satisfactorily have been forced to step down, sometimes accompanied by public humiliation. This was the case with the dismissal of Lim Chee Onn in 1983 and more recently with the resignation of President Devan Nair following a disagreeable international incident and subsequent public disclosure of his alleged alcoholism. Those in office who have transgressed the law are considered to have forfeited their rights just as fully as any criminal—if not more so. Former minister of state Wee Toon Boon was imprisoned in 1976 on four counts of corruption, and former minister for national development Teh Cheang Wan committed suicide in 1986 while under investigation for corruption. Likewise, in 1984, after the collapse of his stock market empire, Malaysian Chinese Association president Tan Koon Swan was charged and later convicted of fraud despite hopes of Malaysian officials for a deal and despite the sensitivity and pragmatism that Singapore normally injects into its relations with Malaysia. A Philippine newspaper feature commented in 1988 that one of the main ingredients of Singapore's success was the government's strict enforcement of rules, with no exceptions or favoritism.[10]

The PAP government has often been characterized as paternalistic. This has been noticeable in the role of PAP ministers as educators and shapers of values, not just through their speeches but also in policies such as the introduction of ethnically mixed government housing and the inclusion of religious philosophy in the school curriculum (the latter, however, is being replaced by enhanced civics and moral education courses). Another manifestation has been through a plethora of national campaigns—a feature now so much associated with Singapore. These campaigns—against littering, spitting, male long hair, and smoking and for courtesy, trees and greenery, road safety, cleanliness, punctuality, and respect for elders, to name a few—have been extensively promoted through wide media coverage, buttons, stickers, posters, songs, films, and prizes. There are also disincentives or penalties for noncompliance. Some Singaporeans scoff at the campaigns, but in fact Singapore is a clean and safe garden city, so much so that some tourists find it holds too little sense of danger and high adventure. As one cynic wrote, "Welcome to Lee Kuan Yew's transistorized, deodorized, air-conditioned, multi-storied city state."[11]

The Role of Ideology

The question as to whether the PAP has an ideology—an integrated and coherent body of ideas and beliefs directed toward action—has often been considered.[12] One answer is that the PAP does have a coordinated set of ideas, plans, and beliefs, drawn from several sources, but these are not traceable to a single, logically consistent, and orthodox dogma.

In the past, it was sometimes said that the PAP had a socialist base. Although the leaders sometimes claimed to be socialists (it was a popular Third World concept in the 1950s–1960s), there was no specific commitment to socialism in the PAP manifestoes, and narrow limits were set to its applicability to policy initiatives. According to Rajaratnam, the PAP government was committed to taking enough from the rich through taxes to provide services such as housing, education, and health for those who could not afford to pay for them. This reflected the PAP commitment to democratic socialism.[13] There was no nationalization, no handouts beyond a welfare state safety net, and equity never replaced growth as the main economic goal. Douglas Sikorski labeled the Singapore economic approach "state capitalism" (or "market socialism"), similar to Japan's "cooperative capitalism," with government allied with business and with unions tame and cooperative.[14]

Nor has the PAP ever desired or pretended to practice any liberal version of Western-style democracy. Singapore is democratic in terms of sets of institutions and to the extent that certain democratic processes are practiced, but the requirements of order are explicitly put ahead of protection of individual freedom. According to Bloodworth

As a democrat, Lee believed that what was important was "to uphold the fundamentals, namely government by free choice of the people, by secret ballot, at periodic intervals." [But Lee] could not afford to put socialist principle before jobs, or freedom before order, or morals before the market, and in a dangerous ecosystem the democratic state of Singapore would evolve in the unorthodox manner of new and small species whose *ad hoc* adaptation to vile circumstance ensured that the fittest survived when dinosaurs died.[15]

Elitism, Confucianism, and Pragmatism

There seem to be three major sources of the PAP beliefs and system of values: elitism, Confucianism, and pragmatism. Elitism as a political concept posits that any society, whatever its institutional form, is—and should be—governed by the few and that the few should be the best, the brightest, and the most capable of organizing society. Lee Kuan Yew and the PAP leaders, including the successor generation, are elitists in the sense of firmly believing that the governors of Singapore should be the most intelligent and talented available and that identifying and nurturing the talented and recruiting them into government service should not be left to chance.

Whereas elitism has generally negative connotations in North America, where it is perceived as denigrating the "common man" and therefore as being antidemocratic, the concept has some grounding in Singapore political culture. Elitism is pivotal to Confucian political philosophy, which holds that people are not born equal but are born possessing different capabilities, a few being born to rule and the rest to be ruled.

As Lee Kuan Yew views it, "You either have the talent or you do not." There has been considerable worry among the leadership about Singapore's limited "gene pool" from which the needed few who can govern must be drawn. Lee has noted that in every society there are about 5 percent "who are more than ordinarily endowed physically and mentally and in whom we must expend our limited and slender resources in order that they will provide that yeast, that ferment, that catalyst in our society which alone will ensure that Singapore shall maintain its preeminent place in South and Southeast Asia."[16] In 1982, Lee estimated that "talented and balanced" Singaporeans—meaning those possessing first class minds and also the right character and personality—amounted to only twelve to fourteen persons a year.[17]

Elitist values among the top PAP leadership have shown themselves in the paternalism and the high moral tone of the government, in its commitment to meritocracy and school streaming, and in policies such as the graduate mother scheme and related population policies. These values are also evident in the PAP leaders' attitude toward governance. As elites, PAP leaders tend to believe that they alone understand the deep complexities and interrelationships of problems and alone have the dedication and ability to devise viable solutions. They are confident that their policies and programs have been rationally arrived at by the best minds in Singapore after careful calculation and recalculation. Therefore, they naturally expect the people to listen, understand, and comply. So, although ministers attend forums, their purpose is more to explain government policies than to listen and respond to public views. There cannot be, as Goh Chok Tong has noted, a national debate on every issue. The PAP leaders, as elitists, believe that participation must necessarily be curtailed. Competitive and conflictual politics is discouraged, and the government really does not accord a legitimate role for wide consultation, public criticism, or bargaining with groups. The government is prepared to listen to "petitions"[18] but not to get into a bargaining situation. In principle, the opposition is viewed as a waste of government time and a waste of scarce talent, but in the eyes of the PAP the latter would hardly apply to the present opposition—Lee has called Jeyaretnam and Chiam "DC-3s operating in the jet age."

Obviously, the Confucianist political tradition is elitist. Although neither a religion nor a unified body of doctrine, Confucianism contains key political concepts that have relevance to the political cultures and systems of East Asia and Singapore.[19] Confucianism dictates a harmonious universe based on hierarchical order—benevolent rule by the most able and virtuous and deference and obedience (*xiao*) to this authority. Confucian society is an ordered hierarchy of unequals, all of whom have necessary functions to perform for the cooperative harmony of all. Obligations and duties are stressed, rather than "rights," which is a Western notion. The Confucian tradition also emphasizes respect for learning, the merit principle, filial piety, and a view of the state as an organic entity, in effect an extension of the family, rather than as a collection of individuals. The entity is a moral order guided by laws, overseen by the bureaucrats (mandarins) and backed by a strong coercive capacity. Confucian political thought encourages paternalism and authoritarianism, but it also holds that to maintain the "Mandate of Heaven" (or legitimacy), rule must correspond to accepted notions of good government and operate for the benefit and welfare of the people. The basic requirements are peace, security, and prosperity, provided by an upright and trustworthy leader worthy of imitation.

The PAP government operates in a primarily Chinese political milieu that, although subject to the impact of Western ideas and modernization, is still influenced by a Confucian ethos (and by Buddhism). Confucianism serves to modify ideas borrowed from the West. The style and policies of the PAP political leadership at the top appear to be aligned closely with the central tenets of the Confucian political and moral tradition. Yet the leaders still manage to function as rational, technologically oriented, secular modernizers.

The key challenge for Singapore's leaders has been to borrow and adapt Western science and technology, jettison values they think might hinder modernization, but still retain a large part of traditional values and cultural identities as a bulwark against negative Western influences associated with the "soft state." It is a difficult balance to achieve and a precarious one to maintain. For example, English is considered the most appropriate language for purposes of modernization, yet the PAP leaders appreciate that culture flows from language. Consequently, the education system gives instruction in English but requires mother-tongue language courses in the hope that students will be functionally bilingual. In fact, the government now believes that the balance has shifted too far in favor of English, and consequently it is attempting to promote more Mandarin literacy in the schools. The balance also includes, of course, promoting elitist and paternalistic (some say authoritarian) values and minimizing notions from the West of societal participation in decisionmaking.

Lee Kuan Yew has been worried about the decline of Confucian values for some time and has warned that if the Chinese lose their Confucian traditions and tendencies, Singapore will become just another Third World state likely to face very difficult times.[20] To counter the impact of Western influences, the government has sponsored a revival of Confucianism. This has taken the form of incorporating moral studies and religious philosophy education in school curricula (although the religious knowledge subject will be phased out because the government now believes that it has been contributing to a revival of Christian evangelicalism) establishing the Institute of East Asian Philosophies, participating in international forums on Confucianism, propagating Confucian values in the media, creating a national ideology, and making exhortations. Some see this as a self-serving attempt to perpetuate a political culture in accordance with PAP authoritarianism, whereas others view it as an attempt (as in Japan) to strike an appropriate balance that will allow further modernization and continued prosperity without incurring a loss of cultural identity.

The final major source of PAP beliefs can be found in political pragmatism. Lee Kuan Yew and the PAP leadership are elitists with particular values, definite visions, and fixed ideas. As political realists and rational calculators, however, they have also been pragmatic and flexible in pursuit of their objectives. They will not bend easily or very far, or for long, on policies they deem to be essential, and they do not want to be seen as having "caved in" to public pressure. But they have been flexible on means, directions, timing, wording, and public presentation of policies. They will zig and zag toward a goal that remains a direct objective. Rarely does the PAP give up on an idea or rescind an important policy permanently. It does so only on rare occasions when experience has shown the policy to be wrong—and costly (for example, the "wage correction" policy).

In 1986, Foreign Minister S. Dhanabalan explained to students that the PAP had a basic principle of pursuing pragmatic and flexible policies, to avoid getting "locked into ideological or hard positions." He said that at one time the government felt very strongly that the CPF contribution rate should not be reduced. But after studying the recessionary economic trends, the government cut the employers' contributions to reduce production costs. On the unpopular taxi fare increases, Dhanabalan told the students that the government had partly changed the policy to reduce prices but had not abandoned the objective. "Ultimately, fares will go up."[21]

There are two aspects to PAP pragmatism; one is simply tactical and the other is a commitment to practical results. The tactical aspect involves prudent political axioms, such as not introducing controversial policies in an election year (not, however, observed in 1984), and methods of attaining public support for policies and programs. One method, employed quite often in the past before the question of succession hastened the tempo of decisionmaking, was to prepare the ground slowly, float ideas, and direct public discussion (for example, by setting up citizen committees and holding public forums) so that the public would arrive at an issue position very close to the position the government held all along. Rajaratnam has explained the PAP approach on sensitive issues involving language, education, religion, or culture: "When you are dealing with emotions . . . you never meet them head on. You work your way around them. People don't keep on pushing a door that is open."[22] Another method, increasingly prevalent, has been to act boldly in setting out a proposition that makes maximal claims or demands on the public and then, after gauging public reaction, to modify the final product somewhat and thereby make it more generally acceptable (for example, changes to CPF regulations).

The other aspect of PAP pragmatism is its commitment to results and the acid test of performance. A parallel can be found in Confucian political thought—a policy has value if it works or succeeds (in accordance with the natural order and moral ends)—and there are still strong pragmatic strains in Chinese mass political culture. Pragmatism has meant that the PAP has not let itself become trapped in dogma; the test has never been ideological consistency at the expense of efficiency.

In this sense, pragmatism has become equated with rationality: If it works, use it; if it doesn't work, discard it and try one of the alternatives.

Elitism, Confucianism, and pragmatism, as sources of the PAP belief and value system, are not only compatible; they overlap. Together they help explain the underlying values behind the process of governance in Singapore under Lee Kuan Yew and the PAP. The composite picture that emerges is perhaps a bit authoritarian for many Western eyes (and for some Singaporeans), but the honesty and effectiveness of the government make Singapore the envy of much of the Third World, and this has tempered the impulse to criticize. Bloodworth summed it up nicely in 1975 when he wrote that Lee's government "has done more than lock up the left wing. It has swept away the slums and given the people towering blocks of low-rental flats, new networks of roads, a new port, a new industrial complex, nearly one hundred new schools, a new social system, a new face and a new future."[23]

Interestingly, in late 1988 the PAP government announced that it proposed to adopt a national ideology to reinforce important Asian values not fully emphasized in existing national symbols. A national ideology would serve to redress the balance against the negative effects of growing Westernization (unrestrained materialism, permissiveness, excessive individualism, and the drug culture) and a preoccupation with individual rights and freedoms over society's rights and entitlements and the concept of obligation. Much can be seen of PAP beliefs in the four core values suggested by the government: (1) communitarianism (community over self); (2) upholding of the family as the basic building block of society; (3) resolution of major issues through consensus instead of contention; and (4) stressing of racial and religious tolerance and harmony.

In the early months of 1989, the government floated the idea more purposively to test public opinion on the concept. The opposition MPs insinuated that it was a ploy to perpetuate PAP power. The public response in the media focused on fears (about democracy, the status of women, minority rights) more than on opposition. A committee headed by B. G. Lee has been empowered to formulate proposals in a green paper to be presented to Parliament sometime in 1990 or later, and the Institute of Policy Studies has been asked to prepare a background paper setting out various options. The government has assured Singaporeans that there will be full public consultation before any national ideology legislation is passed.[24]

THE PROBLEM OF POLITICAL SUCCESSION

Political succession can be an agonizing, destabilizing experience in a young country lacking tested and firmly institutionalized mechanisms for the transfer of power. Recognizing this and believing that leaders such as Mao Zedong and Jawaharlal Nehru hung on to power too long to be able to influence and guide the process, Lee Kuan Yew has, since the late 1960s, been directing considerable energies toward the succession problem in Singapore. A strong believer in the virtue of planning, Lee said in 1986 that although there was not much more that he could personally accomplish, he would like his legacy to be that he passed over power, style, and values intact and with grace to the second generation of leaders.[25]

Finding a successor team from Singapore's small talent "catchment area" has been a deliberate, systematic, and painstaking process of spotting talent emerging from a vast assortment of career streams and recruiting or coopting talented people into the party as parliamentary candidates and potential ministers. The selection process is multistaged; it involves interviews and tests, including a voluntary psychological examination, to gauge intellectual capacity, emotional stability, integrity, honesty, loyalty, and overall suitability.[26] Those accepted are then subjected to an intense process of training to instill proper values, tutoring, and testing of their abilities and dedication on the job. The attrition rate has been high—those who have not measured up to very exacting standards have been dropped, often unceremoniously—and the process of renewal has led to resentment on the part of some of the old guard compelled to stand aside. Furthermore, many of those recruited early on have failed to satisfy Lee and his close government associates, thus lending urgency and worry to the search for suitable successors. The introduction of new candidates for Parliament has been relentless: Between 1968 and 1988, there were 109 new PAP candidates standing in general elections and by-elections. As Lee noted, "I am not sure which is the more difficult task: to start the PAP, and get where we are today, or to ensure a succession by able and dedicated men who can build upon what has been done."[27]

There has been a definite pattern in the type of talent recruited. Lee and his close associates have not sought party organizers or student or trade union activists. Rather, they have selected and sought to coopt well-educated and highly qualified technocratic or professional people in their thirties who have already successfully embarked on a career. Candidates are chosen more for their ministerial potential than as vote getters, although voter appeal is desirable.[28] There has been an emphasis on academic qualifications; however, after some failures, the PAP leaders now recognize that more is needed than a good mind. Lee has stated that he wants men like the original group, only younger. In fact, however, the PAP is not able to recruit people who have been through the political rough and tumble (as Lee likes to say, "on the Long March"), mainly because the PAP, as the dominant party, has faced little political competition since the early 1960s. Singapore is recruiting state-manager politicians, or, as Rajaratnam put it in 1968, the PAP wants "problem-solvers" rather than "word-spinners." Given such people's intelligence, character, teamwork, and demonstrated ability to administer, the PAP leaders hope that experience and a chance to work out their share of errors early will provide political acumen and those indefinable qualities that inspire people to follow.

THE SECOND GENERATION

By January 1980, Lee felt sufficiently satisfied with his second-generation leaders to identify them formally at the twenty-fifth PAP anniversary conference. By 1984, two of this "group of seven" had been dropped, rather abruptly, by Lee, and two more had been elevated. The core of the successor group was now identified as Goh Chok Tong, Tony Tan, Ong Teng Cheong, S. Dhanabalan, and Ahmad Mattar, with Yeo Ning Hong and S. Jayakumar as more recent additions. Of this group, three held Ph.Ds, two had Master's degrees, and one had a B.A. Goh Chok Tong was made campaign organizer at the 1981 Anson by-election, but after the PAP lost (see Chapter 4), Lee noted that the second generation had yet to demonstrate "that sensitive political touch."[29]

Two things happened next. First, the second-generation team was gradually given more responsibility, including running the campaign for the 1984 general election. These team members were also elected to a majority of the seats on the PAP's Central Executive Committee in October 1984. In January 1985, despite the electoral reverses of the previous month, Goh Chok Tong was named first deputy prime minister, and at the same time Lee announced that the successor generation would take over the administration of the country on a day-to-day basis. While most political analysts concurred at that point that Lee still controlled the selection of candidates, the ministerial appointments, and the firings, he let the "group of seven" contend among themselves with the hope that the best man would emerge as leader because his talents would be recognized by his peers (while insisting that they work as a team and strive for consensus). This fit with Lee's conviction that the best team would be closely knit, with a sense of collective responsibility, but also with loyal lieutenants backing the top man. Goh Chok Tong was the unanimous choice of the group as the leader.

Second, the talent search continued, and twenty-six new PAP candidates ran in the 1984 general election. Among these was Brigadier-General Lee Hsien Loong (Hsien Loong is the name of a legendary general and means magnificent dragon)—a thirty-two-year-old multi-

Goh Chok Tong (left), the first deputy prime minister, shaking hands at a Malay celebration in Singapore.

lingual graduate of Cambridge (with a double First Class and star of distinction) and Harvard. A formidable contender for high office by any criteria, he is also the prime minister's eldest son. The prime minister took himself out of the selection process when B. G. was being considered but commented afterward that the selection of B. G. "was so obvious that not to have chosen him would have told me something about the younger ministers."[30] B. G. Lee's candidacy, easy electoral victory, and swift elevation within the party and government have created considerable excitement and speculation in Singapore.

In the eyes of most observers, the succession picture became very much blurred by the new factor of B. G. Lee. Although Lee Kuan Yew indicated that his son must rise by virtue of his performance and with the support and agreement of the younger PAP leaders, the perception in Singapore was that the father was well pleased with the son and that the succession was not settled. Then, in July 1988, Lee Kuan Yew stated that the prime ministership was not his to give away and that he thought it would be bad for his son and for Singapore to have his son succeed him. A few days later, Goh told the press that he had received a fresh vote of confidence from *all* of his colleagues (necessary because B. G. Lee had not been a factor earlier), and the next day B. G. Lee stated plainly that Goh would be Singapore's next prime minister. An editorial commented, "The father has said it. The son has said it. And Mr. Goh

Brigadier-General (Res.) Lee Hsien Loong, minister of trade and industry. B. G. Lee, the prime minister's elder son, is a prominent member of the PAP "successor generation."

Chok Tong has said it. Each in his own way has said it, quickly one after the other. All in the span of the past ten days."[31]

Singaporeans at that point seemed satisfied that the immediate succession issue was settled and that their suspicions that the prime minister was less than totally pleased with the new lineup were groundless. Then, in his National Day speech in August 1988, Lee outlined how he had short-listed and rated five ministers after the 1980 elections, with Tony Tan on top and Goh Chok Tong second. A few weeks later, in a speech at the National University of Singapore forum, Lee made a startling speech that Tony Tan later described as "a very curious speech, a very curious speech." In the speech, Lee gave his blunt assessment of Goh Chok Tong.[32] Much of what he said was complimentary. But, he continued, if a person suffered from one weakness, all that person's virtues would be demolished. Goh Chok Tong, he said, tried to please too many people and spent too much time listening instead of making decisions quickly. Further, Lee stated, "He is unable to convey through television and through mass meetings what he can convey in individual, face-to-face, or small group discussions. . . . He has improved. . . . He needs to improve by more than 100 percent. . . . So, he makes use of other ministers . . . to do the expounding and the explanation. That means more teamwork, more time spent in discussion so that they know exactly which way they are going. Now I watch this with some consternation."

Goh Chok Tong responded in forceful but measured tones. He said that he would not change his style, which was part of his temperament and something he viewed as a strength; he wanted to involve those who could contribute ideas and effort to build a better Singapore. As to his communication skills, he admitted that he was not a rousing public speaker and said it was better for Singaporeans to know him for what he was rather than to expect great oratory from him. On the issue of succession, the second-generation leaders had already decided and that, he said, was that. The prime minister had said that the successor would not be decided by him "and indeed it will not be decided by him."[33]

The issue did not go away, and Goh continued to defend and assert himself throughout the campaign. "I do not know what is PM's ranking of me today in 1988. Maybe I'm still his second choice. Maybe his first choice is Lee Hsien Loong." But, he said, it was a matter for the ministers to decide, and as far as they were concerned he was the first, not the second, choice. "I don't believe that PM was out to undercut me. Neither was he out to raise me in the eyes of the public. He was out to protect his credibility. And so be it. . . . My friends were concerned because they felt that the opposition parties would exploit PM's remarks against me, and so they have."[34]

What was this "very curious speech" all about? Some believed that it was intended to make Goh more forceful and dynamic. Indeed, Lee commented later that his critical remarks were "not a bad gambit. . . . I said: Speak up! Be yourself. If you are angry, say so! The result: He's no longer inhibited."[35] Others believed that Lee had some lingering reservations about Goh and that the speech reflected his earlier dis-appointed hopes that the second-generation ministers would decide to replace Goh as leader. A few even wondered if Lee was hoping for a poor election result so that Goh would be pressured to step aside, whereas others believed it was a ploy to build up a sympathy vote for Goh and the PAP. Certainly in private Lee expressed considerable faith in Goh (except for concerns about his speaking and mobilizing skills) but worried about the successor team in general—that they might not be adept enough street brawlers or schemers, fighters to the death. He knew he picked good men but was not sure if they were the right men, although they were the best available.[36] Lee has stated enigmatically that he had no serious misgivings about Goh, but "I have not chosen him. He has been chosen by his peers. I believe it's the right choice."[37]

After the election, Goh Chok Tong said that he would be ready to take over as prime minister within two years. At the swearing in ceremony for the new cabinet, Lee seemed to confirm the timing and the successor when he said, "Now my duty is to ensure that all will go well in the next two years before I hand over the prime ministership to Mr. Goh Chok Tong."[38]

January 1985 marked the beginning of the transition period that will continue until Lee Kuan Yew does indeed step down as prime minister and, in fact, until Lee is no longer active on the political scene. In the meantime, two questions arise: To what extent have the new leaders been able to make their own decisions? What role is to be designed for the mentally alert, physically fit, and intensely involved Lee, who is finding that it is not so easy, in the end, to step aside? It is clear that the transition has put Lee and the successors in an anomalous situation.

The prime minister is aware that the successor team needs the experience of administering the affairs of state, and it needs to be *seen* to be governing. In June 1988 in Parliament, Lee stated that since 1985 Goh Chok Tong and the younger ministers had taken all the major decisions and that he had not vetoed any of these. As prime minister, however, Lee is still ultimately responsible for the performance of the government. Further, like the concerned parent who cannot quite believe that the child, having learned all that can be imparted, is really ready to go off on his own, Lee continues to offer his ideas and express his views, and these carry enormous weight. In fact, Lee has become the sole guardian, interpreter, and enforcer of values and principles for the second generation. He states regularly that the younger leaders are in charge of the government, yet when Lee says, "The master controls are still with me," this is no idle boast.[39]

THE TRANSITION

In his 1988 National Day speech (in English, Mandarin, and Malay), Lee Kuan Yew stated that those "who believe that when I have left the government as prime minister that I have gone into permanent retirement, really should have their heads examined. . . . Even from my sick bed, even if you are going to lower me into the grave and I feel that something is going wrong, I will get up."[40] There has been considerable speculation in Singapore as to the nature of the role Lee will play after he steps down as prime minister. Lee has said, and it is no doubt true, that he does not need a formal position in order to exert political influence informally.[41] Nevertheless, many observers think that he is interested in a position that would afford him a formal role. The three possibilities that have emerged are that he will become the first elected president, simply retain his position as PAP secretary-general, or be given a position in the cabinet as senior minister in the PMO. Lee has described the kind of role he hopes to play, although this would be decided by his successor, he noted, and would not include any overriding power, even in a crisis. This role should be structured in a way that does not cramp the prime minister but should enable Lee to keep up with the flow of events and make an effective contribution at critical moments. Goh, Lee said, wants him to contribute to the political aspects of government policies—how the agenda could be developed and presented in political terms. "Put simply, it is to help him [Goh] politically. He doesn't need help to succeed administratively. He can administer Singapore as well as I can. But to do it with political savvy so that, at the end of the day, the vote comes out right, that's different."[42]

Throughout 1988, attention centered around the possibility of Lee becoming Singapore's first elected president. Although Lee remained coy about whether he really wanted the job, many Singaporeans believed that the position was being tailored especially for him, and even some PAP members had said that Lee should be the first president in order to set the tone and see the office through the first term. Some problems probably rule out this scenario, however. First, there has been a very long delay in putting the legislation for an elected president together, reputedly due to a lack of agreement on the powers of the office.[43] There is speculation that Lee wanted a stronger presidency but that this was successfully resisted by the younger ministers, after which Lee lost some of his interest in the job. Second, during the 1988 election campaign opposition candidates were able to make their objections to an elected president and to major revisions to the Constitution (just, they contended, to create a position for Lee) a popular issue. Lee responded by saying that the elected president was not being designed for him, that he was not looking for a job, and that if the issue was put to a referendum, he would declare himself out of the race in order to strengthen his moral position for the campaign. In September 1988 Goh Chok Tong announced that he intended to retain Lee in the cabinet as a senior minister in the PMO once he stepped down as prime minister. Further, on August 31, 1989, Parliament reelected President Wee Kim Wee to a second four-year term, indicating that there is no longer the same sense of urgency behind the elected president proposal. In October 1989 Lee confirmed that he did not want to be the first president. He said that he would remain in the cabinet for the remainder of the current parliamentary term, or about four more years.

The younger leaders are in an equally anomalous situation. They know they need to be perceived as "calling the shots" if they are going to build credibility, and they know they must evolve their own style. They proclaim that they have been extensively groomed, have gone through a lengthy apprenticeship, and are ready to meet the challenges ahead. During the 1988 election campaign, various ministers, including Lee Kuan Yew, stated at rallies that cabinet decisions were collective and that the policies of the government since 1985 had been those of the second generation. They are concerned that their contributions may go unnoticed because they are overshadowed by the presence of Lee (they also realize that they are escaping blame for the same reason).[44] Some of the anxiety and frustration over not being perceived as being in charge, even by PAP backbenchers, was illustrated in Goh Chok Tong's letter to the Speaker of Parliament in January 1989. In the letter, Goh wrote,

> The members of cabinet were chosen by me and we are in charge of the day-to-day running of the government, not the prime minister. He chairs cabinet meetings and gives us the benefit of his experience. However, we settle the policies. My colleagues and I are therefore answerable for the performance of this government, not the prime minister. If Members have any questions intended for the prime minister on the actions and conduct of this government, they should address them to me.[45]

To further make his point, in 1989 Goh Chok Tong moved into the center seat on the front bench in Parliament, and Lee Kuan Yew moved two seats away. Yet most are so awed by Lee that they could hardly be expected to oppose with determination any view argued vigorously by him. One has said, "In the night when I sleep, I sleep well knowing that if something goes terribly wrong, the Prime Minister is there to take care of the situation . . . This same feeling is held by other ministers of the second generation."[46]

Nevertheless, the second generation has made an impression. Its members had their way in reversing the graduate mother scheme, modifying the school streaming system, and in postponing and later modifying an unpopular decision on changes to the CPF regulations. They played a key role in managing the economy during the recession, especially in initiating wage restraint and in cost-cutting. They were instrumental in formulating the constitutional changes creating GRCs and town councils, and their views seemed to prevail concerning the role and functions of the proposed elected president. They were also responsible for a number of initiatives intended to promote consulation and more participation as part of a new PAP style. Finally, they took over the task of talent-scouting for possible MPs and ministers, and they organized and ran the campaigns for the general elections of 1984 and 1988. In fact, Lee Kuan Yew acknowledged the new generation's independence after the 1988 election when he commented that he would have fought the campaign a bit differently. "I would have forced the opposition to fight on my issues, and not allowed them to run around and come up with spurious and ridiculous ideas and diffuse the focus. . . . But, perhaps that is the way in which a younger electorate prefers to have issues debated. So be it."[47] At present, an unofficial mutual veto seems to be in operation. Lee appears to be the final arbiter on major issues should he choose to exercise his veto, but the second-generation leaders have stated bluntly that no policies will be enacted unless they agree with them.

A POST-LEE GOVERNMENT

The key consideration in the search for successors was to ensure continuity. The PAP leaders were looking for people with similar social, economic, and political views and with the intellectual capability to manage the state under its prevailing political ethos. Thus, it is not surprising to find the new team espousing similar political views on fundamental issues. Goh Chok Tong has noted, "What we have now, works. Our job is to ensure that the system continues to work and that it is not changed."[48]

The young leaders appear to share some basic views: Singapore is small and vulnerable and to survive requires social discipline among the populace and astute leadership at the top; the Communists have been defeated once, narrowly, but continual vigilance is required to prevent them from threatening the state once again; political stability is a prerequisite for economic growth and prosperity, and stability requires controls and limits on political participation; the opposition is not loyal— it is obstructive at best and destructive at worst; government must be firm, decisive, and willing to make the tough unpopular decisions—it cannot "surrender to the mob" or pander to the voters. "The new generation leaders . . . must go for policies that work, not policies that are popular. After a while, when the policies work, they too will gain the confidence of the people. We must, of course, respect public opinion, but we must remember that popular solutions may not be the right ones to cure some endemic problems."[49] They also appear to believe, although less so perhaps than the prime minister, in the suitability for Singapore of the Confucian gentleman (junzi) as the ideal political leader—someone morally upright and trustworthy. "We believe that leaders must be men of ability and integrity, committed to the public good."[50]

The new leaders also appear to share doubts about the suitability of "democracy," particularly about the ability of the voting masses to understand their own, and Singapore's, best interests, especially during hard times. This weakness of democracy is compounded in Singapore, they believe, by the absence of a naturally conservative rural population that lends stability to democratic practice in many countries. They fear slipping into the quagmire of the Third World pattern of political instability and economic stagnation. They believe that if the PAP ever loses at the polls, all is lost for Singapore. There is no margin for error.

The new leaders do realize that they are about to lead a Singapore citizenry that has grown hungry for more openness in government, increased political participation, and more tolerance toward dissenting views. Consequently, these leaders are attempting to work out a style of leadership that is more open and consultative, that will listen, that appears to offer the possibility of policy accommodation, that seeks to build consensus by coopting the vast middle ground, and that will absorb some level of criticism without retaliation. Goh Chok Tong has stated that he wants to introduce a more participative style of government, but, he cautioned, his job is to "forge consensus, not to encourage dissent."[51] The new leaders cannot appear to believe that they are "always right," yet neither can they appear not to know what they are doing.[52] They must appear competent but not arrogant.

A number of initiatives have been taken to promote a new style. The showpiece is the National Agenda for Action, a government blueprint of national priorities and policy proposals put together after a year of public forums. The introduction to the paper on the agenda presented to Parliament called it "a massive exercise in consultation, public education, and consensus-building."[53] Other efforts include (1) the establishment of a feedback unit to solicit citizen's views; (2) the creation of parliamentary committees, each with resource panels, to give backbenchers a role in policy formulation (these are really PAP caucus committees); (3) the creation of advisory councils on social issues; (4) the establishment of the Institute of Policy Studies as a forum for educated debate; and (5) the proposal to create a new category of nonpartisan, nonelected MPs to contribute to parliamentary debate. Such efforts also include increased constituency work and walkabouts to ensure more exposure of and access to ministers and MPs at the grass roots and a revitalization of the PAP machinery because the second generation may have to increase its reliance on the party organization to mobilize public support.

Chan Heng Chee has added a note of caution, however, about the new style: "If Singaporeans read the new developments as a trend in the liberalisation of PAP governing philosophy, there were regular reminders that core party concerns remained unchanged."[54] The subtle changes that have taken place so far have been those of style rather than substance. It is a strategy aimed at mollifying the young, affluent, and educated. This could be important, however. As one MP notes, the *means* used by the government today to achieve its goals may be just as important as the goals themselves. It is apparently not so easy to break old habits, however. One PAP backbencher in April 1989 expressed dismay over the "mishandling" of a government bill in which there had been no prior public consultation or explanation and which generated a "vehemently negative" public reaction.[55]

One of the most important factors bearing on the future effectiveness of the new generation of leaders is how well they can work together. The original leaders were an uncommonly cohesive group, and there were few challenges to the hierarchy (Ong Eng Guan being the primary exception). This meant that Lee Kuan Yew could function as leader without having to look over his shoulder for a potential usurper, that the PAP did not suffer from any damaging factionalism, and that the principle of collective responsibility could operate smoothly. With the recruitment of a successor group, Lee and his close advisers have stressed the importance of team cohesion, and Lee has fired those not considered team players (or conversely, in the local lexicon, those thought to be "empire-builders").

The new group has been exhorted to function as a team, compelled to choose a leader from among themselves, and ordered not to transgress the strict PAP rules governing intraparty competition. These leaders have gone to some lengths to build a sense of camaraderie and unity among themselves because, unlike the founders, they did not know each other very well prior to government service. They hold precabinet meetings over lunch every week to discuss issues before subjecting their views to the scrutiny of the prime minister, and they have been meeting one afternoon a month as a study group since 1982 to consider long-term issues. If a policy proposal is controversial, the minister responsible circulates a paper, and then the team meets to debate the issue. Once decided, the whole team is collectively answerable for a particular policy. From this, habits of full discussion, trust, accommodation and consensus-building have been developing into an established working style.[56]

B. G. Lee's place in the scheme of things must be considered, however. There is no concrete evidence that an internal rift is developing or that the PAP is becoming factionalized into a Goh Chok Tong/ moderate wing and B. G. Lee/hard-line wing. But the public perceives

B. G. Lee as such a strong challenger for the top post that Goh may not be prime minister for very long (the opposition has called Goh a "seat warmer"). Many believe that the longer Lee Kuan Yew delays his political departure, the more Goh's chances diminish. Indeed, one of the comments about the new PAP candidates in the 1988 election was that a high percentage of them were "pro-B. G." (this situation was partly generational and partly because B. G. recruited them). Also, the most important cabinet readjustment in September 1988, when Wong Kan Seng replaced Dhanabalan as foreign minister, was perceived by many Singaporeans as a B. G.-man moving up the ladder at the expense of a Goh-man.[57] It has been suggested that the number of young (in their mid- or late thirties) and mostly Chinese former Ministry of Defence (MINDEF) bureaucrats and ex-SAF officers moving into politics has been increasing quite rapidly lately. Although it is government policy to direct SAF talent into various areas of government service, the *Far Eastern Economic Review* connects this increase into politics to efforts by B. G. to consolidate his political and administrative power.[58]

Goh tends to dismiss the notion of B. G. as a threat, saying that he has been chosen as successor by the second-generation ministers and that B. G. is "third generation." B. G. Lee, on the other hand, while affirming that Goh is the leader and taking pains to deny that he would allow himself to become a challenger, says that there is no second or third generation, only the founding fathers and all of the rest.[59] The fact that PAP ministers continue to deny publicly any rivalry or friction within the cabinet only reinforces public perceptions that there is. Certainly with B. G. as part of the "inner cabinet" (along with S. Jayakumar, Tony Tan, and Wong Kan Seng, in addition to Goh), the generational lines have become blurred.[60] Goh seems to have the solid support of the second-generation ministers and majority control of the party's CEC and so would be difficult to topple in an overt power play. Such a power play is not likely, however, because this would be so disruptive that the party might split (and it is inconceivable that Lee Kuan Yew would allow this). Rather, it is widely believed that much depends on Goh's first term of office as prime minister. If there are problems, there will be considerable pressure on Goh to step aside voluntarily. Whether these implications and conjectures add up to healthy competition, an internal understanding of the hierarchial order and the timing of any changes in it, or internal divisiveness is hard to predict.

CONCLUSION

Lee Kuan Yew and his close PAP colleagues, most notably Goh Keng Swee, have been nation-builders and modernizers par excellence.

Modern Singapore is thus indelibly identified with them. To a great extent they have indeed created a Third World "miracle" in thirty years. They have done it by combining brainpower and ideas with administrative skills, incorruptibility, inexhaustible energy, great political savvy and cunning, and no shortage of toughness. The founding fathers have fashioned the political parameters for modern Singapore: free enterprise (under limits set by the state) with growth priorities, multinationalism, democracy coupled with constraints on individual freedoms and conscious depoliticization, and meritocracy. The result has been efficient and effective government and a compliant and hard-striving citizenry.

The times, however, are changing. Those Singaporeans who suffered through the political crises, sometimes played out in the streets, and the economic hardships of the 1950s and early 1960s are gone or are graying. Younger Singaporeans now constitute more than half the electorate (in 1988, 69 percent of the electorate was younger than forty-three). Most of these are well educated and have known nothing but security, opportunity, and growing affluence. This had led, expectedly but still rather ironically, to increasing demands for a liberalization of the political process and less state intrusion and regimentation. In 1968, after the PAP had won every seat at an election, Lee Kuan Yew predicted that an opposition would inevitably return, if for no other reason than a desire for change. Years later he remarked that the electors felt that they were missing something and wanted to experience some of the excitement of political combat.

Singaporeans appear to want a broader interpretation of legitimate political activity. A government survey of young Singaporeans showed that the Chinese educated were more supportive of the government than the English educated, especially the professionals.[61] It is perhaps natural for a young, English-educated, middle-class society exposed to Western ideas to yearn for more avenues of political dissent, to feel that the Lee Kuan Yew approach was right for the 1960s but is not for the 1990s. Younger Singaporeans want to participate more and be led by a government that is open, responsive, and fair and that listens and does not overreact to criticism. They want the government to show some faith in their ability to weigh issues carefully and, as voters, to make rational choices in a setting that allows for some diversity. Some are attracted to liberal issues, such as human rights, social welfare, and more extensive assistance to the poor. Some seem to think it "in vogue" to be anti-PAP, although such feelings generally do not run deep. Many others are just annoyed at government arrogance and find it hard to believe that Singapore's survival is any longer "on the line." They do not believe that the government understands or cares about what they want, and they resent what they perceive as government cynicism (such as statements that the young, well educated, and affluent want some opposition but not so much as to cause property values to decline). Some of these are willing to "take our chances come what may" by voting opposition. Few, it would seem, fully appreciate that Singapore might not be able to have all the trappings of a liberal social democracy *and* sustained affluence. One well-informed Singaporean, who estimated that the top 30 percent of the highly educated were to some degree disaffected, pointed out that the problem was that these people did not read, had no perspective, and could not appreciate the difficulties of governing.[62]

Perhaps the biggest change is that Singaporeans are no longer unquestioningly obedient, nor are government explanations automatically accepted. Legitimacy is not an issue, but credibility is. For example, even televised confessions have not ended some public skepticism over the government's contention that the 1987 ISA arrests of various church and social workers for antigovernment activity constituted a conspiracy by Marxists and others. The new leaders certainly agonized over the arrests. Goh Chok Tong, in a statement to Parliament, said that he and others had serious reservations about the evidence presented. It was, he said, the toughest decision that they had ever had to make and the first time they had been required to consider using the ISA. He also noted that the ministers originally reached the conclusion that the group did not represent an immediate threat to state security, but they had eventually been convinced that there was a long-term threat and action was required.[63] One member of the opposition commented that the PAP knows it has a credibility problem vis-à-vis the repressive actions taken between 1986 and 1988, but it cannot seem to change its style for two reasons: Lee Kuan Yew lets his views be known, and the new team wants to "cut its teeth" on some tough issues.[64]

The economic environment is changing as well. Singapore has reached a stage of development where rapid double-digit growth figures are now unlikely to be sustained. Yet decades of spectacular growth have created expectations of more of the same, and consequently there is a danger that these hopes will be frustrated, and the government will be held to blame. As a result, the successors are going to face a new set of challenges, and they will have to do more than simply attempt to maintain the status quo as state managers. They will have to be adept and resourceful politicians with a nose to the ground, capable of adapting where required and of astutely persuading a partially inattentive citizenry.

It is precisely as "politicians," however, that the most concern for the successors' abilities is expressed. They are perceived as technocrats only just in the process of learning political skills useful in dealing with the public and with other states. Techniques can, of course, be learned and language and speaking skills improved. It is possible, with organizational talent, to build up a loyal base of support and with knowledge and experience handle difficult international situations with balance and caution. But politics is a special occupation with demanding requirements. It is not so certain that flair and appeal, the indefinable ability to rouse a generally apathetic citizenry to one's cause, can be taught or that steadfastness in the face of mounting political pressure can be learned on the spot. These have been the concerns of Lee Kuan Yew—that the younger ministers are not skilled enough mobilizers and that they have not been battle tested. Lee has said that in a crisis, it takes the prime minister and at least two others who will not buckle under pressure. "But my worry is this," he said, without naming names, "I can only see two I am sure [will not buckle]."[65] It is not necessary, or desirable, for a governing team to have too many dynamic politicians because this could raise the potential for rivalry and discord. But the governing team should have someone who projects personal appeal, be it through flair or a perception of his trustworthiness, effectiveness, and decency, and he should ideally be the leader.

One way of attempting to evaluate the new team is to look at roles. Some of these roles would include leader, ideas man, troubleshooter, cabinet conciliator, PR man, parliamentary debater, and sectional grassroots mobilizer. These roles are not exclusive; one minister might fill several roles. For example, Tony Tan is considered a brilliant technocrat, a reticent mandarin who is principled and conscientious. He is a cabinet conciliator who is content not to be the leader (formerly a front-runner and Lee Kuan Yew's choice, he took himself out of the leadership race). He is an ideas man and a troubleshooter who quite often takes over portfolios when reform or adjustment is deemed necessary. In many ways, he is the Goh Keng Swee of the second generation.

The new team seems well balanced with respect to the loyal lieutenant roles. Two, however, could fit into the role of "leader": Goh Chok Tong and B. G. Lee. Goh has outstanding leadership and organizational qualities, but reputedly they are those of a corporate chair. He is capable of making tough decisions yet consults his colleagues and tries to build consensus for these decisions. He has the shrewdness of a politician, coupled with natural decency, but little public flair. Articulate in private settings, he is not a dynamic public speaker and has been unable to master Mandarin (he refers questions in Chinese to others) or become very comfortable with Malay—disadvantages in multiracial Singapore. He is viewed positively as not being oversensitive or pompous and as a man who will listen, although he may reply in the end that he does not agree with you. Some Singaporeans see him as a "breath of fresh air" and as the best prospect to oversee some mild liberalization of the political process. Others regard him as tough-minded, committed to a custodian vision of leadership, and not likely to be very liberal.

B. G. Lee is a comparative newcomer to the cabinet inner circles, but he fits the role of leader well. He is a natural politician and he has flair. The first few years he was in politics he was described in such superlative terms (infectious laugh, patrician with a humble demeanor, great communicator, personable, charming, and convincing) that a "most un-Singaporean cult of personality is already germinating."[66] Recently, however, this image has been fading, and others describe him as coldly intellectual, arrogant, hard, and inflexible, a man with a penchant for cutting off subordinates with the order "Do it!" But few would deny that he is an excellent public speaker in several languages, an equally good parliamentary debater, a competent minister, and a very good grass-roots mobilizer. Many consider B. G. Lee the greatest "hard-liner" against any liberalization of the political system among the successors. Ironically perhaps, some of the same Singaporeans who complain that the government is too illiberal seem fascinated by B. G. and the prospect of his one day leading the country—which shows the power of political personality.

It is still premature to compare the new team with the old. The original leaders were strong, tough, and effective but perhaps unacceptably stern and unresponsive for the late-1980s electorate. The new leaders will need to develop a style of rule for the 1990s that takes into account a situation in which the opposition wins sympathy just because it is the opposition. They need to be tough, but not too tough. There is a comparison circulating in Singapore that sums up the situation: The old PAP leaders had brains and guts, the young ones have brains and (almost without exception) heart, and the opposition has heart and guts. The second generation has the "brains" to govern effectively and the dedication to go along with it. It is going to have to summon up the "guts" when necessary so that it can govern wisely, compassionately, and resolutely.

7
A Dependent But Dynamic Economy

Singapore's economy[1] is dictated mainly by its location, size, and lack of natural resources. More than one hundred fifty years ago, its situation on a crossroads of trading routes gave it the opportunity to develop a thriving entrepôt trade that is still important today. The lack of a hinterland and the absence of natural resources, however, have made Singapore's economy extremely dependent on trade. To be sure, Singapore has been so successful in promoting trade that the value of its imports and exports combined is roughly three times the value of its gross national product, although, because of the entrepôt trade, some of these exports are actually reexports. Yet this achievement rests on a precarious base. Even when Singapore was part of Malaysia (its natural hinterland) in 1963–1965, there was no free trade between the two, and later there were even more restrictions because of Malaysia's natural desire to protect its industries and develop its ports. Singapore depends on Malaysia for its water, and any serious disruption of communications in the region could threaten Singapore's oil supply.

Singapore's economic performance has been impressive. Its income per capita (about one-quarter of which goes to resident foreigners) is more than twelve times the 1960 figures in real terms. It is now about $8,000, roughly four times Malaysia's and more than one-third of Japan's. Even allowing for the fact that unlike neighboring countries, its GNP figure is not kept down by the existence of a large, relatively poor agricultural population, this is a considerable achievement. Singapore is no longer considered a developing country but rather a newly industrializing country (NIC). Also, unlike some states that became rich quickly—for example, because of petroleum deposits—Singapore's wealth is accompanied by sophisticated ways of doing business in which modern technology is matched by efficiency and an almost complete absence of corruption.

How has Singapore contrived to do so well economically, given the severe constraints mentioned previously? Apart from location, it has several advantages: The majority of the population are immigrants (mostly Chinese) with a deserved reputation for skill in business, especially trading; Singapore possesses a basic communications structure and an efficient administrative system, both bequeathed to it by Britain; and Singapore benefited from the economic prosperity of neighboring countries and the oil exploration boom in the region in the 1970s. In addition, Singapore's success has rested on its leaders' perception of the country's dependence and their recognition that the world does not owe it a living (a favorite phrase of the prime minister) and that it must adapt quickly and realistically to changing world conditions. Not even the PAP has been consistently successful in making appropriate and quick adjustments, but it has performed better than most governments. Singapore also has leaders dedicated to the pursuit of excellence and the rewarding of merit, and Singapore has a hardworking labor force. Furthermore, the government encourages values that are essential for the successful conduct of trade—honesty, integrity, trust, credibility, and incorruptibility.

THE SINGAPORE ECONOMY, 1959–1989

In spite of Singapore's economic success, a look at the economy since 1959 shows that the economy has undergone a number of ups and downs.[2] The period 1959–1965 was marked by political change and uncertainty. Singapore's internal independence (1959) was followed by divisions in the PAP resulting in the formation of the Barisan Sosialis (and an accompanying rise in strikes) and by Singapore's entry into Malaysia in 1963. This was followed by Singapore's exit from Malaysia two years later without having obtained the Malaysian common market for which it had hoped. Confrontation with Indonesia in 1963–1966 (see Chapter 4) interrupted trade with an important partner. The new government also inherited a high rate of unemployment, more than 10 percent in 1960, and a rapidly growing population, 4.5 percent annually. Consequently, this was a period of relatively slow economic growth, averaging less than 6 percent in 1960–1965, and negative growth (−4.3 percent) occurred in 1964.

To the PAP leaders in 1959 it seemed that even a merger into Malaysia would offer only limited opportunities of expanding the entrepôt trade. They adopted, therefore, a policy of industrialization. Guided by a report from a UN industrial survey mission, they began to set up a system of industrial estates; land clearing for the Jurong estates began in 1961. Manufacturing then accounted for only about 10 percent of the

GNP, so the EDB was created in 1961 with the main object of promoting investment, and various financial incentives were offered.

Although the PAP had identified itself as "socialist," it was aware that the entrepôt trade was an unsuitable candidate for socialization. The PAP also believed that apart from providing a basic economic infrastructure, "state enterprise" was often inefficient.[3] Under the British, local manufacturing had not been encouraged, and for the most part, only small firms were in existence. To obtain quick results from its manufacturing drive, the government looked mainly to foreign investors.

After the separation from Malaysia in 1965, for a short time Singapore followed an import-substitution policy that placed tariffs— some of which replaced previous quotas—on a number of goods (mostly manufactured) so as to encourage their production in Singapore. Given the limits to the use of import substitution in countries with small domestic markets, a substantial switch to production for export soon occurred, with a corresponding reduction of the number of protected items. The move was partly a reaction to an announcement by the British that they would withdraw their remaining military bases by 1971; these accounted for almost one-fifth of Singapore's employment and GNP. Singapore made the logical decision to increase its exposure to and participation in the world economy. In order to do so quickly, it had to encourage investment even more strongly and offer potential investors not only an efficient infrastructure and services but also industrial peace. This was effected through legislation, particularly the Employment Act of 1968, and by an amendment to the Industrial Relations Act. These established rights for workers as well as duties, but the net effect was to strengthen management's powers in respect of hiring, firing, transfers, and so on. Cooperation between the government and labor continued when the National Wages Council was established in 1972. Economic growth had produced an increasing demand for labor, and the idea behind the NWC was to prevent disruptive, rapid rises in wages. The NWC had representatives from government, labor, and business, and each year, until recently, depending on changes in the economy, recommended guidelines for wage increases. These were not mandatory but were followed by the public sector (for the next decade or so) and by most of the private sector. The government also created numerous public enterprises—some intended to facilitate the operations of the private sector and some to undertake activities in fields the private sector was unwilling to enter.

The second half of the 1960s and the start of the 1970s were accompanied by high growth, which in every year from 1966 through 1973 reached double digits. By the early 1970s, unemployment had fallen to 2 or 3 percent and remained at about that level until the start of the

1980s recession. Apart from Singapore's own efforts, these results were helped by world prosperity (including some spin-offs from the war in Vietnam, such as an increased entrepôt trade and spending by U.S. soldiers on leave) and by a decline in the rate of growth of the population. This period of prosperity was cut short, however, by the quadrupling of oil prices and by soaring food prices, which led to high inflation rates in 1973 and 1974 (around 20 percent). A world recession limited growth to about 7 percent in 1974 and 4 percent in 1975. After 1975, although growth was high by world standards, on the average it was less than 10 percent a year and failed to reach the record levels of 1966–1973. By the mid-1970s, in an effort to stimulate growth and create as many jobs as possible, the government had become rather unselective in the type of industry it encouraged. Relatively low wages had led private industry to use labor-intensive techniques even after labor shortages were apparent. Consequently, some firms survived only because wages had been kept artificially low. There was a reaction to this situation in 1978 when the government announced one of its biggest and most contentious switches in economic policy—the wage correction policy. It aimed at allowing wages to rise through the influence of market forces so that labor would move to industries that were more capital intensive and specialized and would be less vulnerable to competition from developing countries, which depended for their competitiveness on the use of unskilled or semiskilled labor.[4] Because Singapore's wages had been kept so low, employers had no incentive before this policy was instituted to move into more capital-intensive industries, adopt more efficient methods, or train workers to acquire new skills. The government wanted to encourage industries such as precision engineering and optics, aircraft component manufacture and repair, higher-value electronics, and computer equipment and parts through tax exemptions, loans, and so on. Sometimes the change was described as a move toward high-tech industries. There was also a feeling that some of the fruits of Singapore's high growth rates should now be passed on to the workers.

To implement the policy, annual wage guidelines were drawn up for 1979, 1980, and 1981. In each of the first two years, wages were to rise by an average of 20 percent and in the third year by 14–18 percent. In later years, increases were to be linked to productivity. Initially, the policy seemed to be working. It led to an increase in inflation in 1980, but prices then leveled out. Workers who were released from industries were for the most part absorbed by others, so unemployment did not increase. Some labor-intensive industries moved, for example, to Malaysia. Local firms suffered more than foreign firms because most of the latter were already upgraded technically or had the means to adjust; moreover, a lower proportion of their costs were labor costs. The hardest-hit firms were small ones that could neither move out nor adjust because they lacked the capital, technology, or necessary management skills. From 1981 to 1984, however, wage increases exceeded the NWC guidelines and also exceeded gains in productivity.[5] Expectations of wage increases remained high, some wage contracts were for a period that had not yet expired, and the demand for labor was intensified by the construction boom in the early 1980s, which arose in part from an accelerated HDB housing construction program. Consequently, in Singapore wages and other costs, such as CPF contributions, had grown much faster than productivity and so firms had performed worse than their counterparts in Hong Kong, South Korea, and Taiwan.[6] By 1985, the effects of the worldwide recession were fully evident in Singapore and led to negative growth, the worst economic performance in twenty years, a decline in exports, and a rise in unemployment to 6 percent.

Some of Singapore's troubles were externally induced—for example, low petroleum prices and the decline in the demand for shipping had affected Singapore's oil refining and petrochemical industries as well as ship repairing and shipbuilding. Falling commodity prices, including oil and gas prices, affected both Indonesia and Malaysia and so resulted in a loss of trade between Singapore and each of these countries. There was a reduction in the U.S. growth rate in 1984–1985 that lessened its demand for electronics imports from Singapore.

The recession, however, was also intensified by internal factors. Costs of production were high and included wages and other labor costs such as employers' CPF contributions as well as rents and charges by statutory boards. The Economic Committee—headed by B. G. Lee and appointed in 1985 to review the progress of the economy and identify directions for future growth—cited these internal factors as having contributed to the recession, terming them "rigidities" in the system, some of which the government had been slow to act on. As short-term measures to meet the recession, the committee recommended proposals to cut employers' costs even below the reductions already made by the government—for instance, wage restraint for two years, cuts in taxes on employers and in their CPF contributions from 25 to 10 percent of an employee's wage or salary, lower statutory board charges, investment allowances, and so on.[7]

Partly as a result of such measures, after only a slight gain in growth in 1986 (almost 2 percent), there was 8.5 percent growth in 1987 and 11 percent in 1988. Growth for 1989 was likely to be around 9 percent, but less than that for 1990.

From 1960 to 1984 (the last "prerecession" year), there was a decided change in the contribution to the economy made by various sectors. The percentage of GDP provided by manufacturing rose by about 80 percent—declining somewhat during the 1980s slump—and financial business services almost doubled. (By 1984, the share of construction had more than doubled, although this was temporary, resulting from the housing boom of the early 1980s, and it quickly dropped during the subsequent recession.) The big loser was commerce—the 1984 share being only about half of the 1960 share. During a quarter century, the Singapore economy had shifted its emphasis from trade to manufacturing and the provision of financial and business services. At the same time, because of the economy's high growth rate, the *absolute* (as opposed to *percentage*) figures for commerce rose substantially—the 1984 figure was more than five times the 1960 total. Smaller sectors, such as agriculture, fishing, and quarrying, showed an absolute increase but a relative decline. As a result of these changes, in 1984 four major sectors accounted for four-fifths of total production: commerce, manufacturing, transportation and communications, and financial and business services.

The last three sectors can be subdivided to show the thrust of Singapore's economic development more clearly. In manufacturing (1985), machinery and appliances led the field in terms of value added, amounting to about two-fifths of the total. New industries, such as electronics and computers, became increasingly important. Next, in order of importance, came chemical products, transportation equipment, and petroleum (its share was dropping).

Although the transportation and communications share was roughly constant between 1961 and the mid-1980s, there were some spectacular advances. Singapore pioneered the use of containers in Asia and quick turnaround for ships. General cargo carried by sea multiplied about six times, and the carriage of mineral oil in bulk rose by slightly more than that. Air traffic increases were even more evident, greater than the worldwide trend, and a second passenger terminal was planned at Changi airport. Similarly, telecommunications (direct exchange lines) increased seventeen times in a little more than twenty years.

Financial and business services also flourished. By 1987, Singapore had 137 commercial banks (both local and foreign), 59 merchant banks, 34 finance companies, 86 insurance companies, and 8 international money brokers. The financial system was strong enough to withstand a severe stock exchange crisis at the end of 1985, when a Malaysian firm with close Singapore links collapsed and the market was closed for three days. Many investors were hurt, and several brokerage firms went under. New regulations and safeguards were adopted, however, and confidence was restored. The market also weathered the rapid decline in share prices in October 1987, although the initial fall was slightly greater than in any other major stock market. In the longer term, share prices could be depressed in the event of a recession in either the United States or Japan.

As had been envisaged for some time, the Malaysian and Singapore governments set a date for the "delisting" (exit) of Malaysian companies from the Singapore stock exchange. They chose December 31, 1989, as the final date for delisting.

The government's aim has been to offer such a wide range of financial services that Singapore can become not just a regional financial center but a "financial supermarket." For example, as early as 1968 an Asian dollar market was established by facilitating the entry of foreign banks and by the operation of offshore dollar accounts. The market's success was facilitated by regional growth and other international factors as well as by Singapore's political stability and the government's policies of permitting a free flow of funds and imposing only low levels of taxation. In 1984, Singapore opened trading in financial futures and extended this trading beyond currencies to include gold, Eurodollar time deposits, the Nikkei index of the Tokyo stockmarket, and U.S. Treasury bonds, although these operations are subject to competition from Tokyo, Sydney, and other financial centers. To conduct such operations, banks have adopted advanced automative and electronic systems. Many of these financial institutions' activities are totally remote from the ordinary person's idea of what banks do. The Development Bank of Singapore's high-rise building contains the offices of dozens of "bankers' banks" from around the world, none of which handles "money" in the ordinary sense. Fortunately for the visitor who wishes to change travelers' checks for a few hundred Singapore dollars, on the ground floor of the building there is a small sundries store willing to undertake such transactions.

In contrast to the expanding modern sector, about 19 percent of the workers in manufacturing are employed in "cottage industries," although these may actually be carried on in a high-rise flat or, in the case of one producer of Malay slippers, a converted chicken coop. The people concerned make artifacts such as auto license plates; mahjong sets; carvings; gold, silver, and tin products; shirt seams; and even electronics parts. Many of these industries provide a living for an entire family, which prefers to live that way, and many industries, although not "high tech," are comparatively highly skilled and/or turn out products intended for the expanding "yuppie" market.[8]

By mid-1989, the manufacturing sector and the finance and business sector each contributed a bit more than 25 percent of the GDP. But although some components of manufacturing were still strong performers, such as machinery, chemicals, and shipbuilding, growth in electronics had slackened. Finance and business was expected to be the fastest growing sector during 1989. The depressed construction sector was reviving at last.

In spite of Singapore's dependence on the outside world, the government has some room to maneuver in its efforts to promote growth and maintain price stability.[9] It can attempt to influence the economy as a whole, mainly through its macroeconomic policies on the exchange rate and taxes, savings via the CPF and the surpluses of bodies in the public sector, and wage and labor policies. The government also carries on business activities and regulates and influences the operations of private business.

GOVERNMENT MANAGEMENT OF THE ECONOMY

The government's economic policies are complex, and only some of the major features of their relation to Singapore's recent problems can be indicated here. The Singapore government, through the Monetary Authority of Singapore, is able to exert some influence on the exchange rate by buying or selling Singapore dollars against foreign currencies. If, for example, Singapore has difficulty selling its products abroad, one way of stimulating sales is to make the Singapore dollar cheaper to foreigners, thus encouraging the demand for its products. Yet, a persistently cheap dollar policy would tend to encourage domestic inflation. Conversely, a higher Singapore dollar would promote stable prices domestically but would make Singaporean goods more costly for foreigners. Generally, the government has tended to tie the value of its dollar fairly closely to the currencies of its major trading partners. During the 1970s, the Singapore dollar appreciated against the U.S. dollar by about 3 percent a year. After 1979, it stood at an almost constant rate as compared with the U.S. dollar (between 2.1 and 2.2 percent). With the decline of the latter in 1986, the Singapore dollar appreciated slightly against it but still tended to follow it. In September 1989, the dollar was worth $1.97.

Unlike larger countries, Singapore—a major offshore banking center with no foreign exchange controls—does not appear to have tried affecting policy by controlling the money supply. For example, during the 1985–1986 recession, liquidity (the supply of money) probably decreased.[10] The government, however, did try to encourage economic activity through reductions in corporate income tax and the payroll tax.

Savings also have considerable effects on the economy. Singapore's domestic savings greatly exceed its foreign savings, amounting to almost 40 percent of GNP, higher than those of Japan, and indeed the highest in the world. Some of these savings are private, but most are public. This high rate of saving makes possible increases in capital that promote growth, thus setting Singapore apart from Third World countries that have to struggle to maintain even a subsistence level for their people. This rate of saving has also helped Singapore to avoid incurring a burdensome foreign debt. Foreign debt is only one-sixth of annual earnings from the export of merchandise, and "official, published" government foreign reserves (the actual total is higher) are about $17.4 billion.

Not all the consequences of this high rate of saving are beneficial,[11] although it does increase opportunities for future consumption. Some reservations about it depend on value judgments. It is hard to say how much "jam" (present consumption) one should forego today in order to have more "jam" tomorrow or ten years from now. Actually, the argument is more complex. Most of the domestic saving is determined by government or quasigovernment agencies, not by individuals. The main sources are government surpluses (of revenue over expenditure), the surpluses of statutory boards, and contributions to the CPF.

The amount of savings resulting from various government decisions may be larger than individuals would have chosen to save if the choice had been left with them. Also, the mere act of saving does not increase the amount of capital in existence until it is invested. A large part of the savings that come into the hands of the government (through revenue and statutory board surpluses and contributions to the CPF) are invested abroad through the Government of Singapore Investment Corporation. (Singapore is now one of the biggest foreign investors in Malaysia, for example.) Thus, the government is making decisions to invest, largely outside Singapore, instead of leaving such decisions to local people who would probably have invested more in the domestic economy.

Wages and Labor

As a result of wage restraint, in 1986 wages rose by only 0.7 percent (2.1 percent in real terms because consumer prices fell by 1.4 percent). The cost of labor to employers fell by about 15 percent because of reduction in CPF contributions and so forth, and productivity rose. As regards the relation between productivity and wages, however, Singapore was behind South Korea, Taiwan, and Hong Kong. A modified version of wage restraint continued in 1987, and by September 1987 Singapore's labor costs were comparable internationally to what they had been six years before.

The NWC mechanism for determining wages provided labor leaders with information and helped to secure their agreement and cooperation. But it was essentially a blunt instrument. One of the great lessons of the 1985–1986 recession in Singapore was the difficulty of adjusting wages downward quickly enough to keep Singapore competitive. Another was the need to distinguish *which* wages needed to be adjusted at a given time and which did not.

A subcommittee of the NWC considered these questions during the recession and late in 1986 made proposals that have been accepted by labor and are being substantially implemented.[12] In future, after a preliminary period, there will be four main components of wages: a basic wage determined according to the value of the job, a service increment of about 2 percent, an annual wage supplement of one month's basic wage, and a variable performance bonus. The size of this last item would depend either on profits or on productivity improvement (which would take profitability into account and would be based on the premise that wage increases would grow less than productivity). This proposal provides for more fine-tuning than the previous arrangements, and in July 1988, in the absence of NWC guidelines, it was put into operation; by the end of April 1989 about 60 percent of Singapore's larger companies had adopted it.

This "flexiwage" system, however, became increasingly subject to trade union pressure. Because the demand for labor was so great, unions began to call for more and more flexibility in the flexiwage arrangement. Wages rose by about 8 percent in 1988 (about half of which took the form of variable bonuses) and were expected to rise by about the same amount in 1989—maybe more if Singapore's growth rate for the year was more than 8 percent.[13]

Because of the falling birthrate, the approaching decline in the labor supply is bound to create a bottleneck. In 1988, even before the decline in supply had occurred, the growing demand for labor had become increasingly evident from the increase in "job-hopping," the more rapid turnover of labor,[14] and the drop in unemployment to about 2 percent. The government is urging, and securing, extension of the retirement age beyond the usual private-sector limit of fifty-five (which is also the age for most of the civil service and most statutory boards). The government is also advocating more employment of older people and more part-time employment, especially of women, although this would seem to conflict with the new government policy of encouraging women to have more children (see Chapter 2).[15] Increasing the *quality* of labor may be a substitute for greater numbers. The Economic Committee pointed out that Singapore lagged behind industrial nations, such as the United States, Japan, and even Taiwan and South Korea, in respect of the percentage of the population educated and trained beyond primary level. There should be more preemployment training by universities and polytechnics (necessitating higher annual intakes) and more postgraduate training directed toward supporting high-tech and research and development (R and D) activities and teaching management skills.[16]

Expenditure on R and D in 1984 was only about 0.55 percent of GNP, about half the percentage for South Korea.[17] The government's aim is to raise the R and D figure nearer its percentage of GNP in developed countries—in the United States and Japan, for example, it is almost 3 percent. Because Singapore's resources are limited, the basic research component of R and D will most likely be smaller than the development component, but it has to be sufficient to allow Singapore to identify and exploit any new ideas in technology. The 1986 budget made a start in providing for the expansion of education and training along these lines and gave tax exemptions for some R and D expenditures. By 1988, R and D expenditure had risen to about 1 percent of GNP.

The government has been able to vary the supply of labor in another way. Like some Western European and Middle Eastern countries. it has employed foreign workers for short periods without any obligation to retain them in Singapore. Thus, when labor is in short supply (in the early 1970s, early 1980s, and in 1988–1989), the deficit can be partly made up by the use of relatively unskilled foreign labor (subject to paying a levy), thereby lessening the pressure for wage increases. At its highest level, foreign labor amounted to about 10 percent of the labor force. In the beginning, foreign labor was recruited mainly from Malaysia but later came mostly from India, Indonesia, Sri Lanka, Thailand, and the Philippines. In 1974–1975 and 1985–1986, the numbers of foreign laborers were reduced. A few years ago, the government had plans to phase out the employment of this type of foreign labor. Now, however, it seems to take the view that such labor should be retained, maybe even increased, although some cultural tensions have resulted from the presence of a sizable number of foreigners in Singapore. Since the end of 1987, the labor market, especially in electronics and the garment industry, has been getting so tight that some U.S. investors have seen it as a serious restraint on future growth. It was also revealed, near the end of 1987, that labor was being hired from China and that several hundred Chinese workers had already arrived.[18] In early 1988, the influx of foreign labor continued and filled more than half of the new jobs available in manufacturing.

A second type of foreign labor consists of highly skilled foreigners who supply deficiencies in available local skills. Such people work not only for private firms but also for the government, and they have ranged from planners and international monetary consultants to authorities on Confucianism. Singapore has no intention of dispensing with such temporary immigrants in the foreseeable future. Additionally, in 1987 the government expressed concern because too many of Singapore's professionals and highly skilled citizens were emigrating.

Singapore will undoubtedly benefit from immigration from Hong Kong. So many qualified persons want to leave Hong Kong that even allowing for emigration to North America, Australia, New Zealand and so on, and taking into account Singapore's requirements for education and experience, it might manage to meet its target for receiving about 25,000 qualified people and their families by the mid-1990s.[19]

The Recession: The Need for Coordination

The 1985–1986 recession provides a good example of the use (or nonuse) of the mechanisms through which the government can influence the economy. With hindsight, critics have identified some actions the government could have taken that would have softened the effects of the recession. It could have diagnosed the approach of the recession sooner and taken earlier action to meet it. It could have checked wage rises more quickly, avoided increasing CPF contributions in 1984, and reduced statutory boards' charges in 1984 and 1985, thereby lessening the burden on employers.[20] It could have controlled the construction boom in the early 1980s, thus allowing it to keep construction in reserve as a weapon for stimulating domestic demand when the recession started.

In fact, the government, both before the recommendations of the Economic Committee were made and also as a result of these recommendations, did take measures to deal with the recession, including wage restraint and cuts in taxes, employers' CPF contributions (from 25 percent to 10 percent of an employee's wage or salary), and statutory board charges. There was some reluctance, however, to give up preconceived ideas. The temporary cut in CPF contributions was much easier to put into effect than a wage reduction. Nevertheless, it represented a big modification in B. G. Lee's thinking.[21] Earlier, he had viewed the cut as a measure of last resort, partly because it might be regarded as diminishing workers' savings and making it more difficult for them to become homeowners. The Economic Committee's report, however, did say that the question of the appropriate long-term rates and structure of CPF contributions should be reviewed.[22] It also recommended that statutory boards lower their charges as much as possible and not aim at maximizing profits and that the board's budget policies be treated as part of the government's total budgetary position (which had not been the previous practice).[23] The report rejected as inflationary the lowering of the value of the Singapore dollar as a way of reducing costs—an opinion that coincided with the government's and was already almost an article of faith because it was firmly held by the influential former finance minister, Goh Keng Swee. In short, the experience of the recession indicated the need for better coordination of government policies,[24] and the report seemed to recognize this, at least in principle.

Obviously, the Singapore government plays a major role in managing the whole economy; "private" business is not so private that it can avoid the efforts of government decisions. Nevertheless, business does enjoy a degree of autonomy, and recently the government has come to believe that some of its entrepreneurial functions would be better performed by the private sector. Consequently it has initiated a process of "privatization."

The Public Sector and Privatization

In many respects, Singapore's economy is closer to a free-market economy than is the case in many other countries. There are very few tariffs, no foreign exchange controls, few restrictions on private enterprise or investment, and no limits on profit remittances or capital repatriation. Nevertheless, economic freedom of action can be exercised only within certain limits because the state plays a major role in managing the economy.[25] The state has been active through a host of statutory boards that promoted economic development and social welfare, such as the EDB, HDB, and CPF Board. The state has provided radio, television, health, and education services and has engaged in commercial operations, including Singapore Airlines, a state trading company, a state investment corporation, the Post Office Savings Bank, and perhaps five hundred wholly or partly owned companies. The government has also exercised control through the NWC and the Employment Act and the Industrial Relations Act, to say nothing of its use of a whole range of financial incentives. Consequently, it can determine what is produced, what is available for export, and what is subsidized (for example, some expenditures on health and education and low-cost housing) and what is not, thus substantially modifying the picture of a free market. The market is "free" to the extent that the government allows it to be free.

When all this has been said, however, the government's role is "primarily market facilitating rather than market inhibiting."[26] Once the government has set the parameters for restrictions on the market, it has encouraged businesspeople to be aggressive and competitive and has been deaf to pleas for help to enable firms to carry on, as, for instance, in the case of a pulp and paper mill.

Some of this vast governmental apparatus—much of it in the form of statutory boards—was necessary in order to create and maintain an economic infrastructure for development, for instance in the form of communications, financial services, and housing. Some government organizations, such as the EDB and the Trade Development Board, still have crucial external functions. The EDB has more than a dozen offices in major world centers. Its duties go far beyond merely providing leaflets and incentives. For foreign investors, it even arranges meetings with possible Singapore-based joint venture partners, and after such a project begins, the EDB maintains contact to facilitate the project and, possibly, to encourage expansion. In fact, it acts very much as a consultant, although it is completely funded by the government.

The government has also acquired ownership of enterprises (such as shipbuilding and the airline) that it runs as government corporations or controls through holding companies. The government originally took on these functions because private enterprise was unwilling and/or unable to do so. Most of the government's economic activities now come under several giant holding companies, the largest of which is Temasek Holdings. In 1985, the holding companies had an interest in about 450 government-owned companies with fixed assets of $10 billion and about 60,000 employees.

Since the early 1980s, as in many other countries including the United States, there has been talk in Singapore about "privatization"— handing state functions over to the private sector. These might even include some welfare functions, such as health care, housing, and education (see Chapter 2). The government sought to increase the efficiency of already efficient organizations, not to transfer inefficient ones into private hands. The entire complex of governmental and quasigovernmental organizations has become unwieldy and difficult to control. According to B. G. Lee, one principal justification for privatization is that it would lessen the pressures on high-ranking civil servants by relieving them of making the decisions currently required of them as directors of statutory boards.[27]

For a long time there has been a feeling among certain business-people, which persists in spite of government disclaimers, that some government enterprises enjoy unfair advantages.[28] The Post Office Savings Bank and some of the trading activities of NTUC-sponsored companies, not formally governmental, have been cited as examples. For these and other reasons, in 1985 the Ministry of Finance drew up guidelines that indicated that the government would invest in new industries only if the private sector did not have the desire or the money to start them and would divest itself of its shares in cases in which it did not have a majority share. There would be exceptions where the government still wanted to be involved for security reasons. The government also established a high-level committee to ensure that government-controlled companies would stick to basic functions and not encroach on areas where they would be in competition with private businesses. (The committee's scope, however, did not seem to apply to the Post Office Savings Bank or to the NTUC cooperatives.)

The process of handing over functions to the private sector has proceeded slowly. The government is determined that there be no "quick killings" on the stock market and that privatization not create private semimonopolies that would hurt consumers. There is a shortage of capital (particularly acute during the recession) and of capable managers. To make good the latter deficiency, in the long run more of Singapore's ablest graduates should enter the private, rather than the government, sector. In the short run, when state-controlled firms are privatized, some of the civil servants who function as directors are likely to stay on for a while. A government-appointed Public Sector Divestment Committee recommended various forms of privatization for some government companies in 1987. It also recommended that further study be given to the future of the statutory boards, including the Port of Singapore Authority, the Public Utilities Board, and the Telecommunications Authority.[29] In April 1989, B. G. Lee announced that the Public Utilities Board's electricity and gas operations would begin to be privatized during the next five years (water would be exempted because its use was too sensitive and strategic). An important consideration for this step was that the public would be given a wider range of companies in which to invest.[30] Seven months later, the government decided in principle that telecommunications would be privatized within the next few years.

Relations with Business: Regulations

The balance between the public and the private sectors depends not only on ownership of resources but also on the degree of control the former exercises over the latter. Until recently, many businesspeople believed that the government too seldom sought their advice or listened to it. This situation changed after the Economic Committee met. The majority of those involved in the committee's work—more than a thousand—were from business, although small business had little representation. They supplied real inputs and did not echo government opinions. In response to businesspeople's complaints about overregulation, the government set up a business enterprise committee to hear appeals against the effects of government regulations,[31] and as a result, a substantial number of these were altered or ended.

INTERNATIONAL LINKAGES

Singapore's prosperity is so dependent on external transactions that a good deal of attention has to be given to international linkages, especially trade and investment.

Trade: The Balance of Payments

Without a high level of exports Singapore could not afford to pay for the imports that enable it to enjoy its high standard of living. As Lee Kuan Yew once remarked, Singapore "has a highly urbanized and complex money economy. If there is any recession, any trade fall off . . . we must all remember there is no going back to the land and living off the land."[32]

Export figures can be misleading, however. Only about 65 percent of total exports are actually "made in Singapore" (the so-called domestic exports). The rest, including rubber, timber, and some machinery and textiles, are produced in neighboring countries, transported to Singapore, and then reexported. They constitute Singapore's entrepôt trade, originally the mainstay of the island's prosperity. Their relative importance is declining now, however. In 1960, these reexports made up about 95 percent of total exports, but by the mid-1980s they constituted only about 33 percent. Confusingly, a sizable proportion of "domestic" exports—about a third—consists mostly of petroleum fuels imported into Singapore but refined there before reexport.

Singapore's largest export market (first quarter, 1989) is the United States, which buys more than one-quarter of its exports; the European Economic Community (EEC) is next, followed by Malaysia and Japan. Machinery and equipment are the major goods items. Within this category, Singapore has been exporting increasing amounts of computer equipment and electronic components to the United States, although exports of these items fell off later in 1989. Mineral fuels are an important export to ASEAN countries and also constitute a prominent export to Japan.

Imports to Singapore may be divided into two broad groups. One consists of items the country needs because it does not produce them in sufficient quantities, such as food, road vehicles, and aircraft. The other consists of raw materials or equipment that Singaporeans use mainly for converting into exports, such as some mineral fuels, rubber, and chemicals.

The principal countries that export to Singapore correspond closely, but not completely, to those that import from it. Japan is followed by the United States, and then by Malaysia, "West Asia" (Iran, Saudi Arabia, the United Arab Emirates, Kuwait, and so on), and the EEC. The imports from West Asia consist mainly of oil. Whereas Singapore's imports and exports do not differ too much in value as regards the United States, Malaysia, and the EEC, this is not so for West Asia and Japan. As regards West Asia, the excess of imports over exports is explained by Singapore's substantial requirements for oil. There is a large imbalance with Japan, whose exports to Singapore are about three times its imports.

Japan provides about one-third of the machinery and transportation equipment; the United States provides about one-quarter. The dominating position of Japanese manufactures is quite striking.

In 1985, as a result of the recession, Singapore's external trade declined and also fell slightly in 1986. But trade grew in 1987 by 23 percent. Total domestic exports were an estimated 20 percent higher than in 1986 (35 percent if oil were excluded), benefiting from the rise in the yen and European currencies. There were higher exports to the United States and Japan and possibilities that Japan and West Germany would transfer some of their manufacturing projects to Singapore companies, which could produce them more cheaply.[33] Reexports, which had fallen slightly in 1986, had recovered, partly because of a rise in commodity prices and higher trade between MNCs in Singapore and Malaysia. Imports grew by 19 percent, the rise being mainly in semi-manufactured goods and in machinery and equipment. Both exports and imports rose sharply in 1988. In 1989, however, the rate of increase in the export of goods slowed down, particularly those to the United States, although the export of services, such as tourism, ship repairing, and banking, was booming.

The yearly value of Singapore's imports is substantially larger than that of its exports. Nevertheless, Singapore has a favorable balance in some types of services, such as tourism. Also, as long as Singapore enjoys the confidence of investors, more capital flows into it than flows out. This was so even during the depression in 1985, with the consequence that the country's foreign exchange resources actually increased.

Trends in Trade

Within Southeast Asia, most of Singapore's trade is with Malaysia. This is largely the result of the close previous historical and political links, and the proportion is declining over time. Singapore's reexports to Malaysia have exceeded its domestic exports to that country, but there are signs that Malaysia (as well as Indonesia) increasingly wishes to trade directly with other countries—in 1985, for example, there was some publicity about its importing mandarin oranges directly from China. In 1987, Singapore still handled an estimated 25 percent of all Malaysia's inbound and outbound trade.

Similar signs of protectionism are found in the trade policies of the United States (see Chapter 8) and the EEC, and if this trend continues, Singapore will have to fight hard to maintain its share of a world market that grows only slowly, if at all. Much depends on the degree to which future negotiations under the General Agreement on Tariffs and Trade can liberalize world trading. Singapore's exports to the United States are frighteningly dependent on U.S. economic health, competence in dealing with its budget and trade deficits, and avoidance of extreme protectionist policies. Since 1980, Singapore's export performance would have been poor if the U.S. demand for its exports had not risen. Prospects of Japanese cooperation with Singapore to lessen Japan's favorable trade balance (higher in 1987 than ever before) may improve given a 1988 Japanese decision to expand quotas for imports from NICs, including Singapore. On a positive note, China is likely to expand its imports in the future, although at a rather slow rate, and its market is potentially so vast that even if Singapore could obtain only a small proportion of the increase, it would gain considerably. Singapore already exchanges machinery for Chinese canned foods, and this type of "countertrade" could expand. At present, however, the balance of trade between the two countries is much in China's favor, and prospects of greater trade suffered a setback after China's internal disturbances in 1989. There are also possibilities of greater exports to Taiwan, South Korea, and Hong Kong. To be sure, these are competitors of Singapore, but they are also growing markets, and their trade with Singapore has increased during the last few years.

Services

Services as a whole have grown considerably in the past few years and amounted to more than 30 percent of gross domestic product in 1984, as compared to about 23 percent in 1970. There are several reasons why an expansion of the services sector represents good export opportunities for Singapore. The Economic Committee observed that world exchanges of services had been growing faster than world merchandise trade. Services are also less vulnerable to protectionist pressures than trade is.[34] Singapore's productivity in the sector has been high, as might be expected from its advantages in transportation and communications and its English-speaking labor force. For Singapore, the value added per worker was higher for services than for goods.[35]

The committee recommended, in particular, that financial and banking services be extended, although both face stiff competition, mainly from Tokyo. The committee also noted the importance of computer services and of newer fields such as agrotechnology, robotics, management and business consultancy, hotel management services, business services, and information technology in general. The committee suggested that Singapore try to attract more exhibitions and that it concentrate on persuading companies to locate their regional headquarters in the city, as the Deutsche Bank, Sony, and other MNCs have recently done.[36] The latter would produce numerous spin-offs in services. (If companies decided to reduce their representation in the region, the headquarters would be more likely to survive than a branch would be.)

The committee stressed the importance of tourism, pointing out that 6 percent of GDP and 16 percent of the country's foreign exchange came from this source. It deplored the fact that the growth in visitor arrivals had been checked 1980–1985 and had fallen to only about 40 percent of the increase for the previous five years. In perhaps the only part of the report that bordered on lyricism, the committee suggested that to improve Singapore's appeal to tourists, "We should maintain some of our oriental charm and mystique."[37] The growth of tourism revived in 1986; the numbers reached 3.7 million in 1987, reached more than 4 million in 1988, and continued to rise in 1989.

Trade, whether in goods or in services, is clearly a major aspect of Singapore's external economic policy. Foreign investment, however, is equally important, because it provides a basis for successful export policies.

Foreign Investment

More than 80 percent of investment in Singapore is financed by Singaporeans. Foreign investment's share of Singapore's capital formation is more important than its relatively low arithmetical value would suggest, however. It accounts for more than 70 percent of manufacturing output and more than 80 percent of manufacturing exports. It also contributes the know-how and the entrepreneurship that Singapore must encourage if it is to continue improving its standard of living by moving toward more sophisticated and more capital-intensive methods of production. The PAP has always been concerned with encouraging foreign investment through efficiency and lack of corruption in government, attractive and predictable wage policies (although not through cheap wages); with building an excellent economic infrastructure in communications and finance; with promoting the widespread understanding of English; and with encouraging party activists to be aware of what rival countries offer potential investors.[38] It is a tribute to Singapore's advantages that whereas in the Third World potential investors usually have to approach government through intermediaries, in Singapore they can get in touch with government directly and secure help without undue delay or without bribes.

The government does offer inducements to foreign investors, mostly administered by the EDB, and these were stepped up during the recent recession. Even before the recession, there were provisions for grants, investment allowances, the advantages that accompanied "pioneer status," and so on. The firms that benefited most were those that engaged in projects of strategic value to Singapore's industrial development—for example in precision engineering, advanced electronics products, and robotics.

Studies done a few years ago indicated that investors were attracted by Singapore's political and economic stability even more than by specific financial advantages. B. G. Lee observed, "We are hoping that . . . companies come here and put in fresh investments, and they don't do that because this year's CPF is down. They do that if they think for the next five years, the next ten years, this is a good place to do business."[39] The March 1988 issue of *Fortune* gave Singapore "A's" for receptivity to foreign investment in Singapore, political stability, and income distribution, placing it ahead of Japan, South Korea, Taiwan, and Hong Kong.[40]

In 1985, foreign investment declined by about one-third but substantially recovered in 1986, rose further in 1987, and continued to grow in 1988. It faltered at the beginning of 1989. The United States was Singapore's main source of investment (excluding petrochemicals) until 1985. It was replaced by Japan, but regained the leading position in the first quarter of 1989. The EEC is now second. Disturbances in Hong Kong in 1989 led to an influx of investment, mainly in property, from the Crown colony to Singapore. In terms of *cumulative* investment, the leaders are the United States and the EEC countries. U.S. investment is now equivalent to more than $2,000 for each Singapore citizen.

At one time, the highest foreign investment was in petroleum and petroleum products (mainly by Japan). The United States and Japan are now concentrating increasingly on more capital-intensive, technologically advanced products, such as electrical and electronics components, metal products, and engineering, mechanical, and office equipment. Investment in services has recently been growing, for example, in information technology activities, leisure services, and medical services.[41] Yet Singapore (like many other countries) is dependent on U.S. prosperity and on its protectionist policies being restrained. Additionally, too great a decline in the U.S. dollar would encourage U.S. companies to produce more at home rather than to invest abroad. Although Japan became the main source of foreign investment in 1986, 1987, and 1988 and a continuing source of high investment since then—partly because of the appreciation of the yen—long-term investment trends may be less favorable for Singapore. Japan, as well as some other manufacturing countries, may be moving away from supporting labor-intensive manufacturing ventures in developing countries and toward setting up high-tech factories (often with robots) in the United States and Europe. Increasingly, to Singapore's detriment, Japan is establishing factories in the countries where the goods will be sold (thus surmounting their tariff and trade barriers) rather than in the countries where the goods can be most economically produced.[42] Singapore has stepped up its investment in Malaysia (mainly Johor) and in other ASEAN countries. Recently, the government has been exhorting local industries, which have ample funds but are restricted from domestic expansion by the small market, to invest in high-technology businesses, especially in the United States. This advice is being followed. In June 1989, Yeo Hiep Seng Ltd. formed a joint venture with Temasek holdings to acquire a U.S. food operation for $52 million.[43]

Multinational Corporations: Local Entrepreneurs

Much of Singapore's foreign investment has been by MNCs; at the end of 1986, of twelve MNCs, each had more than $11 billion invested in Singapore, more than any local firm's investments. (Ironically, considering the recession, in the previous year there were only eight.) Singapore, along with Taiwan, Hong Kong, South Korea, and other similar states, has worked hard to attract MNCs. Such countries have been heavily criticized by writers who believe that they should not have sold out to foreign interests and are therefore in a condition of "dependency." The main thrust of the argument (which has been applied to many areas of the Third World)[44] is that the MNCs are more powerful than governments and so can dictate to them. The MNCs ally themselves with those in power and promote the interests of the rich or the bourgeoisie (sometimes called their compradores) against the workers and the small local firms. By encouraging corruption, they strengthen the grip of those in power over the masses, who are deprived of necessary social reforms. Additionally, economic development is retarded because MNCs do not pass on information about sophisticated techniques or allow the Third World countries to compete against them by producing high-tech items.

Yet Singapore is a particularly ill-chosen target for such arguments. If MNCs were to act collectively against the government of Singapore, they might indeed be more powerful than it is. Nevertheless, the government, being competent, noncorrupt, and united, can play MNCs off against each other, particularly by ensuring that those admitted are not drawn predominantly from a single country. The government is able to do this not just because of its political strength but also because it has economic attractions to offer. It has been strong enough to turn down conditions that investors have requested—for instance, that their employees not be compelled to join a trade union. Consequently, "there has never been any doubt in the minds of the people at both ends of the relationship [the government and the foreign firms] as to who has the sovereign authority."[45] Singapore has achieved what in the 1970s one of its most carping critics envisaged as only a remote fantasy: "It is possible that Singapore can achieve a *balance* of foreign interests, whereby political independence is assured at the same time as economic growth is spurred by outside enterprise and technology."[46] Additionally, the presence of MNCs has not shut Singapore off from high-tech operations; its problems with high technology lie elsewhere. Neither have MNCs prevented Singapore from providing a high level of social services (see Chapter 2). Indeed, Singapore's position vis-à-vis the MNCs is so strong that it has sometimes been referred to as an example of "dependency reversal."

How does the high profile of MNCs affect local business?[47] Some small local entrepreneurs believe that the government favors MNCs over them. They may be correct to the extent that the government believes that the country badly needs the presence of foreign firms because of the technological knowledge and marketing links they can provide. These firms have to be wooed away from rival countries; they are not "captives," as are the local firms. Additionally, foreign firms can afford to pay higher wages and thus drive up the costs of employing local skilled labor. Nevertheless, those who own and work for local firms are important politically, and government leaders, as good politicians, recognize this. B. G. Lee remarked, "Local business men are the pillars of our society. They are important supporters in the grassroots associations. . . . If the Singapore economy consists only of MNCs and the Government, and if our domestic structure is not strong, then our society will be weakened."[48] In fact, the EDB now administers schemes to help small and medium local businesses (as well as foreign investors). The government also plans to raise the proportion of local investment in manufacturing from a little more than 20 percent to 40 percent. In 1988, the government even established a new EDB unit to help larger local firms expand their overseas services so that eventually they might develop into multinational corporations.[49]

Although foreign firms may appear to have dominated the economy, the government has not acted directly to protect local firms (by imposing quotas on foreign firms, encouraging takeovers, and so forth). As is shown by the experience of many developing countries, the mere fact of protection does not of itself create successful entrepreneurs. MNCs are not substantially in direct competition with small and medium (often Chinese) local firms, which produce mainly for the domestic market. MNCs help to upgrade the operations of some local firms by training people who may later become entrepreneurs on their own. Singapore also benefits from the transfer of technology from MNCs, which helps to give it an edge over Hong Kong, which has fewer MNCs. The government encourages linkages, tying small business into profitable relations with MNCs through, for example, subcontracting. A scheme was announced in 1987 to allow MNCs to apply for grants to upgrade the technology and management skills of their local suppliers. Other measures for helping local business—less regulation, better financing, and taxation changes—were recommended by the Economic Committee.[50]

New openings for local business will also be provided when, in accordance with its privatization policy, the government ceases to perform and no longer takes up activities that could be better left to the private sector. In some developing countries, governments' feelings about MNCs are mixed; the MNC presence is perceived as being necessarily accompanied by disadvantages. Such attitudes are a little reminiscent of those of two elderly ladies discussing their recent unsatisfactory meal. "It wasn't really very appetizing," said one. "Yes, and there wasn't enough of it," replied the other. In contrast, the Singapore government likes foreign investment and wants more of it.

CONCLUSION

Soon after 1959, the Singapore government made wise choices in directing industrial policy. It picked a high proportion of "winners" in deciding what sectors to emphasize.[51] It diversified instead of putting all its eggs in one basket. It also provided sound communications and financial infrastructures, which gave it an edge over most competitors, through its airport (and later its airline), its ports, and its postal and telecommunications services.

Although Singapore picked some early winners, such as shipping and ship repairing, the government later realized that, because of the effects of trade-cycle fluctuations, it had concentrated too much on some sectors and that there had to be drastic retrenchment. Simultaneously, Singapore's hitherto successful petrochemical industry was depressed, not only by a fall in demand during the recession but also by new competition from Saudi Arabia and Kuwait. Consequently, although the petrochemical industry still constitutes a major component of the manufacturing sector, at one time it was dubbed a "white elephant" by the prime minister. Also, the contribution of oil refining, which was a mainstay of the economy, now faces competition from Indonesia and the Middle East, although it seemed to adapt well in 1987–1988. Picking winners in industry has much in common with the corresponding process in horse racing and on the stock market. There are few *permanent* winners. A country such as Singapore needs a niche—an area of concentration that is just right for its stage of industrial development and capabilities and in which competition from other countries is relatively weak. But, as with winners, in the industrial context there are no permanent niches.

Indeed, a newspaper headline summarized a B. G. Lee comment in the words, "Get out of our present niche or we're finished!"[52]

In the late 1970s, the switch to more capital-intensive production—a result of the apparent belief that high technology was the "only game in town"—was quite widely criticized. Critics argued that other economic sectors, such as services, should also be encouraged and that the single-minded concentration on high technology constituted a reversal of Singapore's previously successful policy of diversification. Furthermore, proponents of a move toward high technology seemed to assume that it would somehow, almost by itself, help to insulate Singapore's industries from competition. But such a move might actually expose firms to more intense competition. Later, in referring to high-tech investment in Singapore, B. G. Lee asked some pertinent rhetorical questions: "Do you think that the newly-industrializing countries are not strenuously upgrading education; upgrading their infrastructure; raising their technical competence level; developing into substantial economic entities in their own right? Do you think that other countries, equally desperate for such investments, are not going all out to get them to come, offering all kinds of inducements?"[53] This message was not intended as a criticism of a high-tech policy, which B. G. Lee endorsed in principle, but it was an indictment of those who believed that the adoption of such a policy would in itself make the struggle for economic success any less unrelenting. In any case, it was not clear that Singapore would have all that great an advantage over other countries intent on entering the high-tech field in a big way. Its domestic market was comparatively small; in the early 1980s its labor force lacked some required skills; and it had a shortage of high-tech entrepreneurial ability. In sum, the faith in high technology seemed unjustified, the product of a mystique rather than a rational strategy.

The Singapore government, while still engaged in picking winners, also realistically believes in playing the odds. The government calculates that if only, say, one in five of the exciting new prospects turns out to be a real winner, its strategy will have paid off. Finance Minister Richard Hu has stated that the government accepted that it could pick winners only in broad terms. For instance, in biotechnology it could not pick specific winners, but it did set up the Institute of Molecular and Cell Biology to train people and encourage expertise which in time would produce winners in one field or another.[54]

The government learned from the 1985–1986 recession the importance of dealing effectively with "rigidities" and the need for greater education, training, and R and D. In 1988, the government announced that all clerks and secretaries in Singapore were to be taught how to use personal computers and that 25 percent would be qualified to do so by 1990. By the 1990s, Singapore aspires to find a new niche as a developed country "with an edge."[55] Constantly, it has to convert its training programs into productivity gains that will surpass those of its industrialized and industrializing competitors, particularly the other three "little tigers"—South Korea, Taiwan, and Hong Kong.

At the same time, in spite of improved performance from 1987 to 1989, the government has to persuade its citizens to live with lower expectations than those prevailing in the heady days of the early 1980s. It also has to operate in a world in which exchange rates may fluctuate more violently than in the past and in which protectionism may seem increasingly attractive to Singapore's chief trading partners.

8

Defense and
Foreign Policy

When Singapore ceased to be part of Malaysia in August 1965, it became responsible for its own defense and foreign policy, which had previously been handled by Britain and then by Malaysia. Whereas many other Third World countries struggled to gain independence, Singapore was a reluctant beneficiary. Apart from the problem of managing to survive when separated from its hinterland, peninsular Malaysia, it had to defend itself by building up its tiny armed forces and by winning friends—particularly among its neighbors and among the great powers—through an appropriate foreign policy. Singapore's location at the southern tip of the Straits of Malacca, a crossroads of strategic trade routes, provided it with solid commercial advantages but also exposed it to many dangers. Consequently, in 1965, Singapore's leaders, unlike those of most newly independent countries, were sober rather than jubilant. The new foreign minister, S. Rajaratnam, showed his awareness of the realities of independence in an understated comment: "Our sovereignty is real enough, even though we have to exercise this sovereignty with wisdom and with regard to the facts of political life."[1] Singapore's elites clearly understood that deterrence and defense capabilities necessarily worked in tandem with political and economic development (stability and prosperity) and astute diplomacy.

DEFENSE

At independence, when relations with both Malaysia and Indonesia were strained and the Vietnam War was escalating alarmingly, Singapore's armed forces consisted of two battalions of the Singapore Infantry Regiment, which comprised 1,000 men and 50 officers, most of whom were Malays and many of whom were not Singapore born. The navy consisted of two small vessels, and there was no air force. Initially,

National Day parade, August 9, 1984, with government leaders on the steps of City Hall
watching the Singapore Armed Forces march past.

however, Singapore was given a breathing space in which to build up
its defense forces by the presence of British, Australian, and New Zealand
troops.[2]

In the aftermath of separation, the government decided, first, that
Singapore's small size and population meant that the country could not
depend on a traditional territorial defense with a large standing army.
Instead, Singapore would need a small but well-equipped and highly
mobile military force backed up by reservists and civil defense units.
The aim was to create a deterrent force that could inflict a very high
cost on any aggressor and deny potential aggressors any certainty of
success. The analogy used at first was that of the poisonous shrimp:
Swallow it and you die (the analogy nowadays is the porcupine, which
has a better chance of surviving attacks). The models adopted were at
first from Israel, which sent military advisers to Singapore in 1965–
1966, and then from Switzerland, with its huge citizen reserve force,
the latter being diplomatically much more acceptable to Singapore's large
Muslim-majority neighbors.

Second, the government decided that the SAF should reflect the
ethnic composition of the state rather than being dominated by an ethnic
minority that also happened to be the majority race of surrounding
states. In colonial times, Malays comprised about 80 percent of the
military and police forces and relied heavily on these occupations for

employment and upward social mobility. Conversely, the Chinese traditionally avoided these occupations and accorded them very low status—
a promising son was wasted by soldiering (you should not use good
iron to make nails). The answer to this unacceptable situation, initiated
in 1967, was compulsory national service for twenty-four to thirty-six
months (a number of volunteer careerists, including women in noncombat
roles, constituting about 8 percent of the total regulars, were also
recruited).

The sensitive ethnic dimensions of this policy could not be made
public. All able-bodied males were required to register before their
eighteenth birthday (it is not possible to gain legal employment without
a card showing either completed national service or exemption from it),
and the shared experience of integrated military service was hailed as
a contribution to nation-building. In fact, Malay youths, with only a
few exceptions, were not called up for service until the ethnic composition
of the SAF approximated that of the population.[3] The policy was also
politically daring, given the Chinese dislike for uniforms and the un-
successful attempt of the British to impose conscription in the early
1950s. Nevertheless, the PAP had enough political dominance and
determination to make it work, and there are now no serious problems
with compliance.

Third, the government decided that the practice of "citizen soldiers"
would be adopted. After active service, a soldier became a reservist for
thirteen years or until his fortieth birthday (fifty for officers), whichever
came first. A reservist was required to spend up to forty days a year
at a rugged refresher camp (virtually no exemptions) and to participate
in emergency mobilization exercises. In 1987, the law was amended to
allow key appointment holders (KAHs), the top 100 commanders of the
reserve, to train for more than forty days. In all cases, the civilian jobs
of the reservists were protected, and they were given full monetary
compensation. Additionally, in 1982, the Singapore Civil Defence Force
(SCDF) was formed, comprising regular SAF officers and national ser-
vicemen, including reservists, as well as civil volunteers. In 1986, the
SCDF became an independent organization with operational units in
each parliamentary constituency. The SCDF learns and practices skills
such as fire-fighting, food and water distribution, first aid, and evacuation
procedures and participates in civil resource mobilization exercises. In
March 1986, the SCDF played an important role in the rescue operations
following the collapse, during construction, of the Hotel New World.

Finally, to compensate for the SAF's relatively small numbers,
Singapore's leaders believed that their soldiers must be "better" than
enemy soldiers and that the way to do this was to stress strategy,
brainpower, and organization; to purchase state-of-the-art computerized

technology; and to emphasize expertise in engineering and signals. Starting in 1966, the scholar-officer program (which now accepts about twenty-five entrants a year) was introduced and was complemented in 1974 by an additional program destined to spot promising officer material. The scholar-officer program was intended to attract people with the highest talent to the SAF and then educate them abroad, train them intensively, and give them demanding military responsibilities. The promotion system was altered from one based on age and seniority to one based on potential, talent, and performance, and salaries were made commensurate with those of the private sector. Possibly with some negative effects, brains and technology took precedence over field experience. Also, the idea of the "thinking army" was encouraged, with a modified "management approach" to commands instead of blind obedience and with distinctions in ranks blurred by such devices as having a common mess.

Unlike its counterpart in peninsular Malaysia, the SAF does not have a significant internal security role (although the army did in the turbulent mid-1950s to mid-1960s, especially in terms of riot suppression and control). There are no guerrilla movements operating in Singapore, and there are no substantial areas of jungle. Nevertheless, the government is deeply concerned about internal security—especially against threats from communism and Islamic fundamentalism—and has armed itself with draconian laws to combat subversion. It is primarily the responsibility of the seven-thousand-strong Singapore Police Force, especially the plainclothes Special Branch, to penetrate and cripple subversive organizations and arrest their leaders.

The fifty-five thousand-strong SAF is today one of the best-designed militaries in the region. The army is highly mobile, bristling with technological expertise, and in possession of fully modern equipment; the air force is the most formidable in ASEAN (and is soon to be further strengthened by the acquisition of eight sophisticated F16A and F16B fighter planes on order in 1988); and the navy, although small, has full coastal waters capabilities. SAF reservists now number about two hundred thousand.

The monetary cost of maintaining this deterrent posture is high. Defense spending in Singapore constitutes 6 percent of GDP and around 23 percent of total government spending (amounting to nearly $1.5 billion by 1989), and its per capita cost (about $450 per person) ranks among the highest in the non-Communist world (the costs per capita for small states are always high). This is the price that must be paid for deterring aggression, as is often reiterated by the government.

Singapore's leaders have had two lingering worries about internal aspects of defense: the image of the SAF (affecting recruitment and morale) and the complacency of the population in the absence of any immediate threat (contributing to criticism of high defense expenditure and compulsory national service). Many steps have been taken to counter these problems—higher salaries; special military programs for top academic achievers; promotions for reservists; the retention of rank for those moving into civilian employment; help in securing employment for those leaving active service; opportunities for officers to make lateral transfers to senior civil service posts (thus enhancing the interchangeability of elites); a constant media barrage on the merits and worthiness of the SAF; and the presence of the prime minister's two highly talented sons in the army.

The most extensive defense program in the last few years has been the development of the concept of "total defense," which comprises the psychological (the collective will); the social (ethnic cohesion and harmony); the economic (resilience); the civil (voluntary civil defense functions); and the military (the SAF).[4] The idea behind the total defense program, adapted from the Swiss and Swedish models, is that the task of protecting the homeland is not the SAF's alone; everyone must play a part because modern warfare is all encompassing, and pressure is exerted on all facets of the life of a country. A crucial consideration in national defense is the character, nerve, and resolve of the civilian population in a crisis and its understanding and appreciation of the stakes involved and its support for the military.[5] The most noticeable aspects of the program have been the well-publicized mobilization exercises, already conducted in most constituencies, covering food and water conservation and distribution, blood collection, traffic control, and the transportation of vital supplies (involving, for some exercises, the requisitioning of vehicles and the voluntary use of gas rationing coupons). The government has also armed itself with a law allowing for the requisition in an emergency of cranes, tractors, bulldozers, trucks, and so on and the mobilization of skilled civilian professionals, such as doctors, for purposes of civilian welfare.

The SAF's image appears to be slowly improving, and recruitment picked up during the recession (thus probably forestalling an earlier suggestion, made because of Singapore's graying population, that women be included in the national service scheme). Nevertheless, national service is still not popular among many parents, youths, and employers, and Singaporeans remain somewhat complacent about defense. Either they do not believe that there will be any armed aggression directed against Singapore in the near future, or else, as a Ministry of Defence survey revealed, one in two Singaporeans believes that Singapore could successfully defend itself against most countries other than the superpowers.[6] Clearly, Singapore has made good use of its limited resources in its strategies for building up its armed forces. It has been equally skillful in devising a foreign policy to meet its particular needs.

SINGAPORE'S FOREIGN POLICY: REQUIREMENTS AND STRATEGIES

In spiritual terms, it may be true that "no man is an island." But in 1965, Singapore actually was one and had to build "bridges" in order to lessen its isolation. Nevertheless, it started with a few advantages. Because of its location and its importance in international trade, there already were thirty foreign consulates and missions in Singapore in 1963.[7] Lee Kuan Yew and others had extensive contacts with foreign politicians, particularly with those who belonged to democratic socialist parties. By the early 1960s, they had traveled extensively in order to win support for the proposed formation of Malaysia and to rebut Indonesia's case against it.

Nor were they hampered by the need to accommodate themselves to local public opinion. As in most Third World countries, very few individuals or groups were at all concerned about foreign policy. There was little discussion of it in Parliament, and no parliamentary bodies performed any functions remotely resembling the congressional hearings on foreign affairs that are held in the United States. Nor, by 1965, did the views of other political parties count for much. Essentially, the sole voice on foreign policy was that of the PAP leaders. Moreover, there were no major divisions of opinion among the leadership on this issue, even after a new generation of leaders emerged in the late 1970s.

Nevertheless, Singapore was hampered by its smallness. Small states' resources are too limited to buy support or to compel fear. Usually their "talent pools" are restricted, although Singapore uses its pool to the limit. If fighting did occur, its size would rule out a "scorched earth" policy, as was practiced by the USSR against Germany in World War II.

For a year or two after 1965, Singapore's foreign policy reflected strong influences that pulled it in different directions. It wanted to reap the benefits of attracting as many friends and trading partners as possible. With this in mind, it wooed nonaligned Asian and African countries and their prestigious leaders, such as Prince Norodom Sihanouk (Cambodia), and Ne Win (Burma). Singapore also concluded trade agreements with the USSR and East European countries. Its actions were restrained by its links to Malaysia and Britain, however. Malaysia, because of its proximity to and close ties with Singapore, would not permit the new (and smaller) country's foreign policy to conflict substantially with its own. Also, Singapore wished to retain the British armed forces base, both for protection and for its substantial contribution to the local economy. At the same time, because British troops would probably soon be withdrawn, Singapore probably saw the United States as the most likely anti-Communist stabilizing force in the region.

In 1989 these competing forces did not persist in exactly the same form. But translated into current terms, they were not all that different. The then foreign secretary, S. Dhanabalan, said in 1981 that there were four "fundamental precepts" of Singapore's foreign policy:

> 1. We will be friends with all who want to be friends with us;
> 2. We will trade with any state for mutual benefit, regardless of ideology or system of government;
> 3. We will remain non-aligned with regard to the rivalries of great-power blocs; and
> 4. We will cooperate closely with ASEAN members to achieve regional cohesion, stability, and progress.[8]

The first two points expressed Singapore's continued desire to win and keep friends and trading partners. The third needed careful interpretation. The fourth indicated the importance of ASEAN.

As a catchall term, "nonalignment" retains much of the appeal of "motherhood." Nevertheless, B. G. Lee, in listing strategies for security, stated under the heading of "diplomacy" that nonalignment was "more a slogan than a specific policy prescription" and demonstrated its imprecision by remarking that Cuba was reported to be "nonaligned."[9]

B. G. then analyzed other possible strategies. He considered both neutrality and a policy of alliances as unpromising strategies. While recognizing that (unfortunately for a small power) diplomacy was no substitute for strength, he leaned toward a balance-of-power policy as offering the best prospects for Singapore's security. The competing great powers in an area might keep each other in check so that no one dominated, thus enabling small states to survive "in the interstices between them." Additionally, although a small power could not manipulate the big powers, it might manage to influence their policies a little in its favor. If possible, the big powers' self-interest must be invoked so as to support the small state's survival. For example, the larger the number of countries that invest in Singapore, the greater the support that can be mobilized to help it resist a threat. These views are rather far away from nonalignment, as the term is commonly understood. Yet the notion of balance indicates that although in a general way Singapore is "Western leaning," it is nonaligned in the sense that any alignment it may adopt is subject to the overriding balance-of-power principle. At the same time, because of its small size, it is compelled to have good relations with its close neighbors—hence, its attachment to ASEAN.

SINGAPORE AND ASEAN

Singapore was a founding member of ASEAN (along with Indonesia, Malaysia, Thailand, and the Philippines), established in 1967. ASEAN's aims were predominantly economic, social, and cultural. Although there was no ASEAN-wide collaboration on defense, there were exchanges of information, plans for dealing with internal subversion, and attempts to standardize weapons. Among other activities, Singapore has taken part in joint exercises with Malaysia and Indonesia and has nationals of other ASEAN countries attend its six-month staff college courses.

ASEAN is not a federation or even a structured alliance; it is only an association. The members have not surrendered any sovereignty, nor are there any formal mechanisms for obtaining agreement or bringing a deviating member into line. ASEAN members attempt to reach consensus—for example, on the relative importance of various threats—but if no agreement arises, the result is an agreement to differ.

Initially, ASEAN was not very active. Curiously, in view of its previous socioeconomic emphasis, its main thrust in the early 1970s was toward achieving neutrality in the region. But the Communist victories in Vietnam, Cambodia, and Laos (1975) acted as a stimulus, and after a "summit" meeting of heads of state in Bali (Indonesia) in 1976, cooperation was pursued more seriously. Accordingly, a central secretariat was set up, regular meetings of foreign ministers were scheduled, and machinery was established for settling disputes among members by the Treaty of Amity and Cooperation (1976). The potential "dominoes" had affirmed their determination to remain standing.

Singapore, in particular, increased its commitment to ASEAN from the mid-1970s onward. As a small country with a mainly Chinese population, surrounded by countries with large "indigenous" populations, it was sometimes regarded by them as "an odd man out" or even as a "second (or third) China." Economically, Singapore was indeed different because of its greater dependence on and expertise in industry and trade, the almost complete absence of an agricultural sector, and its greater prosperity. But since the mid-1970s, Singapore has increasingly worked through and identified with ASEAN while remaining aware of itself as distinctive in some respects. For their part, the other ASEAN countries have come to regard Singapore as an acceptable and respectable neighbor and partner. Nevertheless, this relationship is based on national interests coinciding—Singapore does not strive to be liked.

Singapore's early skepticism about some ASEAN projects, because they were (in the words of Rajaratnam) "airy-fairy," was illustrated by its reservations about "neutralization." In the early 1970s, the growing importance of China and the U.S.-China rapprochement under Richard Nixon encouraged ASEAN—largely inspired by the Malaysian prime minister, Tun Razak—to promote the idea of a zone of peace, freedom, and neutrality in the region.[10] This concept was the basis for a November 1971 declaration that called for a neutral Southeast Asia, "free from any form or manner of interference from outside powers." This was an eloquent symbolic expression of the ASEAN leaders' desire to keep the region from becoming an arena of great-power conflicts, although their hopes that the region's neutrality would be guaranteed by the great powers was not fulfilled. Singapore believed that the neutralization approach, although acceptable in principle, was unrealistic and preferred a version of the balance-of-power strategy.

Since its foundation, ASEAN has acquired an additional member, newly independent Brunei (January 1984). At various times, Burma and Sri Lanka have seemed possible recruits to ASEAN, but neither has become a member. The idea of a wider grouping—a Pacific Basin community—has been mooted since the early 1980s; it would consist of the ASEAN states and the United States, Canada, Japan, Australia, and New Zealand. Meetings attended by representatives of these countries have been held about the formation of such a group, but the outcome is still uncertain. The subject was raised again by Australia in July 1989, when it proposed an "Asia-Pacific Cooperation" organization. The intended membership was the ASEAN states, the United States, Japan, Canada, Australia, New Zealand, and South Korea. The group met in November 1989 but without resolving what its membership or its relationship to ASEAN should be. The Soviet Union is firmly opposed to such a scheme, seeing it as a "closed economic grouping" from which the USSR would be excluded. For many years, the USSR has been advocating its own pan-Asian collective security agreement to oppose the interests of China, Japan, and the Western nations.

ASEAN's Economic Activities

A primary ASEAN objective is to promote economic growth. But although ASEAN countries have one of the highest growth rates in the world, this is attributable mainly to the actions of individual members, not to collective policies. Promoting economic growth by means of trade agreements is difficult because some of the countries' more important products—tin, rubber, oil, and palm oil—are competitive rather than complementary. Even twenty years after its foundation, ASEAN is not within sight of being a free-trade area (with no tariffs on trade within the region); still less is it near to being a common market (with uniform tariffs applying to imports from outside countries). Nevertheless, the ASEAN countries have successfully cooperated in working out common negotiating positions for most of the questions they discuss with the EEC, Japan, the United States, Canada, Australia, and New Zealand. This has strengthened their bargaining power. To cite just one example: In June 1985, the second Japan-ASEAN Economic Ministers Meeting resulted in Japanese tariff cuts on eighteen hundred products.

The margin of preference on most items has hitherto been too small to allow fellow ASEAN exporters a decisive competitive edge. One major factor has been Singapore's distinctive role in the region's trade. More than 80 percent of ASEAN's internal trade consists of Singapore's trade with Malaysia, Indonesia, and, to a lesser extent, Thailand. It follows that other trade between ASEAN members is small. Additionally, many of Singapore's manufactures are more efficiently produced than those of its fellow members. Therefore, it would benefit most from tariff reductions inside ASEAN because the markets of the other members (particularly Indonesia, with a population of about 175 million) would then be opened up to Singaporean products. On the other hand, Indonesia wishes to limit free trade inside ASEAN in order to protect its domestic market for the goods its own less efficient industries produce.

In ASEAN as a whole, the *number* of items with reduced tariffs for other members has increased to tens of thousands. But many of these items are not traded very often; the Philippines, for example, has reduced its tariff on snow plows! Sadly, tokenism has often been the order of the day. Nevertheless, Singapore would be opposed to a common market for ASEAN because it would then be under pressure to impose tariffs to conform to those imposed by the other members, which would damage Singapore's historic free-trade status vis-à-vis the rest of the world. ASEAN, however, is still considering ways of moving toward diluted versions of a free-trade arrangement and a common market.

Other attempts at industrial cooperation have included industrial "complementation" projects and joint ventures involving more than one ASEAN country. To date, however, progress has been slow, although at the Third Meeting of ASEAN Heads of Governments (in Manila, December 1987), commitment to economic growth was reaffirmed and four economic pacts were signed.[11]

ASEAN's Relations with Kampuchea

In the last few years, ASEAN has attracted greater world attention by its diplomatic activities regarding Kampuchea (Cambodia) than by its solid, but less spectacular, economic efforts.[12] After Communist forces took over Vietnam, Cambodia, and Laos in 1975, it seemed for a year or two that ASEAN might be able to come to terms with Vietnam, the most powerful of the three (with the third, or fourth, largest army in the world), but also, after thirty years of struggle, possibly anxious to concentrate on economic reconstruction. There even seemed to be a chance that Vietnam might join ASEAN or that an enlarged zone of peace might be designated to include Vietnam, Laos, Cambodia, and, perhaps, Burma. But the overt hostility of the Kampuchean Pol Pot regime to Vietnam, combined with Vietnam's centuries-old dream of completely dominating Kampuchea, led to a Vietnamese invasion in December 1978. China promptly reacted, partly because most of the refugees from Vietnam (the "boat people") had been ethnically Chinese, but mainly because Vietnam had recently concluded an agreement with the USSR, whose influence in the region China was determined to check. After administering a "lesson" to Vietnam by invading it, the Chinese withdrew, but Vietnam maintained its existing puppet government in Kampuchea, supported by the troops it had stationed there.

ASEAN was in a disturbing predicament. It had no liking for Pol Pot, whose Khmer Rouge had been responsible for more than 1 million deaths. Yet ASEAN had to argue (and convince others, particularly the United Nations) that the coalition government of Democratic Kampuchea, which included the Khmer Rouge, was still the legitimate government of Kampuchea. ASEAN maintained that in strictly legal terms, human rights violations could not be an excuse for the violation of national sovereignty and therefore that Vietnam's invasion constituted unacceptable international behavior. Only by doing so could ASEAN register effectively its disapproval of aggression and expansionism. An ASEAN spokesperson summed it up in 1981 by saying that stopping Vietnamese expansion in Southeast Asia was more important than bringing up the past history of the Khmer Rouge.

ASEAN was unhappy to see all Indochina under Vietnamese occupation, with a consequent threat to ASEAN's "frontline" member, Thailand. The ASEAN countries worked out a joint policy, which they pursued at the United Nations and in other diplomatic negotiations and conferences, notably at a 1981 International Conference on Kampuchea. At the U.N., ASEAN succeeded in preventing the new Vietnamese-backed government of Kampuchea from gaining recognition. At the same time, in order to prevent the Khmer Rouge from appearing to be the only alternative to a Vietnamese-controlled regime, ASEAN managed to set up a coalition (September 1981) composed of the Khmer Rouge and two other groups, one of them headed by Prince Sihanouk, who had ruled Kampuchea until 1970. Each of the three groups maintained guerrilla forces in Kampuchea, but their strengths were unequal; the Khmer Rouge, partly because of help from China, was decidedly the most powerful.

The ASEAN strategy was well explained by Tommy Koh, former Singapore ambassador to the U.N.[13] The objective, according to Koh, was not to attempt the almost impossible task of defeating Vietnam and its Kampuchean ally in the field but to increase the military, economic, and human costs of Vietnam's occupation in order to make it willing to come to the negotiating table. Pressure was to be maintained by political, diplomatic, and economic means, particularly by restricting economic assistance to Vietnam or its Kampuchean ally. At the same time, Vietnam should be offered "an attractive diplomatic exit from the quagmire." Three principles would apply. Vietnamese forces should withdraw, in phases; the Cambodian people should be allowed to hold elections, but the Khmer Rouge would be excluded from these; Cambodia should become neutral and nonaligned and would be neither an ally of China nor a vassal state of Vietnam. Obviously, ASEAN lacks the power to achieve these aims by itself. Its task is to persuade other countries to support these aims.

In 1988, it seemed that a solution to the problem might be possible, mainly because relations between the principal backers of Vietnam and the Khmer Rouge—the Soviet Union and China, respectively—had recently improved. In August, talks were held in Bogor (Indonesia) among representatives of Vietnam, the ASEAN countries, and four Kampuchean groups—the three components of the coalition and the Vietnam-backed government. The importance of Prince Sihanouk as the possible symbolic head of a new government of Kampuchea became increasingly evident, and in July 1988 Japan volunteered to fund an international peacekeeping force in Kampuchea as well as send civilians to form part of an international team to supervise elections there. No answer has yet been found to the basic question, however: How can Vietnamese troops be removed from Kampuchea without handing over effective power to the Khmer Rouge, by far the strongest of the three components of the coalition and by far the most detested?

A further meeting of the four Kampuchean groups in Paris (July-August, 1989) ended in a stalemate. Although Vietnamese troops "withdrew" from Cambodia by September 1989, there was skepticism that all of them had actually done so; Singapore believed that the withdrawal should be confirmed by a UN inspection. Singapore still proposed that there should be elections in Kampuchea. It now agreed that the Khmer Rouge should take part in these, but that there should be supervision by a UN peace-keeping force. It still maintained that a coalition government was desirable, but that the Khmer Rouge should not play a dominant, or even equal, role in it. By December 1989, the Vietnamese "withdrawal" did not seem to have had much effect on the military situation in Kampuchea.

Singapore's views on the complex Kampuchean tangle are not completely in line with those of the other ASEAN states (nor are the other states all in agreement). Singapore has been particularly active and outspoken about Vietnam's behavior, in contrast to its low profile on some earlier international issues. Its viewpoint is probably based mainly on its desire to uphold international law and protect the integrity of small nations[14] as well as on its opposition to the Soviet bases in Vietnam. Singapore's strong stance against Vietnam contrasts with the Indonesian position, which is to some extent based on Indonesia's perception of China as a more serious long-term threat. Nevertheless, in spite of such differences, in public the ASEAN states have presented a reasonably united front on the Kampuchean question. The main recent exception has been Thailand. Under the Chatichai government (1988–) it has given priority to establishing closer economic relations with Vietnam rather than to taking a tough line with Vietnam on the future of Kampuchea.

Singapore's Relations with Other ASEAN Countries

Obviously, Singapore has most opportunities for cooperation or conflict with those countries that are closest, either geographically or because of numerous previous contacts, especially Malaysia and Indonesia. The three countries differ, for example, on the status of the Straits of Malacca and Singapore and on the rights of international shipping to pass through them. Another possible source of dispute is the smuggling that occurs between Singapore and Java and Sumatra (Indonesia) and Singapore's refusal to sign an extradition treaty with Indonesia concerning fugitives accused of "economic crimes."

Relations with Malaysia are of particular importance because of proximity, defense considerations, and close previous ties. Religious tensions, too, are never far below the surface. In November 1986, there were protests from pro-Palestinian Malaysia, including the mainly non-Malay Democratic Action Party (as well as in Indonesia and Brunei), against a visit by the president of Israel to Singapore. Occasional disagreements between the two countries have not prevented the continuance of strong economic ties, however. In 1987, Singapore's investment in Malaysia (mainly in Johor, the Malaysian state closest to Singapore) was fourteen times what it had been in 1982. In 1988, one of Singapore's vital economic and strategic concerns, an increased supply of water to meet the needs of its growing economy, was ensured when a package deal with arranged. Through it, Singapore would also purchase natural gas from Malaysia, and communications between the countries would be improved by a widening of the existing causeway or by the building of a second link. Fortunately, two possible threats from Malaysia have been kept in check. Successful Malaysian policies have defused Communist subversion and militant Islam and helped to prevent their spread to Singapore.

Singapore's leaders have also worked hard to establish and maintain good personal relations with leaders in the other ASEAN countries, especially Malaysia and Indonesia, and to ensure that such bilateral relationships are paralleled at lower levels. Singapore also had close links with Brunei even before that country joined ASEAN. In general, ASEAN's members, partly because they *are* members of the organization, have tended to play down minor issues, such as ownership claims to tiny islands, instead of inflating them.

RELATIONS WITH THE GREAT POWERS

Because of its strategic location, Singapore lives in a volatile international environment and is greatly affected by the changing relationships among the great powers: the United States, China, the Soviet Union, and Japan. Singapore strives to avoid being the victim of tensions and imbalances among these four. Its relations with each cannot be "symmetrical" because of the vast disparities in size and strength. Nevertheless, Singapore's small size and economic role as a global city make a balance-of-power strategy essential.

Singapore's preferences among the great powers are also plain. As Lee Kuan Yew has remarked, "There are four major powers in the Pacific between whom the balance of power has to be maintained—the United States, Japan, China, Soviet Union. . . . I have no doubts who we should have as the dominant power."[15]

The United States

For Singapore, the United States is a unique great power, strategically and economically. It embodies "the West" (in spite of the fact that Singapore English is closer to English English than to American English). The links between the two countries are numerous, including extensive trade, a general belief in the virtues of free enterprise (the United States extols Singapore as a model of successful capitalism), the sharing of aspects of Western culture (including McDonalds and popular Western music), and a large number of personal contacts, particularly the presence of U.S. tourists in Singapore and Singaporean students in the United

States. Other similarities are a belief in pragmatism and a heritage of recent ancestors who were hardworking immigrants.

On the other hand, some cynics have observed that the United States does not know or care much about Southeast Asia (including Singapore), except in relation to threats to the area from outside. Furthermore, many Singaporeans believe that U.S. foreign policy is subject to shifts of opinion as well as of personnel that render it inconsistent and unreliable. Singapore's confidence in the military power of the United States in the region (as the main component of the Western part of a "balance") was shaken after the Vietnamese and Cambodian debacle. Nevertheless, a main element in enabling Singapore, and other ASEAN countries, to adjust to the post-1975 situation was a continuing U.S. naval presence and increased economic relations. Consequently, during the Carter and Reagan administrations and in view of the reduced Communist threat as a result of the Sino-Soviet split, Singapore's confidence was somewhat restored. Yet balances are always precarious, and "the most terrifying thought" for Lee Kuan Yew would be a Japanese alignment or understanding with China, the Soviet Union, or both.[16]

In August 1989, Singapore offered to establish naval and air force facilities for the United States. In the Philippines, there had been domestic criticism of the U.S. bases, and it was possible that a U.S. withdrawal would create a power vacuum in the area. The Singapore offer was limited. It did not include setting up bases and was confined to an extension of existing bunkering, repair, and other services for ships and aircraft until a zone of peace, freedom, and neutrality existed in the region. Nevertheless, it was criticized by some Malaysian sources, although the Malaysian prime minister stated that he had no objections provided that U.S. troops, warships, or aircraft were not stationed in Singapore.[17]

Economically, the United States is a major (in many years, the principal) trader with and investor in Singapore, and U.S. firms provide about seventy thousand jobs there. Singapore has a major grievance against the United States, however: its protectionism. In 1986, while Singapore was importing 95 percent of its goods from the United States duty-free, pressures for protectionism were growing in the United States. Lee Kuan Yew explained the Singapore point of view in a 1985 speech in the United States. He extolled the advantages of dismantling existing trade barriers as opposed to putting up new ones. He also pointed to the obstacles that greater U.S. protectionism would present to China's entry into the international trading system and contended that measures aimed at retaliating against Japanese protectionism would hurt other countries, including the ASEAN countries, more than they would damage Japan. He predicted that the consequences would be not just economic but also—through lowering living standards and creating unrest—political and could eventually include conflict and war. Nevertheless, in 1988 the United States announced that beginning in January 1989 Singapore (as well as South Korea, Taiwan, and Hong Kong) would no longer qualify for U.S. tariff concessions under the Generalized System of Preferences because it had been running trade surpluses with the United States. Singapore protested vigorously, asserting that it had in fact met the requirements necessary to quality under the Generalized System, but to no avail.

China

China is of great importance in Singapore's foreign policy by virtue of its size, large population, growing industrial strength, and ethnic attraction for Singapore Chinese. By the start of the 1950s, it was clear that Singapore and the other ASEAN nations could no longer ignore China, and diplomatic visits and trade talks took place. Although a closer relationship with China makes sense because of its growing importance in the world, Singapore is concerned that China could become too powerful. Singapore is within China's sphere of influence geographically, although China has not yet been able to take advantage of this, whereas the United States and the Soviet Union are much farther away. In the long run, China could become the dominant power in the region. To be sure, ASEAN and China share the wish that Vietnamese expansionism be restrained, but ASEAN (and Singapore) wants a neutral Kampuchea, rather than the dependent Kampuchea that China would like to see.

Economically, Singapore, like the other ASEAN countries, would like China to concentrate on economic development, with a consequent increase in trade with ASEAN. Another surge of concern with ideology in China would be harmful to ASEAN, not so much because it might be "exported" to ASEAN but because it would damage trade and investment. China's internal disturbances in summer 1989 have resulted in a decrease in Singapore's trade with China. Unless further unrest and violence occur, it is likely that trade will soon resume its upward trend.

The danger that Singapore's large Chinese population might be unduly swayed by its emotional links to China seems—at least for some time to come—no longer of major importance.[18] Indeed, Singapore's "Chineseness," added to its understanding social and economic achievement, has impressed China's leaders sufficiently for them to ask Singapore for cooperation and advice on, for example, banking, tourist promotion, and managing Shanghai airport, and for them to appoint a former leading cabinet minister, Dr. Goh Keng Swee, as economic adviser for the development of the Chinese coastal cities. The prevalence of Mandarin in Singapore should also give it an edge over other countries in trading and cooperating with China.

Although Singapore's leaders are conscious of the dangers of China's being too powerful, they nevertheless regard it as being now concerned primarily with its own economic development. They also see China as a necessary check on Vietnamese expansionism and Soviet ambitions and as useful protection for Thailand against Vietnam. Indonesia, with some support from Malaysia, has made the assessment that in the long run, China presents a greater threat than Vietnam. Yet in the short run, ASEAN members are agreed in opposing Vietnam's Kampuchean aggression, and all wish to expand their trade with China.

The Soviet Union

Unlike China, the Soviet Union is not geographically near Singapore. It does not have any vital interests in the area, but it is concerned about threats to itself and Vietnam from China and wishes to put pressure on Japan (especially as regards its rearmament), and counter the U.S. presence in the Pacific. The Soviet Union is interested in communications in the Pacific Basin, especially the route through the Straits of Singapore and Malacca, which allows access between the Pacific and Indian Oceans for both military and trading purposes. Soviet naval and air bases, especially in Cam Ranh Bay and Danang, are useful in "filling the vacuum" left by the U.S. withdrawal from Indochina and in preventing China from occupying it. There are some signs of Soviet restraint because in an area that is not of vital importance to it, the Soviet Union does not wish to push the United States or China too far and thus risk a major war. Nor does it want to drive ASEAN countries into the arms of either of these two powers. The Soviet Union has also used its influence over Vietnam (which it supplies with food and almost all its oil and whose armed forces it supports financially) to prevent it from attacking Thailand on a larger scale than its recent "hot pursuit" incursions and to seek a solution in Kampuchea.

Nevertheless, Singapore has been apprehensive—more so than the other ASEAN countries—about the role of the Soviet Union in Kampuchea, believing (at least until the Gorbachev era) Soviet actions there[19] and in Afghanistan in 1979 to be indicative of aggressive long-term ambitions. Singapore has been alert to the Soviet naval buildup in the area and to the consequent possibility that the Soviet Union could block the sealanes through the Straits of Malacca and Singapore almost at will. Yet, in keeping with the principles on which it conducts its foreign policy, Singapore is the most active trading partner of the Soviet Union among the ASEAN countries, although the scale is relatively small because the Soviets do not have all that much to offer. But although Singapore has allowed Soviet merchant ships to use its dry dock facilities, it has drawn the line at letting Soviet naval vessels use them.

After Mikhail Gorbachev's accession to power in 1985, the Soviet Union became more active diplomatically in the region; among other activities, the USSR promoted the creation of a nuclear-free zone in Southeast Asia and advocated reductions in naval activity in the Pacific and in conventional arms in the region. The aim, apparently, was to make the Soviet image less threatening. Gorbachev's Krasnoyarsk speech on Asia (September 16, 1988) contained seven major points.[20] Of particular relevance was Gorbachev's offer to stop using Soviet bases in Vietnam for the USSR's fleet if the United States agreed to scrap its bases in the Philippines—by far the larger facilities. The speech was welcome as indicating that détente might spread to the region. Less reassuringly, it confirmed that the Soviets intended to play a more active role there than previously.

Japan

There are two major differences between Singapore's (and ASEAN's) perception of Japan and its perception of other great powers. First, Japan, unlike the others, invaded and occupied Singapore during World War II. Second, at present, Japan is a great power only economically. Even if Japan rearms above its current level (about 1 percent of national income), thus relieving some of the U.S. expenditure for Japan's defense, its political and military power will still be limited.

Older Singaporeans still remain distrustful of Japan, on the basis of wartime experiences. Popular unrest flared up in 1971 after the discovery of large numbers of bones of Singapore Chinese who had been slaughtered by the Japanese during the war. Also, like other ASEAN countries, Singapore has been unhappy that Japan has not kept its promises about aid and more liberalized trade. Nevertheless, Japanese investment in Singapore has recently been increasing, and trade between the two countries has been the highest per capita in ASEAN—although consistently in Japan's favor. Japan must therefore be given credit for having contributed to Singapore's spectacular economic progress.

Singapore has probably been the ASEAN member most in favor of Japanese rearmament and of extending the defense perimeter for which Japanese forces should be responsible. Although Singapore's leaders have reservations about Japanese rearmament and would be most reluctant to see Japanese forces supplied with nuclear weapons, they still think that it is worth the risks involved.

RELATIONS WITH OTHER COUNTRIES

Relations with other countries can be referred to only briefly. Britain, along with Australia and New Zealand, has special links with Singapore (and Malaysia) through membership in the British Commonwealth and in the Five-Power Defence Arrangement. Britain, Australia, New Zealand, and Canada share the use of the English language with Singapore, and schools and universities in these countries, like those in the United States, attract many students from Singapore. The disputes between these countries and Singapore are not frequent or deep. They often concern tariffs—recent examples have involved textile tariffs (the EEC) and New Zealand's claim that Singapore had become too high income a country to qualify for the tariff exemptions for "developing countries."

In the mid-1980s, Singapore's perspective on nonalignment differed from its mid-1960s view. Singapore was no longer so desperately in need of friends and was disillusioned with the inconsistencies and illogicalities of some so-called nonaligned countries. Nor did Singapore feel it necessary to retain membership in international bodies in which, PAP leaders felt, its contribution was not being usefully spent, as in the United Nations Educational, Scientific, and Cultural Organization and the International Labor Organization. Nevertheless, Singapore does maintain good relations with developing countries generally and in particular with some Arab oil-producing countries, and with geographically close countries such as Sri Lanka, Papua New Guinea, and Bangladesh.

CONCLUSION

Singapore's defense and foreign policies have been specifically designed to maximize its chances of survival in the international jungle. Ethnic and ideological sympathies are subordinated to self-interest, as shown by the government's rejection of "boat people" from Vietnam who were Chinese. Singapore's defense aims are limited but are calculated to make any attack, unless in overwhelming force, costly for the aggressor. Through its membership of ASEAN and its policies toward countries that are important to it, Singapore has earned credibility and widespread respect.

9

Prospects for Stability and Change

In any country, a government's first task is to govern. Unless it can exercise effective control, its policies are doomed to remain ineffectual aspirations. The special problems that Singapore faces suggest that its government may need to exercise quite a high degree of control, and its leaders make a point of emphasizing this frequently in their public pronouncements. Among these problems are the potential traditional and cultural attractions of China and of Malaysia and Indonesia to the Chinese and Malays, respectively; the difficulties of dealing with pressures from contending superpowers and of defending a small country from possible external attack; and Singapore's extreme reliance on foreign trade and investment. Singapore has to offer economic advantages, based on political stability, that will be more attractive to prospective economic partners than those offered by competitors such as Hong Kong, Taiwan, and South Korea.

Consequently, unlike some developed countries, Singapore cannot rest content with simply "muddling through"; planning and calculation are needed to maintain Singapore's status as an NIC. "Any fool in charge can ruin Singapore. But it requires a special kind of genius to maintain a mere 224 square miles of territory without natural resources of any kind as a successful and thriving nation."[1] The official view is that Singapore needs a government that, while dedicated to the long-term interests of the people, is not committed to satisfying their short-term desires. To make the political system operate in such a way, two conditions are necessary. First, the government must be intelligent and tough. Second, the people must have faith in the government and be willing to forego some immediate benefits in the interests of achieving future goals. Under the PAP, the system has worked so far because most people in Singapore are convinced that in return for their sacrifices the government can deliver the goods. But in the second half of the 1980s, the situation began to change. The handing over of power to a new generation of political leaders is coinciding with growing pressures for more openness and participation in government. The problem—from the government's point of view—is to discover how such changes can be brought about without destroying what has hitherto been a proven recipe for successful governance.

Preceding chapters indicated that the government has indeed exercised a high degree of authority. It attempts to control, mostly very successfully, the loyalty of the citizens and the promotion of national unity through a variety of means, including language policy; relations with neighboring countries, particularly Malaysia and Indonesia; and the stimulation of trade and investment. Through its education policies, the government seeks to promote values, especially regarding discipline, competitiveness, elitism, and duties toward parents. Indeed, although Chapter 2 focused on society, it contained frequent references to the state or the government because in fact the state penetrates and controls many aspects of social life. "We wouldn't be here, would not have made the economic progress, if we had not intervened on very personal matters—who your neighbor is, how you live, the noise you make, how you spit [or where you spit], or what language you use. . . . It was fundamental social and cultural changes that brought us here."[2] In the last quarter century, a "low-rise" society, dependent substantially on an entrepôt trade, has been replaced by a high-rise society supported mainly by the export of increasingly sophisticated goods and services.

A high degree of state control has been possible because the government knows what it wants and takes steps to get it, in conjunction with an efficient civil service, a tightly organized party, extensive grass-roots organizations, periodic "campaigns" on particular issues, and control of the mass media. The government also seeks to maintain its power through constitutional and institutional changes, as described in Chapter 5. Singapore's small size, although raising economic and defense problems, greatly facilitates control. No part of the country is too remote to escape the government's attention, and the number of higher civil servants (or higher-ranked military officers) is too small for any of them to be anonymous to the top half-dozen political leaders.

At the same time, although the government exerts authority over a wide range of activities, there are limits to its authoritarianism. Increasingly, electors can, and do, express dissatisfaction through the ballot box. In the late 1980s, the government became increasingly receptive to the need for consultation and feedback, as was evident from the setting up of town councils to link MPs with constituents, the new powers of parliamentary committees, and the discussions on the National Agenda.

In the past, the Singapore government has been capable of adapting. It met the challenges of creating a new state at short notice in 1965, dealt with the effects of the withdrawal of the British bases a few years later, and coped with the economic recessions of the mid-1970s and mid-1980s. Nevertheless, adaptability (or pragmatism?) has to be seen in terms of the *kind* of adaptation required. The PAP has shown that it can adapt appropriately to changes in external circumstances, but it is reluctant to act if adaptation involves giving up the cherished principles it believes have formed the basis of its success. Prominent among these is a belief in the ability of elites and their qualifications to rule and control. Additionally, the older PAP leaders believe in toughness and fear newer generation Singaporeans may lack the ruggedness of their predecessors. As survivors of a contest with Communists, the older leaders are determinedly anti-Communist. They also place their trust in financial soundness, the maintenance of adequate reserves, the strength of the Singapore dollar, and a high rate of saving, especially through CPF contributions. Singapore is the only country in the world that proposes to change its president's functions so that his main responsibility will be to safeguard its financial reserves (see Chapter 5). In the eyes of the PAP leaders, to compromise such principles would constitute a betrayal of principle, not adaptability. They cannot believe that any alternative government would be sufficiently dedicated to such essentials or sufficiently tough in implementing them. Communist opponents can be dealt with by using security regulations, but the PAP leaders probably have a greater fear of a time when "democracy" would include the concept of changes of government through the use of the ballot box, which could lead to a fairly elected government made up of muddled and ineffectual do-gooders—Jeyaretnams.

To the PAP leaders, "representative" government is less important than "responsible" government, in which electors are not simply given what they want but are led by elites along the lines most appropriate for Singapore's long-term development. This is not to say that people's opinions and feedback are ignored. But the government believes that it alone should be responsible for laying down the broad lines of policy.

As far as it is able, the government draws a line in foreign policy beyond which foreign pressures and influences are firmly resisted. True to its "porcupine" image, the government becomes "prickly" beyond a certain point. In 1986, for example, it underlined its sovereignty by putting Tan Koon Swan, the leader of a Malaysian government party, in jail for crimes committed in Singapore, in spite of demonstrations and pressures in Malaysia urging more lenient treatment. The government also follows a hard line toward foreign journals accused of infringing on its sovereignty (see Chapter 2).

Consequently, given the PAP leaders' worldview, contemporary pressures for more participation and openness in government, combined with the government's own programs for reducing the number of things it does or regulates, may present a real dilemma. For instance, if changes in the role of citizens in the grass-roots organizations are to be more than cosmetic, the whole style of governing will need to be altered. Methods that have worked well in the past—although now they seem to be slightly dated—may be replaced by others that the older leaders may fear will endanger stability or entail giving up the party's basic principles.

Changes in the style of ruling are occurring at the same time as changes in the leadership. Some of the new leaders may prove to be more adaptable than the old, but they may also prove to be *too* adaptable and may sacrifice some of the PAP's cherished ideals. On the other hand, while Lee Kuan Yew is still on the scene, they may be inhibited from making changes because of wondering what "he" will think.

Above all, there remains the question, How competent are the new leaders compared with the old? Even if some are indeed "clones," it remains to be seen if they have been programmed to deal with the problems of the 1990s and beyond rather than with those of the 1960s or 1970s.

To take the argument further, can Singapore's determined pursuit of economic and social development be easily reconciled with instilling a civic spirit, a capacity for enjoyment, or a quest for culture? Can Singaporeans be taught to be courteous as a way of life rather than just as a way of encouraging tourism? Are some of the PAP's visions of the future society unrealistic? Will it really be possible "to make living in Singapore fun" or to have Singapore become a "knowledgeable well-read society, a society culturally vibrant"?[3] In short, can the city-state successfully combine the civilization of Athens with Spartan discipline?

Singapore's National Day celebrations (August 9, 1988) seemed to indicate that the PAP leadership had become more fun-minded. Dancing that had been planned for the Orchard Road area had to be called off because of the danger of overcrowding. But Lee Kuan Yew and Goh Chok Tong insisted that the "party" (Swing Singapore) be rescheduled a few weeks later on a larger scale. It was a huge success, attracting about 250,000 people. Undoubtedly it also helped the PAP vote among younger Singaporeans at the elections a few days later. The idea was so popular that in 1989 the government decided to hold a similar party on the last Sunday of every month.

Demands for continuing political change may be hard to contain, especially if they are accompanied by reforms in the education system that have the effect of stimulating enquiry—for example, the recent policy of having schoolchildren study Edward de Bono's principle of "lateral thinking." At some point the government may try to draw the line, which could provoke adverse reactions.

Indications of dissatisfaction with the government and desires for change (often only vaguely specified) should not obscure the fact that the government is generally regarded as legitimate. Those foreign observers who think that the main basis of the government's rule is organized repression and that Singapore is a police state are wide of the mark. Most people do not question the government's right to rule. The PAP enjoys support, not only from a wide range of bureaucrats, technocrats and local big businesspeople but also from blue- and white-collar workers, lower-ranking civil servants, teachers, and medium and small businesspeople. Even intellectuals, in the broad sense, although sometimes critical of the government, quite often vote for it. Some Malays, of course, may withhold recognition that the government is legitimate until a Singaporean identity is more fully established. There is also an emotional gap between the government and some of the younger electors. The latter wish material prosperity to continue but want to be free of control and the need to support all major government policies. Such people, for example, may be skeptical about the need to take strong measures against the revival of communism because they are not convinced that nowadays there is a real communist threat comparable to that of the early 1960s.

At the same time, because Singapore is a relatively new state and has an ethnically diverse population, much of the support for the government may lack really deep roots, although there are intense social interactions and "Singaporeans are caught by multilayered webs of intense social obligations and regulations."[4] Much of the support for the government depends on its effectiveness. Electors, as well as politicians, are usually pragmatic and will back the government as long as it delivers the goods. Hitherto, for example, most citizens have accepted the government's contention that restrictions on civil liberties are necessary in order to provide the stability essential for high economic performance. Nowadays, however, this argument is being questioned more than formerly.

It is widely acknowledged that government policies have been highly effective, particularly on racial harmony, language, and economic progress, at times when even the country's survival was in question. The government has achieved good relations with neighboring states, has managed labor unions, has built housing, and in general has provided fair, efficient, and noncorrupt rule. The government was disturbed by the recession of the mid-1980s but in the end met the challenge resolutely and capably.

The PAP has also made mistakes, which should convince skeptics that its leaders are human. These have included political miscalculations, such as the decision to field candidates in the Malaysian 1964 elections and the muddle over the Israeli president's visit in 1986. Also, some social and economic policies have been maintained after it was plain that they needed to be changed—for example, the wage correction policy and the accompanying concentration on high technology, the continuation of the population-limiting policy into the mid-1980s, and the destruction of areas of "old Singapore," which, among other things, damaged tourism. The PAP's record indicates, however, that the leadership's habits of calculation, reason, generally placing of realism above emotion, and insistence on the proper implementation of policy have paid massive dividends. Above all, Singapore is an almost unique example of a country where "national interests, albeit defined by a narrow elite, are consistently placed ahead of any particular benefits for the rulers."[5] These features are rarely found in other countries, which suggests that Singapore would be a difficult model to copy. Its success has been due to its leadership skills rather than to the use of any particular techniques for economic development.

Singapore's future is hard to predict, partly because of global and regional uncertainties and partly because it is difficult to foresee the effects of changing relations between the government and the people combined with the handing over of power to a new generation of leaders. The new leaders' general objectives do seem to be similar to those of their predecessors even if the style of government is changing. Furthermore, it is hard to believe that Lee Kuan Yew will not have an important say on policy for a long time to come. Yet, once the new leadership is entirely on its own, there may be changes in direction, the leadership may be less cohesive and less monolithic than in the past, and government policy may reflect more pressures from public opinion.

Singapore's history since 1959 is often cited as an example of successful modernization. But two features distinguish it from most other examples. First, in modernizing, the government has not abandoned tradition but has attempted to draw inspiration and strength from Confucianism. Second, it has not just matched the West in providing the "conveniences" of daily living or even excelled it, as Singapore Airlines and Changi Airport testify. Singapore has also consciously rejected certain Western values and features of "Western democracy" that it considers counterproductive for Singapore. Instead, it has followed Plato in starting from a vision of the society it wished to build and has striven to realize it mainly through education and the example of its leaders. In trying to do so, it has benefited from continuity of leadership, although the effects of outside influences are probably too strong for the leaders to realize their vision completely. Observers of this experiment in elitism are usually either enthusiastic admirers or, less often, resolute critics. Few can fail to be moved, one way or the other, by the Singapore story.

Notes

Chapter 1

1. Simon Winchester, *The Sunday Times* (London), December 8, 1985.
2. *Straits Times*, July 29, 1986.
3. Report of the Economic Committee, *The Singapore Economy: New Directions* (Singapore: Ministry of Trade and Industry, 1986), pp. 194–195.
4. David Bloom, "The English Language and Singapore: A Critical Survey," in Basant K. Kapur, ed., *Singapore Studies: Critical Surveys of the Humanities and Social Sciences* (Singapore: Singapore University Press, 1986), pp. 337–458.

Chapter 2

1. Saw Swee Hock, *Population Projections for Singapore, 1980–2070* (Singapore: Institute of Southeast Asian Studies, 1983).
2. *Straits Times*, March 2, 1987; *Far Eastern Economic Review*, March 5, 1987, pp. 45 and 120. Another version was "At least two. Better three. Four if you can afford it."
3. Nathan Glazer and Daniel P. Moynihan, eds. *Ethnicity* (Cambridge, Mass.: Harvard University Press, 1975).
4. *Far Eastern Economic Review*, August 10, 1989, p. 14.
5. *Straits Times*, January 20, 1989.
6. Lee Kuan Yew, "The Twain Have Met" (East-West Center Dillingham Lecture delivered at the University of Hawaii, Honolulu, Hawaii, November 11, 1970).
7. *Far Eastern Economic Review*, June 16, 1978, p. 24.
8. Catherine Lim, *The Serpent's Tooth* (Singapore: Times Books International, 1982), pp. 84–85.
9. David Bloom, "The English Language and Singapore: A Critical Survey," in Basant K. Kapur, ed., *Singapore Studies: Critical Surveys of the Humanities and Social Sciences* (Singapore: Singapore University Press, 1986), p. 381.
10. *Far Eastern Economic Review*, March 22, 1984, p. 24.
11. For a detailed explanation of the Goh Report, see Seah Chee Meow and Linda Seah, "Education Reform and National Integration," in Peter S.J.

Chen, ed., *Singapore: Development Policies and Trends* (Singapore: Oxford University Press, 1983), pp. 240–267.

12. *Asiaweek,* February 5, 1982, pp. 11–12.

13. See *Straits Times,* November 1, 1988, January 11, 20, 1989; *Straits Times* (Weekly Overseas Edition), March 25, April 22, May 6, June 3, June 10, July 1, and August 12, 1989.

14. *The Asia Magazine,* August 3, 1969, p. 15.

15. *Straits Times,* March 21, 1987.

16. *Straits Times,* June 21, 1988, October 31, 1988.

17. *Straits Times,* June 10, 1971.

18. *Asiaweek,* July 27, 1984, pp. 36–37.

19. Lee Kuan Yew, *Straits Times,* June 1, 1986. See also Lee Kuan Yew, "Conversations," in Raj K. Vasil, *Governing Singapore,* rev. ed. (Singapore: Times Books International, 1988), pp. 222–223.

20. "Singapore: Lee's Creation and Legacy," *The Economist,* November 22, 1986, p. 3.

21. Goh Chok Tong, *Petir* (the PAP journal) (May 1986).

22. *Straits Times,* October 19, 1988.

23. *Straits Times* (Weekly Overseas Edition), June 10, June 24, July 1, October 28, and November 4, 1989.

24. "Singapore: Lee's Creation," p. 15.

25. *Straits Times* (Weekly Overseas Edition), March 25, 1989.

26. *Straits Times,* October 11, 1988.

27. In 1985, for every 1,000 births in the United States, 10.6 babies died before the age of twenty-one ("Too Many Babies Are Dying, Panel Says in Call for Action," *Los Angeles Times,* August 15, 1988.

28. Barrington Kaye, *Upper Nanking Street, Singapore* (Singapore: University of Malaya Press, 1960), p. 5; T.J.S. George, *Lee Kuan Yew's Singapore* (London: Andre Deutsch, 1973), pp. 100–101.

29. By 1979, however, it was not clear that less ethnic segregation was resulting in greater ethnic integration. One survey showed that Malays in flats were associating mostly with other Malays and not mixing very much socially with non-Malays. In early 1989, the government was disturbed by the presence of "racial enclaves" in some housing estates (*Straits Times,* January 31, 1989). Later in 1989 the government imposed limits to prevent any one race's preponderance in a group of flats.

30. Sharon Siddique and Hirmada Puru Shotam, *Singapore's Little India* (Singapore: Institute of Southeast Asian Studies, 1982).

31. *Vancouver Sun,* October 22, 1983.

32. "The Twain Have Met."

33. *Asiaweek,* February 12, 1982, p. 16.

Chapter 3

1. For a comprehensive and annotated list of historical books, articles, and documents, see Edwin Lee, "The Historiography of Singapore," in Basant K. Kapur, ed., *Singapore Studies: Critical Surveys of the Humanities and Social*

Sciences (Singapore: Singapore University Press, 1986), pp. 1–32. A sophisticated early history is also presented by Barbara Watson Andaya and Leonard Y. Andaya, *A History of Malaysia* (London: Macmillan, 1982). Also see P. Wheatley, *The Golden Khersonese: Studies in the Historical Geography of the Malay Peninsula Before A.C. 1500* (Kuala Lumpur: University of Malaya Press, 1961); C. E. Wurtzburg, *Raffles of the Eastern Isles* (London: Hodder and Stoughton, 1954); Carl Trocki, *Price of Pirates: The Temenggongs and the Development of Johore and Singapore, 1784–1885* (Singapore: Singapore University Press, 1979); N. J. Ryan, *A History of Malaysia and Singapore* (Kuala Lumpur: Oxford University Press, 1969); Yen Ching-hwang, *Coolies and Mandarins* (Singapore: Singapore University Press, 1985); James Francis Warren, *Rickshaw Coolie: A People's History of Singapore, 1880–1940* (Singapore: Oxford University Press, 1986); C. M. Turnbull, *A History of Singapore, 1819–1975* (Kuala Lumpur: Oxford University Press, 1977); W. L. Blythe, *The Impact of Chinese Secret Societies in Malaya* (Kuala Lumpur: Oxford University Press, 1969); C. D. Cowan, *Nineteenth Century Malaya: The Origin of British Control* (London: Oxford University Press, 1961); and *Road to Nationhood: Singapore, 1818–1980* (Singapore: Archives and Oral History Department, 1984).

2. Raymond Flower, *Raffles: The Story of Singapore* (Beckenham, England: Croom Helm, 1984), pp. 5–6; and Andaya and Andaya, *A History of Malaysia*, pp. 32–34. In the latter book, the authors pointed out that the Malay Annals (*Sejarah Melayu*) do "not purport to adhere to a strict chronology or provide a precise rendering of events in the past" (p. 32). They are more in the nature of folk stories. For example, no evidence of a great city of Singapura as described in the Malay Annals has yet been found in any other source (p. 34).

3. For the same reasons that Raffles was instructed to find a suitable trading station near the Straits of Malacca, the EIC had earlier obtained the island of Penang to the north, when in 1791 Francis Light secured it by treaty from the sultan of Kedah. Penang failed, however, to fulfill trade and security expectations (primarily because of its geographic location). Malacca first came under British control in 1795 during the Napoleonic Wars (previously, the influential Malacca sultanate had been captured by the Portuguese in 1511 and was then seized by the Dutch in 1641). The British, believing that they would have to return Malacca to the Dutch when peace was restored, destroyed its famous fortress and most of its strategic value. Ironically, when the EIC inherited Malacca as a result of the Anglo-Dutch Treaty of 1824, it was no longer considered an ideal trading station or a suitable post from which to safeguard EIC trade routes. Singapore, however, fulfilled both trade and strategic expectations. In 1826, the three territories, lying nearly in a north-south line, were put into a single administrative unit called the Straits Settlements.

4. N. J. Ryan, *The Making of Modern Malaysia and Singapore* (Kuala Lumpur: Oxford University Press, 1969), p. 112.

5. See C. M. Turnbull, *The Straits Settlements, 1826–1867: Indian Presidency to Crown Colony* (London: Athlone Press, 1972).

6. Dennis Bloodworth wrote that the Chinese schools were the source of seven out of ten party members and also of paid union officials. Because the ex-students were "literate, numerate and educated," they rose quickly through

the party and union ranks (*The Tiger and the Trojan Horse* [Singapore: Times Books International, 1986], p. 76).

7. A nationwide state of emergency (known as "the Emergency") was declared by the Federation of Malaya in June 1948 in response to the escalation of violence and open rebellion of the (mainly Chinese) Communist guerrillas attempting to seize power by force of arms. The fighting was of a jungle warfare variety, although there were incidents of urban terrorism. The Emergency ceased to be a serious threat to the security of Malaya after the mid-1950s, and it was officially declared over in 1960. With the conclusion of the Emergency, a number of tough security measures also lapsed. Nevertheless, splintered Communist remnants still operate along the Thai-Malaysian border and perpetrate the occasional act of sabotage and assassination. Also, a number of security regulations have since been reenacted under the Internal Security Act. See A. Short, *The Communist Insurrection in Malaya, 1948–60* (New York: Crane Russak, 1975); and R. L. Clutterbuck, *Riot and Revolution in Singapore and Malaya, 1945–1960* (London: Faber and Faber, 1973).

8. For a detailed political analysis of the 1948 election and PP, see Yeo Kim Wah, *Political Development in Singapore 1945–55* (Singapore: Singapore University Press, 1973), especially pp. 98–105 and 260–266. The PP was a conservative multiethnic party led mostly by monolingual English-educated professionals and businessmen who had graduated from British universities. The party supported colonial policies on the expansion of English education and on English as the sole official language of the legislature, and it opposed citizenship for the China-born Chinese aliens in Singapore (pp. 100–101). Also see Yeo Kim Wah, "A Study of Three Early Political Parties in Singapore," *Journal of Southeast Asian History* 10, no. 1 (March 1969):115–141.

9. Bloodworth, *The Tiger*, p. 123.

10. For an objective but sympathetic view see Chan Heng Chee, *A Sensation of Independence: A Political Biography of David Marshall* (Singapore: Oxford University Press, 1984), especially p. 91. For a somewhat harsher judgment on Marshall, see Bloodworth, *The Tiger;* and John Drysdale, *Singapore: Struggle for Success* (Singapore: Times Books International, 1984).

11. Drysdale, *Singapore: Struggle for Success*, pp. 202, 339; and Bloodworth, *The Tiger*, pp. 156, 229. Also see Alex Josey, *Lee Kuan Yew* (Singapore: Donald Moore, 1971), rev. ed., p. 15.

12. Chan, *A Sensation*, pp. 165–176. Drysdale (*Struggle for Success*, pp. 147–149) noted that Lee was the real winner of the first talks because he deflected British doubts as to his true ideological colors (convincing most that he was not a Communist) and showed himself as a capable, sensible, restrained, and shrewd politician and a skilled negotiator.

13. See Bloodworth, *The Tiger*, p. 141; and Drysdale, ibid., p. 154.

14. The Middle Road Unions and unionists were named after MCP headquarters in a shophouse in Middle Road.

15. Drysdale, *Singapore: Struggle for Success*, pp. 183–184; and Bloodworth, *The Tiger*, pp. 162–163.

16. T.J.S. George, *Lee Kuan Yew's Singapore* (London: Andre Deutsch, 1973), pp. 43–44. Also see Bloodworth, *The Tiger*, p. 181.

17. Drysdale, *Singapore: Struggle for Success*, pp. 212–214.

18. Bloodworth, *The Tiger*, p. 194.

Chapter 4

1. Lee Kuan Yew in *People's Action Party, 1954–1979* (Singapore: Central Executive Committee, PAP, 1979), p. 34.

2. "At the end of our term of office, the people will judge us not on the basis of our capacity for slogan-shouting . . . but on whether we have been able to protect the livelihood of the people . . . and to expand the social, health, housing, educational and cultural services for the people" (CEC Policy Statement, December 31, 1960, quoted in Raj K. Vasil, *Governing Singapore*, rev. ed. [Singapore: Times Books International, 1988], p. 10).

3. The term *pro-Communist*, although widely used in Singapore historically and now, is vaguely defined. It is used narrowly to describe Communist believers who are not under party discipline. It is used more widely to describe Communist sympathizers, supporters of radical leftist politics, and Communist dupes. We use the term in the latter sense in this book.

4. T.J.S. George, *Lee Kuan Yew's Singapore* (London: Andre Deutsch, 1974), p. 52.

5. Fong Sip Chee, *The PAP Story—The Pioneering Years* (Singapore: Times Periodicals, 1979), p. 93.

6. Apparently, at the "Eden Hall tea party" with Lord Selkirk on July 18, 1961, several of the PAP's pro-Communists were told what they had wanted to hear: Britain would not intervene in the constitutional processes of self-governing Singapore unless there was a threat to people's lives. Dennis Bloodworth wrote that this meant the PAP's pro-Communists no longer needed the moderates as cover, and Selkirk "omitted to caution them" (*The Tiger and the Trojan Horse* [Singapore: Times Books International, 1986], pp. 235–236). John Drysdale noted that Lord Selkirk "had overlooked the political implications of his response" (*Singapore: Struggle for Success* [Singapore: Times Books International, 1984], p. 278). Some have implied that the British knew exactly what they were doing and wanted to flush the Communists and pro-Communists out of the PAP. See Alex Josey, *Lee Kuan Yew* (Singapore: Donald Moore, 1971), rev. ed., pp. 141–142; and George, *Lee Kuan Yew's Singapore*, pp. 163–164.

7. Bloodworth, *The Tiger*, pp. 243–244.

8. See Thomas J. Bellows, *The People's Action Party of Singapore: Emergence of a Dominant Party System* (New Haven, Conn.: Yale University Southeast Asia Series, 1970), p. 80. Also see Bloodworth, *The Tiger*, p. 261.

9. Bloodworth, *The Tiger*, p. 287.

10. See R. S. Milne, "Singapore's Exit from Malaysia: The Consequence of Ambiguity," *Asian Survey* 6, no. 3 (1966): 175–184; Milton E. Osborne, *Singapore and Malaysia* (Ithaca, N.Y.: Cornell University Press, 1964); Nancy M. Fletcher, *The Separation of Singapore from Malaysia* (Ithaca, N.Y.: Cornell University Press, 1969); *Separation* (Singapore: Ministry of Culture, 1965); and *Singapore Breakaway* (Kuala Lumpur: Department of Information, 1965). Also see four sets of published speeches by Lee Kuan Yew: *The Winds of Change* (Singapore: PAP

Political Bureau, 1964); *The Battle for a Malaysian Malaysia, Towards a Malaysian Malaysia;* and *Are There Enough Malaysians to Save Malaysia?* (all published in Singapore by the Ministry of Culture in 1965).

11. Dennis Bloodworth, *An Eye for the Dragon: Southeast Asia Observed, 1954–73* (Harmondsworth, England: Penguin Books, 1975), p. 342.

12. See J.A.C. Mackie, *Konfrontasi: The Indonesia-Malaysia Dispute, 1963–1966* (Kuala Lumpur: Oxford University Press, 1974); and Donald Hindley, "Indonesia's Confrontation with Malaysia: A Search for Motives," *Asian Survey* 4, no. 6 (1964): 904–913.

13. See, respectively, *Separation* (Singapore: Ministry of Culture, 1965), p. 12; and Chan Heng Chee, *The Politics of Survival, 1965–1967* (Singapore: Oxford University Press, 1971), p. 6.

14. See Bellows, *The People's Action Party,* p. 65. The Alliance denied all such allegations. Also see George, *Lee Kuan Yew's Singapore,* p. 80.

15. Drysdale, *Singapore: Struggle for Success,* p. 182.

16. Bloodworth, *The Tiger,* pp. 292–293.

17. The PAP takes pride in its domestic achievements and points out that to a considerable degree this is the result of the government's ability to attract foreign investment and to sustain Singapore's "competitive edge."

18. Drysdale, *Singapore: Struggle for Success,* p. 403.

19. Lim Joo-Jock, "Singapore in 1985: Signs of Change in Leadership Style and the Emerging New Problems," *Southeast Asian Affairs 1986* (Singapore: Institute of Southeast Asian Studies), p. 268. Also see Chan Heng Chee, "The PAP and the Nineties: The Politics of Anticipation," in Karl D. Jackson, Sukhumbhand Paribatra, and Soedjati Djiwandono, eds., *ASEAN in Regional and Global Context* (Berkeley, Calif.: Institute of East Asian Studies, 1986), pp. 163–182; and *Asiaweek,* January 4, 1985, pp. 7–10.

20. *Straits Times,* January 1, 1985.

21. *Far Eastern Economic Review,* July 11, 1985, p. 34.

22. Based on conversations and interviews with Singaporeans and on the authors' observations.

23. Speech by Goh Chok Tong prepared for the conference on Singapore and the United States into the 1990s, Fletcher School of Law and Diplomacy, Tufts University, Medford, Massachusetts, November 6, 1985, pp. 19–21.

24. *Far Eastern Economic Review,* March 26, 1987, pp. 22–23.

25. The Select Committee comprised thirteen MPs, including Prime Minister Lee and opposition member Chiam. The committee received ninety-nine submissions and held a number of hearings, which were extensively televised.

26. *Asiaweek,* February 5, 1988, p. 21. As early as August 1987, however, the prime minister had stated that the team MP proposal was a way of ensuring the continued representation of minority races, particularly the Malays, in Parliament (*Straits Times,* August 17, 1987).

27. For example, Anson, which had voted opposition since 1981, was split and divided among four constituencies, and some other constituencies that had been held by PAP old guard stalwarts about to be dropped by the party and who possibly were contemplating running against the PAP, such as Rochore

(Toh Chin Chye) and Teloh Ayer (Ong Pang Boon), were split up and absorbed into other constituencies.

28. In 1984, thirty of seventy-nine PAP candidates were returned unopposed.

29. *Straits Times*, September 1, 1988. A scenario was presented in the *Straits Times* as follows: The rubbish is piling up in your estate because the contractor is not doing his job. What will your town council do? The Housing Board will not be around to help. Everything depends on the ability of the people who make up the council—and on the leadership of one man, its chairman (ibid.). Also the government promised extra grants for special projects to town councils that qualified as being managed competently and honestly.

30. See *Asiaweek*, May 6, 1988, p. 18; and poll results published in the *Straits Times*, May 18 and 23, 1988. One poll showed that only 19 percent of those questioned doubted that those arrested in 1987 under the ISA were involved in a Marxist conspiracy (but nearly one-third of the twenty to twenty-nine age group did), and only 22 percent believed that the detainees were mistreated while in custody. In another poll, 76 percent agreed with the government's version of events concerning the Hendrickson affair (see Chapter 5).

31. *Straits Times*, August 24, 1988.

32. *Straits Times*, September 1, 1988. The PAP performed well in the debates but inadvertently antagonized Malay opinion because B. G. Lee overshadowed Ahmad Mattar, the other PAP minister (a Malay), during the debate in Malay.

33. *Asian Wall Street Journal*, September 2–3, 1988; and *Christian Science Monitor*, September 6, 1988.

34. After the election, Goh Chok Tong singled out the Malay community for not supporting the PAP electorally and mentioned that the government would have to rethink its programs to help the Malays. This, analysts believed, only fueled resentment. See *Far Eastern Economic Review*, October 13, 1988, pp. 24–25.

35. *Straits Times*, September 5, 1988. Afterward, Lee said that he was "fairly satisfied" with the campaign, although he would have done some things differently. But, he concluded, "perhaps that is the way in which a younger electorate prefers to have issues debated. So be it."

36. See the *Asian Wall Street Journal*, September 5, 1988; and the *Far Eastern Economic Review*, September 15, 1988, pp. 14–16.

37. *Sunday Times*, September 4, 1988. The *Business Times* (Malaysia) reported that analysts had expected that the PAP would lose a handful of seats or more but that its percentage of total vote would climb slightly. The outcome was the other way around (September 5, 1988).

38. *Far Eastern Economic Review*, February 9, 1989, p. 32.

39. *Asian Wall Street Journal*, September 2–3, 1988.

40. Speech by Goh Chok Tong, p. 11.

Chapter 5

1. Raj K. Vasil, *Governing Singapore*, rev. ed. (Singapore: Times Books International, 1988), p. 183.

2. Many of these criticisms were made and replied to in a parliamentary debate (*Straits Times*, August 12 and 13, 1988).

3. See Chan Heng Chee, "Legislature and Legislators," in Jon S.T. Quah, Chan Heng Chee, and Seah Chee Meow, *Government and Politics in Singapore* (Singapore: Oxford University Press, 1984), Chapter 4, for instances of dissent in Parliament by PAP members. During the 1978 budget debate, some PAP backbenchers were quite outspoken, including one who said that in the last few years there had been disturbing trends toward "rank capitalistic practices with no corresponding counteracting action to maintain our socialist objectives" (*Straits Times*, March 14, 1978).

4. See Goh Chok Tong, *Straits Times*, (Weekly Overseas Edition), June 3, 1989.

5. The scope of appeals to the Privy Council was greatly restricted early in 1989, however. The government believed that the council had been "interventionist" in reviewing the actions of the executive, particularly on the issue of preventive detention (*Straits Times*, January 24, 1989). See also *Straits Times* (Weekly Overseas Edition), April 1 and April 29, 1989.

6. Appeals to the judiciary (except on procedural grounds) were ended by an amendment to the Internal Security Act in February 1989 (retroactive to July 1971) (*Far Eastern Economic Review*, February 9, 1989, p. 14).

7. Vasil, *Governing Singapore*, pp. 235–236.

8. Lee Kuan Yew, *Straits Times*, November 22, 1962.

9. This policy was successful, not only because of strict legislation (which required, for instance, that those convicted of corruption be required to pay back all the money received in addition to their court sentence) but also because the government acted with determination to enforce it. The government set a good example and minimized temptation by paying civil servants well.

10. Some doubts have been expressed about the ability of the younger leaders to stand up to top civil servants. But one such leader had no doubt that they would and that civil servants had better do what they were told (interview with Brigadier-General [Reservist] Lee Hsien Loong, August 1986).

11. Jon S.T. Quah, "The Public Policy-Making Process in Singapore," *The Asian Journal of Public Administration* 6, no. 2 (1984): 115. To quote examples, Lee, backed by the cabinet, took the initiative in promoting national courtesy campaigns and schemes for improving the quality of the population (see Chapter 2), whereas civil servants recommended action to check the dangerous practice of glue sniffing.

12. See Chan Heng Chee, *The Dynamics of One Party Dominance: The PAP at the Grass-Roots* (Singapore: Singapore University Press, 1976), pp. 3–6; Thomas Bellows, *The People's Action Party of Singapore. The Emergence of a Dominant Party System* (New Haven, Conn.: Yale University Southeast Asia Studies, 1970), pp. 1–5; Maurice Duverger, *Political Parties: Their Organization and Activity in the Modern State*, trans. Barbara and Robert North (London: Methuen, 1962), pp. 307–312.

13. *Petir* (December 1982).

14. Bellows, ibid., p. 4. He used Otto Kirchheimer's classification from "The Transformation of the Western European Party Systems," in J. LaPalombara

and M. Weiner, eds., *Political Parties and Political Development* (Princeton, N.J.: Princeton University Press, 1966), pp. 184–187.

15. Yeo Kim Wah, *Political Development in Singapore, 1945–55* (Singapore: Singapore University Press, 1973), p. 118.

16. Dennis Bloodworth, *The Tiger and the Trojan Horse* (Singapore: Times Books International, 1986), p. 84. The British were not certain where Lee stood politically in the mid-1950s. In the legislature on May 16, 1955, Chief Secretary Sir William Goode said that if Lee was against communism "let him say so loud and clear, with no quibble and no clever sophistry. He has deplored violence after hell was let loose and men were killed." Lee replied, "I will not fight Communists to support colonialism. . . . But give us our rights and we shall fight anyone . . . to defend our freedom" (John Drysdale, *Singapore: Struggle for Success* [Singapore: Times Books International, 1984], pp. 109–111).

17. Vasil, *Governing Singapore,* pp. 27–56. Also see Pang Cheng Lian's classic book, *Singapore's People's Action Party: Its History, Organization and Leadership* (Singapore: Oxford University Press, 1971).

18. Samuel P. Huntington, *Political Order in Changing Societies* (New Haven, Conn.: Yale University Press, 1968), p. 409.

19. *Far Eastern Economic Review,* November 19, 1982, p. 14. Also see Chan Heng Chee, "The PAP and the Nineties: The Politics of Anticipation," in Karl D. Jackson, Sukhumbhand Paribatra, and Soedjati Djiwandono, eds., *ASEAN in Regional and Global Context* (Berkeley, Calif.: Institute of East Asian Studies, 1986), pp. 163–182.

20. Chan Heng Chee, "Internal Developments in Singapore," *Indonesian Quarterly* 15, no. 1 (1987); 128–138. Also see *Petir* (May 1986).

21. Interview with Brigadier General (Reservist) Lee Hsien Loong, August 1986; and *Petir* (April 1986). Goh Chok Tong was asked if future MPs would be drawn from the Youth Wing. He replied, "Yes, but not all. The party must cast its talent net wide" (*Petir* [March 1986]).

22. See *Straits Times,* December 12, 1988, and *Straits Times* (Weekly Overseas Edition), July 8, 1989.

23. *Straits Times,* January 17, 1987. The idea of a new manifesto was first announced by Goh Chok Tong in October 1986. Also see *Petir* (February and May 1987).

24. Huntington, *Political Order,* pp. 429–432.

25. Interview, August 1986.

26. See Chan, *The Dynamics,* pp. 185–220.

27. See *Far Eastern Economic Review,* January 8, 1987, p. 63.

28. *Straits Times,* January 23 and February 28, 1987. In March 1987, the Committee of Privileges found Jeyaretnam guilty on a further two complaints and fined him $1,000 (*Straits Times,* March 20, 1987).

29. See *Straits Times,* May 26 and August 20–22, 1987.

30. The notable acts were the Employment Act (1968) and the Industrial Relations Act (1968). See Vasil, *Governing Singapore,* pp. 127–140. For an interpretation of Singapore as an "authoritarian corporatist" state, see Frederic C. Deyo, *Dependent Development and Industrial Order* (New York: Praeger, 1981).

31. C. V. Devan Nair, "The PAP-NTUC Symbiosis," in Devan Nair, ed., *Not by Wages Alone* (Singapore: NTUC, 1982), p. 70. In fact, the PAP is first among equals to the same extent that Lee is first among equals in the cabinet— that is, he is *first*.

32. *Sunday Times*, August 13, 1967.

33. Lim Chee Onn, Speech at Pre-University Seminar, *Trade Unions in Singapore*, June 16–20, 1980 (Singapore: Ministry of Education and St. Andrews Junior College, 1980), p. 8.

34. Chan Heng Chee, "The Role of Intellectuals in Singapore Politics," in Wee Teong-Boo, ed., *The Future of Singapore—the Global City* (Singapore: University Education Press, 1977), pp. 41–46.

35. Seah Chee Meow, "Parapolitical Institutions," in Quah et al., eds., *Government and Politics of Singapore*, pp. 173–174. Also see "Role of the Grassroots Organizations," *PAP, 1954–1984: Petir 30th Anniversary Issue* (Singapore: People's Action Party, 1984).

Chapter 6

1. Dennis Bloodworth, *An Eye for the Dragon* (Harmondsworth, England: Penguin Books, 1975), p. 375.

2. Reported in the *Straits Times*, April 23, 1983. In 1988, Barker conceded that opposing the prime minister was easier said than done but that the older generation could do it. *Straits Times*, August 8, 1988.

3. *Straits Times* (Weekly Overseas Edition), June 10, 1989.

4. James Minchin, *No Man Is an Island* (Sydney: Allen and Unwin, 1986), p. 22.

5. "Singapore: Lee's Creation and Legacy," *The Economist*, November 22, 1986, p. 3.

6. Minchin, *No Man Is an Island*, p. 23.

7. *Far Eastern Economic Review*, January 8, 1987, p. 45.

8. See the *Straits Times*, January 7, 1980.

9. Raj Vasil, *Governing Singapore*, rev. ed. (Singapore: Times Books International, 1988), pp. 166–168.

10. *Business World* (Manila), reprinted in the *Straits Times*, August 5, 1988.

11. Pendennis in *The Observer*, August 10, 1980.

12. For example, see Thomas J. Bellows, *The People's Action Party of Singapore* (New Haven: Yale University Southeast Asia Studies, 1970), pp. 12–18; Vasil, *Governing Singapore*, pp. 56–65; Chan Heng Chee, "Singapore: The Ideology of Survival," *Commentary* (University of Singapore Society) 2, no. 1 (May 1969): 1–3; Minchin, *No Man Is an Island*, pp. 74, 243.

13. From Vasil, *Governing Singapore*, p. 64. Lee Kuan Yew once noted that the "democratic socialist is less ruthless and consequently less efficient, torn between his loathing for regimentation and mass coercion and his inhibition to making more effective use of the carrot by his desire to distribute the rewards more fairly and equally too soon" (p. 60).

14. Douglas Sikorski, "Development Versus Idealism: Can Singapore Reconcile the Conflict?" *Contemporary Southeast Asia* 7, no. 3 (December 1985): 172–192.

15. Dennis Bloodworth, *The Tiger and the Trojan Horse* (Singapore: Times Books International, 1986), pp. 198–199.

16. T.J.S. George, *Lee Kuan Yew's Singapore* (London: Andre Deutsch, 1974), p. 186.

17. S. Jayakumar, ed., *Our Heritage and Beyond* (Singapore: SNTUC, 1982), p. 21.

18. Chan Heng Chee, *The Dynamics of One Party Dominance* (Singapore: Singapore University Press, 1976), p. 232.

19. For excellent discussions of Chinese political culture in Singapore, see ibid., pp. 228–233; and *Far Eastern Economic Review*, May 7, 1982, pp. 19–23, and December 20, 1984, pp. 104–105.

20. See, for example, *Far Eastern Economic Review*, January 8, 1987, p. 74; *Straits Times*, September 1, 1987.

21. *Sunday Times*, August 3, 1986.

22. Vasil, *Governing Singapore*, p. 163.

23. Bloodworth, *An Eye for the Dragon*, p. 375.

24. See especially *Straits Times*, January 12, January 17–21, 1989; and *Far Eastern Economic Review*, February 9, 1989, pp. 30–34, 40–41. Also see *Straits Times*, October 31, November 12, November 17, and November 28, 1988; and *Straits Times* (Weekly Overseas Edition), March 11, April 1, June 24, and July 22, 1989.

25. Interview, August 4, 1986. In the *Straits Times*, September 14, 1988, Lee said that leaders are judged, first, by how effectively they have exercised their authority in the interests of their people; second, by the way they have provided for continuity; and third, by the grace with which they leave office and hand over to their successors.

26. See *Straits Times*, June 3–July 1, 1984, special series, "The Making of a Candidate."

27. *Sunday Times*, January 6, 1980.

28. Interview with S. Rajaratnam, August 4, 1986.

29. Thomas J. Bellows, "Big Fish, Small Pond," *Wilson Quarterly* (Winter 1983): p. 81.

30. *Straits Times*, October 12, 1984.

31. *Straits Times*, July 23, 1988. Also see *Straits Times*, July 16, 19, and 21, 1988; and *New Straits Times*, July 20, 1988.

32. *Straits Times*, August 24, 1988.

33. Ibid. Also see *Far Eastern Economic Review*, September 1, 1988, p. 21; and *Asiaweek*, September 16, 1988, p. 40.

34. *Straits Times*, September 2, 1988.

35. Ibid.

36. Interviews with Lee Kuan Yew, August 4, 1986, and July 15, 1988.

37. *Straits Times*, September 14, 1988.

38. Ibid.

39. *Straits Times*, April 5, 1986.

40. *Straits Times*, August 15, 1988.

41. Interview, July 15, 1988. Also see ibid.

42. *Straits Times*, September 14, 1988.

43. Interview with a diplomat, July 1988.

44. Minchin, *No Man Is an Island*, p. 334.

45. *Straits Times*, January 17, 1989.

46. Vasil, *Governing Singapore*, p. 163.

47. *Straits Times*, September 5, 1988.

48. Vasil, *Governing Singapore*, p. 192.

49. Goh Chok Tong, question and answer session in *Petir* (December 1984).

50. *Straits Times*, June 1, 1988 (Goh Chok Tong).

51. *Straits Times*, July 30, 1988.

52. Interview with B. G. Lee, August 7, 1986.

53. See *Straits Times*, February 20, 1988.

54. Chan Heng Chee, "Internal Developments in Singapore" (Paper presented CSIS-SIIS Indonesia-Singapore Bilateral Conference, Bali, Indonesia, July 23–24, 1986), p. 10. She noted the Newspaper and Printing Presses (Amendment) Bill, for example.

55. *Straits Times* (Weekly Overseas Edition), April 15, 1989. The speaker was Dr. Hong Hai. The controversy was over the "half-tank" bill requiring motorists traveling to Johor to have at least a half tank of gasoline in their cars. Gasoline is cheaper in Malaysia, and the PAP government estimated that it was losing $1 million a month in revenues from Singapore motorists filling up in Johor.

56. Interview with S. Jayakumar, July 11, 1988. Also see *Far Eastern Economic Review*, March 26, 1987, p. 23; and *Straits Times*, January 21, 1989.

57. Officially, Dhanabalan, who retains his national development portfolio, asked to have his workload lightened. It is difficult to believe that Dhanabalan would have wanted to step down as foreign minister. It has been rumored that Lee Kuan Yew was unhappy with the way Dhanabalan handled the visit of Israeli President Herzog and that Dhanabalan disagreed with the way the government reacted during the Hendrickson affair. During the summer of 1988, it was widely rumored that Wong Kan Seng was after Dhanabalan's job.

58. *Far Eastern Economic Review*, April 20, 1989, pp. 33–34.

59. Interview, August 7, 1986.

60. *Straits Times*, January 21, and January 28, 1989; and *Straits Times* (Weekly Overseas Edition), August 26, 1989.

61. *Straits Times*, July 7, 1988.

62. Interview, July 13, 1988.

63. *Far Eastern Economic Review*, October 22, 1987, p. 22.

64. Interview, 1988.

65. *Straits Times*, August 16, 1988.

66. *Far Eastern Economic Review*, January 8, 1987, p. 51.

Chapter 7

1. Most of the data for this chapter were taken from Singapore government publications, especially the annual *Economic Survey of Singapore* (Singapore: Ministry of Trade and Industry); the yearbooks, for example, *Singapore 1989* Ministry of Communications and Information; and the annual reports of the Economic Development Board. Other main sources of data were You Poh Seng and Lim Chong Yah, eds., *Singapore: Twenty-five Years* (Singapore: Nan Yang Xing Zhou Lianhe Zaobao, 1984); and the "Intelligence Reports," issued by *The Economist*.

2. Lee Soo Ann, "Patterns of Economic Structure in Singapore," and Augustin Tan, "Changing Patterns of Singapore's Foreign Trade and Investment Since 1960," in You and Lim, eds., ibid., pp. 13–37 and 38–77.

3. On socialism and the PAP's industrialization policy, see Goh Keng Swee, *The Economics of Modernization* (Singapore: Asia Pacific Press, 1972), pp. ix–x, 9–18, 209–211, and Chap. 6.

4. Speech by Richard Hu, Minister for Finance, at Kreta Ayer National Agenda Seminar, Singapore, May 24, 1987 (Release no. 37/May-08-1/87/05/ 24, 6). Garry Rodan, *Singapore's Second Industrial Revolution: State Intervention and Foreign Investment* (Kuala Lumpur: ASEAN-Australia Joint Research Project, 1985).

5. Report of the Economic Committee, *The Singapore Economy: New Directions* (Singapore: Ministry of Trade and Industry, 1986), p. 5 (hereafter referred to as REC).

6. Ibid., p. 9.

7. Ibid., pp. 51–54.

8. *Far Eastern Economic Review,* June 20, 1985, p. 81.

9. Lee (Tsao) Yuan, "The Government in Macro-Economic Management," in Lawrence B. Krause, Koh Ai Tee, and Lee (Tsao) Yuan, eds., *The Singapore Economy Reconsidered* (Singapore: ISEAS, 1987), Chap. 6.

10. Ibid., pp. 132–136.

11. Koh Ai Tee, "Saving, Investment and Entrepreneurship" in ibid., pp 79–87.

12. *Far Eastern Economic Review,* January 1, 1987, pp. 54–55.

13. *Straits Times* (Weekly Overseas Edition), June 10, and August 12, 1989.

14. *Straits Times,* August 25, 1988.

15. *Straits Times,* October 21, 1987.

16. REC, pp. 113–119.

17. REC, p. 148.

18. *Asian Wall Street Journal,* November 17, 1987.

19. *San Francisco Chronicle,* July 13, 1989.

20. These criticisms were contested by Finance Minister Richard Hu (*Straits Times,* November 7, 1987). Most of Singapore's neighbors were also slow to react.

21. *New Straits Times,* October 28, 1985; *Singapore Business,* February 13, 1986. On Lee Kuan Yew's views, see *Far Eastern Economic Review,* January 16, 1986, pp. 82–83.

22. REC, p. 52. From July 1, 1988, the employer's share for pensionable employees was raised to 12 percent and the employee's share reduced to 24 percent. The contribution rates for workers older than fifty-five were lowered. In July 1989, the employers' contributions were raised to 15 percent and the employees' share lowered to 23 percent.

23. REC, p. 53.

24. Lee (Tsao) Yuan, "The Government in Economic Management," in Krause et al., *The Singapore Economy,* p. 169.

25. Linda Y.C. Lim, "Singapore's Success: The Myth of the Free Market Economy," *Asian Survey* 23, no. 6 (1983): 754ff.

26. Hal Hill, "Has Planning Really Helped Asia's NIC's?" *Far Eastern Economic Review,* March 20, 1986, p. 135.

27. Interview, August 7, 1986. The Economic Committee, which he headed, also supported privatization.

28. *Business Times,* August 8, 1978; *The Mirror,* July 4, 1977.

29. Ng Chee Yuen, "Privatization in Singapore: Divestment with Control," *ASEAN Economic Bulletin* 5, no. 3 (1989): 300–316. Also see Linda Low, "Privatization in Singapore," in Paul Cook and Colin Kirkpatrick, eds., *Privatization in Less Developed Countries* (New York: St. Martin's Press, 1988), pp. 259–280.

30. *Straits Times* (Weekly Overseas Edition), April 8, 1989.

31. REC, pp. 71 and 83.

32. Lee Kuan Yew, *The Mirror,* October 10, 1966.

33. *Straits Times,* October 28, 1987.

34. REC, p. 12.

35. Lawrence B. Krause, "Industrialization of an Advanced Global City," in Krause et al., *The Singapore Economy,* p. 57.

36. Singapore is already benefiting from the business exodus from Hong Kong, reportedly including Japan's "Big Four security houses" (*Straits Times* [Weekly Overseas Edition], July 29, 1989).

37. REC, p. 195.

38. *Petir* (April 1986).

39. *Straits Times,* March 1, 1986.

40. *Straits Times,* March 26, 1988.

41. "A new medical centre for the region's rich and famous—both the doctors and their patients—is to be built on prime land at Orchard Boulevard" (*Straits Times* [Weekly Overseas Edition], July 29, 1989).

42. REC, pp. 60–61.

43. *Straits Times* (Weekly Overseas Edition), June 24, 1989.

44. For work on dependency, see Ronald H. Chilcote, ed., *Dependency and Marxism* (Boulder, Colo.: Westview Press, 1982); Martin Staniland, *What Is Political Economy?* (New Haven, Conn.: Yale University Press, 1985), especially Chap. 5; and Tony Smith, "Requiem or New Agenda for Third World Studies?" *World Politics,* 37, no. 4 (1985): 544–561.

45. Theodore Geiger, *Tales of Two Cities: The Development Progress of Hong Kong and Singapore* (Washington, D.C.: National Planning Association, 1973), pp. 30–31. For arguments asserting Singapore's relative independence of MNCs,

see Lau Teik Soon, "The New Left View of Southeast Asian Economic Development," and Augustin H.H. Tan, "Foreign Investment and Multi-national Corporations in Developing Countries," in C. V. Devan Nair, ed., *Socialism That Works: The Singapore Way* (Singapore: Federal Publications, 1976), pp. 70–76 and 86–96. For a view that is, on the whole, anti-MNC, see Hafiz Mirza, *Multinationals and the Growth of the Singapore Economy* (New York: St. Martin's Press, 1986).

46. Iain Buchanan, *Singapore in Southeast Asia: An Economic and Political Appraisal* (London: Bell, 1972), p. 63.

47. See Koh Ai Tee, "Saving, Investment and Entrepreneurship," in Krause et al., *The Singapore Economy*, pp. 87–98. Also see "Two Factors That Hinder Entrepreneurship," *Straits Times*, September 22, 1987, which quoted Professor Assar Lindbeck as saying that the public sector and large foreign corporations drain highly qualified people from small and medium firms in the private sector and that public sector savings lessen the amount of private equity capital available, thus damaging entrepreneurship.

48. *Petir* (September 1985).

49. *Straits Times*, September 24, 1988.

50. REC, pp. 134–138.

51. "Singapore: Lee's Creation and Legacy," *The Economist*, November 22, 1986, pp. 4–6.

52. *Straits Times*, March 1, 1986.

53. Ibid.

54. "Singapore 1987," *Far Eastern Economic Review*, January 8, 1987, p. 70.

55. REC, p. 11.

Chapter 8

1. *Straits Times*, August 31, 1965.

2. These were withdrawn in 1971. A Five-Power Defence Arrangement was concluded by Australia, Malaysia, New Zealand, Singapore, and Britain in 1971. The countries concerned still hold joint defense exercises.

3. In addition to being contrary to Singapore's policies of multiracialism and meritocracy in other spheres, the National Service situation in the early years caused employment hardships to Malay youths who lacked exemptions or had not completed service. See Stanley S. Bedlington, "Ethnicity and the Armed Forces in Singapore," in DeWitt C. Ellinwood, and Cynthia Enloe, eds., *Ethnicity and the Military in Asia* (New Brunswick, N.J.: Transaction Books, 1981).

4. See *Q and A on Defence, One: Defence Policies and Organization*, (Singapore: MINDEF, 1985); and *The Mirror*, January 1, 1987, pp. 17–18. On the SAF, also see Patrick M. Mayerchak, "The Role of the Military in Singapore," in Edward A. Olsen and Stephen Jurika, Jr., eds., *The Armed Forces in Contemporary Asian Societies* (Boulder, Colo.: Westview Press, 1986); and Patrick Smith and Philip Bowring, "The Citizen Soldier," *Far Eastern Economic Review*, January 13, 1983, pp. 26–32.

194

NOTES

5. Speech by First Deputy Prime Minister Goh Chok Tong, Singapore, September 25, 1984, Singapore Government Press Release, no. 51/Sep. Also see *Asiaweek*, December 7, 1984, p. 23.

6. *Straits Times*, May 9, 1985.

7. Obaid ul Haq, "Foreign Policy," in Jon S.T. Quah, Chan Heng Chee, and Seah Chee Meow, eds., *Government and Politics of Singapore* (Singapore: Oxford University Press, 1985), p. 278. In 1985, there were fifty foreign embassies and missions in Singapore and another twenty-two to Singapore but not resident in Singapore (*Facts and Pictures in Singapore* [Singapore: Information Division, Ministry of Communications and Information, 1986], p. 206).

8. S. Dhanabalan, "Why Singapore Needs an Active Foreign Policy," cited in Robert O. Tilman, *Singapore's Foreign Policy* (Paper prepared for the conference on Singapore and the United States into the 1990s, Fletcher School of Law and Diplomacy, Tufts University, Medford, Massachusetts, November 1985), p. 8.

9. *Straits Times*, November 8, 1984. On general strategies, also see Michael Leifer, "'Overnight, an Oasis May Become a Desert,'" *Far Eastern Economic Review*, January 8, 1987, pp. 52–55.

10. *Foreign Affairs, Malaysia* 3, no. 2 (1970): 13–19, and 4, no. 1 (1971): 9–16. Recently, ASEAN has been studying the possibility of a nuclear-weapon-free zone in Southeast Asia—an extension of the zone of peace, freedom, and neutrality.

11. Donald Crone, "The ASEAN Summit of 1987: Searching for a New Dynamism," *Southeast Asian Affairs 1988* (Singapore: Institute of Southeast Asian Studies, 1988).

12. See Khaw Guat Hoon, "ASEAN in International Politics," in Diane K. Mauzy, ed., *Politics in the ASEAN States* (Kuala Lumpur: Marican, 1984), pp. 236–255.

13. Tommy T.B. Koh, "Speech Delivered to the Asia Society" (December 4, 1984, mimeo).

14. Obaid Ul Haq, "Foreign Policy," pp. 297–298. It was also outspoken on events in Iran and Afghanistan (p. 305).

15. *Straits Times*, June 2, 1988.

16. *Straits Times*, November 12, 1987.

17. *Straits Times* (Weekly Overseas Edition), August 19, 1989; and *Far Eastern Economic Review*, August 31, 1989, pp. 9–10.

18. Previously, this may have been a reason against entering into diplomatic relations with China. Singapore's official view was that although Thailand, Malaysia, and the Philippines had established such ties, Singapore would wait until after Indonesia had done so. But, additionally, Rajaratnam stated that if a Chinese embassy were set up in Singapore, the government had to be sure that it would not be treated "as something special" (*New Straits Times*, July 9, 1975).

19. Khaw, "ASEAN in International Politics," pp. 238–239, quoting *New Straits Times*, September 11, 1982.

20. "A Siberian Serenade," *Asiaweek*, September 30, 1988, pp. 18–23.

Chapter 9

1. Devan Nair, *Not by Wages Alone* (Singapore: NTUC, 1982), p. 67.

2. "Singapore: Lee's Creation and Legacy," *The Economist*, November 22, 1986, p. 3.

3. Chong Lee Choy, "Development Management in Singapore," *Southeast Asian Affairs 1985* (Singapore: Institute for Southeast Asian Studies, 1985), p. 311, referring to the PAP's Agenda for Action, outlined in Goh Chok Tong's statement, "Singapore, City of Excellence—A Vision for Singapore by 1999," *Straits Times*, December 12, 1984.

4. Seah Chee Meow, "Political Change and Continuity in Singapore," in You Poh Seng and Lim Chong Yah, eds., *Singapore: Twenty-five Years of Development* (Singapore: Nan Yang Xing Zhou Lianhe Zaobao, 1984), p. 252.

5. Thomas J. Bellows in a review of Frederic C. Deyo, *Dependent Development and Industrial Order: An Asian Case Study, Third World Quarterly* 7, no. 4 (1985): 1096.

Annotated Bibliography

Bellows, Thomas J. *The People's Action Party of Singapore: Emergence of a Dominant Party System.* New Haven, Conn.: Yale University Southeast Asia Series, 1970. A classic account of the turbulent state of politics in postwar Singapore and the emergence and initial years of PAP rule.

Bloodworth, Dennis. *The Tiger and the Trojan Horse.* Singapore: Times Books International, 1986. A very readable, and sometimes personal account of how the PAP "rode the tiger" of communism but later subdued it. He shows how the intensity of the struggle contributed to PAP leaders' present attitude of determined anticommunism.

_____. *The Eye of the Dragon: Southeast Asia Observed, 1954–1986.* Singapore: Times Books International, 1987. The book's scope is Southeast Asia–wide, but the sections on Singapore include many acute comments.

Braddell, Roland. *The Lights of Singapore.* Kuala Lumpur: Oxford University Press, 1982. An easy-to-read book (first published in 1934) that gives basic facts about Singapore's history and describes British colonial life shortly before World War II.

Chan Heng Chee. *The Dynamics of One-Party Dominance: The PAP at the Grassroots.* Singapore: Singapore University Press, 1976. This excellent book explains much at two levels. Generally it analyzes the sources of the PAP's hegemony, while it also provides a detailed study of the organizations at local level that facilitate PAP control and contribute to its legitimacy.

_____. *David Marshall: A Sensation of Independence.* Singapore: Oxford University Press, 1984. A well-written account of the political life of David Marshall, Singapore's first and brief-tenured chief minister. The book gives a good sense of political background.

Chan Heng Chee and Obaid ul Haq, eds. *The Prophetic and the Political: Selected Speeches and Writings of S. Rajaratnam.* New York: St. Martin's Press, 1987. A selection of Rajaratnam's speeches, ably edited. Although Rajaratnam was foreign minister for a long time, the speeches collected here have a wide range. There are also transcripts of three long interviews with the editors.

Chen, Peter S.J., ed. *Social Development Policies and Trends.* Singapore: Oxford University Press, 1984. The best recent broad survey of social developments in Singapore.

Deyo, Frederic C. *Dependent Development and the Industrial Order: An Asian Case Study.* New York: Praeger, 1981. An analysis of Singapore's economic policy, with valuable insights on government-labor relations, trade, and investment.

Drysdale, John. *Singapore: Struggle for Success.* Singapore: Times Books International, 1984. A well-written, well-documented account of Singapore's political struggles focused on the period 1950–65. There is also an outline of later events—in a somewhat uncritical vein.

Economic Survey of Singapore. Singapore: Ministry of Trade and Industry, quarterly and annually. The best handy source for data and commentary on current economic trends.

Fong Sip Chee. *The PAP Story—The Pioneering Years.* Singapore: Times Periodicals, 1979. A useful account of the early days of the party (1954–68) by a longstanding member who participated in its struggles and triumphs.

George, T.J.S. *Lee Kuan Yew's Singapore.* London: André Deutsch, 1974. Contains much information and many anecdotes. Critical of PAP policies and personalities but sometimes showing grudging admiration.

Goh Keng Swee. *The Economics of Modernization.* Singapore: Asia Pacific Press, 1972. Essays on economic and other topics by the former finance minister, the main architect of Singapore's economic infrastructure and success.

Josey, Alex. *Lee Kuan Yew,* vol. 1. Singapore: Donald Moore for Asia Pacific Press, 1968. Vol. 2. Singapore: Times Books International, 1980. Excerpts from Lee Kuan Yew's speeches, with some scene setting but minimal analysis. Few other politicians' remarks would be worth reproducing at such length.

Kapur, Basant K., ed. *Singapore Studies: Critical Surveys of the Humanities and Social Sciences.* Singapore: Singapore University Press, 1986. Contains a wide range of references on history, sociology, social work, political science, geography, economic development, literature, and so on. The chapter on the English language in Singapore by David Bloom is a work of art.

Krause, Lawrence, Koh Ai Tee, and Lee (Tsao) Yuan. *The Singapore Economy Reconsidered.* Singapore: ISEAS, 1987. An insightful examination of the economy in 1987 in the light of the 1985–1986 recession, with particular attention to the role of the government. The authors make some persuasive policy recommendations on the macroeconomic level.

Lim Chong Yah, ed. *Policy Options for the Singapore Economy.* Singapore: McGraw Hill, 1988. Twenty-six economists from the University of Singapore look at options for various aspects of the economy, including the role of government, population, labor, wages, savings, foreign investment, the exchange rate, income distribution, poverty, and monetary and fiscal policy. A useful background for understanding *The Singapore Economy: New Directions.*

Minchin, James. *No Man Is an Island: A Study of Singapore's Lee Kuan Yew.* Sydney: Allen and Unwin, 1986. Partly a political history but also contains much information about Lee Kuan Yew as a person. The Malayan/Malaysian background is sometimes inadequately explained.

Nair, Devan, ed. *Socialism That Works—The Singapore Way.* Singapore: Federal Publications, 1976. Especially useful for the contributions on the economy, Southeast Asian development, and foreign investment and multinational corporations, by Goh Keng Swee, Lau Teik Soon, and Augustine Tan, respectively.

Pang Cheng Lian. *Singapore People's Action Party: Its History, Organization and Leadership.* Singapore: Oxford University Press, 1971. This study, concentrating on the 1957–1965 period, tells us more about the workings of the party than the title might suggest. The analysis of the 1961 split in the party is brilliant.

Quah, John S.T., Chan Heng Chee, and Seah Chee Meow, eds. *Government and Politics of Singapore.* Singapore: Oxford University Press, 1985. What this book covers, it covers well. Unfortunately, some major topics, such as how the PAP operates and how it governs Singapore, are missing.

Report of the Economic Committee. *The Singapore Economy: New Directions.* Singapore: Ministry of Trade and Industry, 1986. This committee, drawing on the experience of hundreds of businesspeople, economists, and so forth and headed by B. G. Lee, proposed both short- and long-term measures, most of which have been or are being adopted.

Road to Nationhood: Singapore, 1818–1980. Singapore: Archives and Oral History Department, 1984. A product of the oral history unit. Contains illustrations, including photographs of documents and newspaper extracts.

Rodan, Garry. *The Political Economy of Singapore's Industrialisation: National, State and International Capital.* London: Macmillan, 1989. Discusses the reasons for Singapore's high rate of economic growth. In particular, it deals with the government's attempts in the late 1970s to introduce higher value-added industries to Singapore by raising wages.

Salaff, Janet W. *State and Family in Singapore: Restructuring the Industrial Society.* Ithaca, N.Y.: Cornell University Press, 1988. The author examines the impact of industrialization on both poor and reasonably well-off families through case studies that compare 1974–1976 with 1981.

Sandhu, Kernial Singh, and Paul Wheatley, eds. *Management of Success: The Moulding of Modern Singapore.* Singapore: Institute of Southeast Asian Studies, 1989. This monumental book (over 1100 pages and correspondingly priced) provides analytical reflections on almost every aspect of life in Singapore, written by acknowledged authorities.

Saw Swee Hock and R.S. Bhathal, eds. *Singapore Towards the Year 2000.* Singapore: Singapore University Press, 1980. Suggests possible future trends in numerous features of Singapore society. On the whole the authors play safe in their predictions.

Singapore: An Illustrated History, 1941–1984. Singapore: Information Division, Ministry of Culture, 1984. The text summarizes the main events during this period, but the large collection of photographs is the book's main feature.

Singapore 1989. Singapore: Information Division, Ministry of Communications and Information, 1989. The latest edition of a yearbook covering all aspects of life in Singapore and including a good bibliography and statistical appendix.

Tilman, Robert O. *Southeast Asia and the Enemy Beyond: ASEAN Perceptions of External Threats.* Boulder, Colo.: Westview Press, 1987. The data were obtained from interviews supplemented by writings, speeches, and other sources. Tilman asks how the perceptions of the various ASEAN countries on such threats differ and why.

Turnbull, C. M. *A History of Singapore, 1819–1975.* Kuala Lumpur: Oxford University Press, 1977. *The* standard short history of Singapore. Indispensable.

Vasil, Raj K. *Governing Singapore,* rev. ed. Singapore: Eastern Universities Press, 1988. A hard look at the problems of governing Singapore and the ways in which the PAP has tackled it. Contains transcripts of the author's interviews with Lee Kuan Yew and Goh Chok Tong.

Yeo Kim Wah. *Political Development in Singapore, 1945–55.* Singapore: Singapore University Press, 1973. An authoritative and thorough treatment of a critical period in Singapore's politics.

You Poh Seng and Lim Chong Yah, eds. *Singapore: Twenty-five Years.* Singapore: Nan Yang Xing Zhon Lianhe Zaobao, 1984. Especially strong on economic aspects, including many useful tables, and on population and labor.

Index

A&W (restaurant chain), 39
Abortion, 10, 11, 12
Abortion Bill (1969), 14
Advisory councils, 90, 124
Advisory presidential council, 78
Afghanistan, 172
Africa, 161
Aging, 33, 34, 40, 160
Agriculture, 136
Agrotechnology, 148
Air force, 159
Airport. *See* Changi International Airport
Albar, Syed Jaafar, 61
Ali-Abrar Mosque, 5
Alliance, 47, 48, 51
Alliance (Malaysia), 59–60, 61
All-Party Constitutional Mission to London (1956), 48
    Second (1957), 49–50
    Third (1958), 50
Amnesty International, 80, 81
Amusement parlors, 39
Anglo-Dutch Treaty (1824), 43
Ang Mo Kio New Town, 36(illus.)
Anson (constituency), 56, 65, 66, 67, 116
Anticolonialism, 86
Anticommunism, 80–81, 177
    crackdown on communists (1956–1957), 49
Anticorruption agency, 83
Armenian Church, 5
ASEAN. *See* Association of Southeast Asian Nations
Asia, 161. *See also individual countries*
Asian dollar market, 137
Asian Wall Street Journal, 26

Asiaweek, 26
Association of Southeast Asian Nations (ASEAN) (1967), 3, 92, 95, 159, 164–168, 171, 172. *See also under* Singapore
Australia, 2(fig.), 4, 157, 164, 165, 174, 197(n2)
Authoritarian trend, 73, 112, 114, 176, 179
Autos, 6, 31, 35, 40
"Awakening, The" (television soap opera), 25
Azahari, Mahmud (sheikh), 58

Baboo, M.K. bin M., 72
Badminton contest (1980), 7
Balance of power, 162, 164, 169
Balhetchet, Robert, 20
Bangladesh, 174
Banishment, 49
Banks, 136, 137, 143
Barisan Sosialis, 31, 57, 58, 59, 61, 63, 64–65, 72, 87, 132
Barker, E. W., 104
Bencoolen, 42
Bilingualism, 18, 19, 20, 21, 22, 63, 112
Biotechnology, 154
Birth rate, 11, 12, 51, 140
Bloodworth, Dennis, 49, 52, 59, 104, 109, 114
Borneo, 3, 57, 60
Botanic Gardens, 1, 5, 39
Brunei, 2(fig.), 3, 57, 168, 169
    and ASEAN, 164
    GNP, 4

independence (1984), 164
revolt (1962), 58
Buddhists/Buddhism, 7, 111
Bugis, 43
Bugis Street, 5
Buildings, 3(illus.), 5, 38
Bureaucracy, 54–55, 77, 82–83, 84, 85,
    111, 140, 176
Burma, 161, 164, 166
Buses, 35
Business groups, 97, 99
Business Traveller, 4
Byrne, K. M., 86

Cabinet, 48. *See also under* People's
    Action Party
Cambodia/Kampuchea, 5, 161, 163, 165–
    168, 170, 171, 172
Cam Ranh Bay (Vietnam), 172
Canada, 164, 165, 174
Cane lashings, 8
Cantonese, 7, 56
Catholic organizations, 14, 81
Catholic social workers, 81, 128
CCCs. *See* Citizens' Consultative
    Committees
CEC. *See* People's Action Party, Central
    Executive Committee
Census
    1824, 43
    1980, 11
Central Council of Malay Cultural
    Organizations, 23, 28
Central Provident Fund (CPF), 32–33, 34,
    40, 66, 113, 122, 135, 138, 139, 142,
    143
Chambers of commerce, 99
Changi International Airport, 4, 136, 153,
    180
Changi jail, 45, 51
Chan Heng Chee, 30, 125
Cheng, Vincent, 81, 82
Chettiars, 37
Chiam See Tong, 67, 69, 71, 74, 91, 92,
    94–95, 111
Chia Tye Poh, 82
Child-care centers, 11
China, 24, 44
    People's Republic of (1949), 2(fig.), 7,
        46, 141, 148, 164, 166, 167, 168, 170,
        172, 175. *See also under* Singapore

Chinatown, 5, 37, 38, 56
Chinese, 7, 12, 13, 16–17, 27, 43, 45, 52,
    53, 56, 66, 82, 86, 112, 127, 171, 173,
    174, 175
    businesses, 99
    Communists, 46, 47, 51–52
    education, 16, 17, 18–19
    fertility rate, 12, 23
    in government, 78
    immigration, 13, 44, 48, 132
    income, 31
    and Japanese occupation, 45
    and the military, 158
    musical instruments, 24
    opera, 24
    secret societies, 44
    students, 18–19, 47, 48, 49
    value changes, 40
    See also Chinatown; Democratic Party
Chinese (language), 16–17, 19, 21, 46
    newspapers, 26
    See also individual dialects
"Chinese Dialect Groups" (oral history),
    24
Chinese texts, 42
Christians, 7, 14
    evangelical, 21, 112
Citizens' Consultative Committees
    (CCCs), 55, 100–101
Citizenship, 50
City Council, 50
    abolished (1959), 53
    See also Town councils
City Hall, 3(illus.), 5, 157(illus.)
Civil resource mobilization exercises, 158,
    160
Civil servants, 31, 54, 82–83, 144, 176
    expatriate, 82
    salaries, 31, 83
    See also Bureaucracy
Class differences, 13, 31–32
Cocaine, 8
COMFORT (trade union cooperative), 35
Commerce, 136
Common market possibility, 60, 132
Communications, 16, 131, 132, 136, 143,
    149, 153
Communists, 4, 26, 31, 46, 47, 51–52, 55,
    56, 80–81, 82, 86, 97, 100, 101, 123,
    159, 170
    in Cambodia, Laos, and Vietnam, 163,
    166

in China, 44
in Malaya/Malaysia, 45, 169
pro-, 47, 49, 50, 53, 55, 58–59, 86, 97, 98, 187(n3)
See also Anticommunism; People's Action Party, Communist wing
Communitarianism, 114
"Communities of Singapore" (oral history), 24
Community centers, 55, 85, 100, 101
Community Development, Ministry of, 34
Company unions, 98
Complementation projects, 165
Compradores, 151
Computers, 146, 148, 154
Confucianism, 20, 40, 110, 111–112, 114, 123, 180
Confucianists, 7, 104
Confucius, 8
Conrad, Joseph, 6
Consensus, 114, 124
Conspicuous consumption, 40
Construction industry, 135, 136, 138, 142
Consumer prices, 139
Container use, 4, 136
Contraception, 10
Coolie immigration, 44
Cooperative capitalism (Japan), 109
Cooperatives, 35, 99, 145
Corruption, 8, 51, 83, 108, 131, 149
Corrupt Practices Investigation Bureau, 54
Cottage industries, 137
Council of Education for Muslim Children (MENDAKI), 23, 29
Court of Appeal, 80
Court of Criminal Appeal, 80
CPF. *See* Central Provident Fund
CPM. *See under* Malayan Communist Party
Crime, 8
Cuba, 162
Cult of personality, 130
Cultural activities, 23–25, 34
Culture, Ministry of, 24

Danang (Vietnam), 172
Dance, 24
Death sentence, 8
De Bono, Edward, 179
Decentralization, 84
Defence, Ministry of (MINDEF), 126, 160

Defense, 156–161, 174
spending, 159
total, concept, 160
See also Security
Democracy, 106, 114, 124, 177, 180
Democratic Action Party (Malaysia), 168
Democratic Party, 47, 48
Democratic socialism, 51, 86, 92, 109, 161
Dependency mentality, 40
Deregistration, 49
Detention without trial, 4, 49, 80–82
Dhanabalan, S., 113, 116, 126, 162, 194(n57)
Dietary patterns, 13
Disneyland, 5
Doctors, 6
Drama, 24, 25, 81
Drugs, 8, 28
Drums, 23
Drysdale, John, 49

Earthquakes, 36
Eastern Europe, 161
Eastern Sun (newspaper), 26
East India Company (EIC), 1, 42, 43
Economic Committee (1985), 135, 140, 142, 145, 148, 153
Economic Development Board (EDB) (1961), 99, 133, 143, 144, 149, 152
EDB. *See* Economic Development Board
Education, 6–7, 12, 13, 18–23, 40, 55, 109, 140–141, 143, 144, 154, 176, 178–179, 181
British/American model, 21
centers (PAP), 89, 100
dropouts, 19, 22
exams, 22
German/Swiss model, 21
Goh Report, 19–20
income, and fertility, 11, 12, 23
language of, 16, 18, 20, 21
moral, 20, 21, 22
new education system, 22
primary, 19–20, 21, 22
private, 18, 21
registration, 10, 11–12
religious, 112
setting, 23
Special Assistance Plan, 21
standardized, 18
streaming, 22–23, 67, 110, 122

superschools, 21, 22
university, 23, 33, 72
See also under Chinese; Indians; Malays;
    Women
EEC. *See* European Economic Community
Efficiency, 131, 132, 144, 149, 176
EIC. *See* East India Company
Elections, 4, 77, 84, 87, 95–96
    1948, 1949, 1951, 46
    1955, 47
    1957, 50
    1958 and 1959, 51
    1961 (by-election), 56
    1963, 32, 58, 59, 60, 82
    1965 (by-election), 61
    1968, 1972, 1976, and 1980, 65
    1981 (by-election), 37, 88, 91, 116
    1984, 12, 33, 66, 67, 88, 90, 91, 95, 96,
        116, 123
    1988, 29, 72–75, 95, 121, 122, 123, 126,
        178
Electoral system, 69–71, 77
Electorate, age and education, 127
Electronic Road Pricing, 35
Elitism, 107, 108, 110–111, 112, 114, 176,
    181
"Emergency." *See under* Malaya
Emergency mobilization exercises, 158,
    160
Employers' groups, 99
Employment, 19, 31, 133
    of older people, 140
    part-time, 140
    pre-, training, 140
    quotas, 13, 28
Employment Act (1968), 133, 143
English (language), 13, 16, 17, 18, 19, 20,
    21, 23, 25, 27, 39, 40, 46, 63, 68, 75,
    86, 112, 127, 149, 174
    newspapers, 26
    See also Singlish
Ethnic groups, 1, 6, 7, 10, 12–14, 27, 37,
    47, 179
    and occupations, 13
    and population, 12–13
    riots (1964), 28, 61
    See also specific groups
Eunos (constituency), 72, 74, 94
Eurasians, 78
Eurodollar time deposits, 137

Europe, 1. *See also* Eastern Europe;
    France; Great Britain; Holland;
    Switzerland; West Germany
European currencies, 147
European Economic Community (EEC),
    146, 147, 150, 165, 174
Exhibitions, 24, 148
Exports, 98, 131, 133, 135, 143, 146, 147–
    148, 149
    domestic, 146
    entrepôt, 146, 147

Fabian socialist, 104
Family obligations, 8, 114, 176
Family planning, 10–12, 67
Far Eastern Economic Review, 26, 126
Fast-food restaurants, 39
Federation of Chinese Chambers of
    Commerce and Industry, 99
Feedback unit, 102, 124, 176
Festivals, 6
Finance, Ministry of, 144
Financial business services, 4, 136, 137,
    143, 147, 148, 149, 153
First Merdeka Talks. *See* All-Party
    Constitutional Mission to London
Fishing, 136
Five-Power Defence Arrangement (1971),
    174, 197(n2)
Flag, 62
Folk culture, 23–24
Food prices, 134
Foreign debt, 139
Foreign exchange, 138, 143, 147, 149, 155
Foreign financial reserves, 4, 139
Foreign policy, 161–174, 176, 177. *See also*
    individual countries
Foreign residents, 131. *See also* Labor,
    foreign
Fortress Singapore naval base (British),
    45, 161–162, 177
Fortune, 150
France, 1, 24, 43
"Freeing the white pigeon," 52
Free trade, 165

Gambier, 43
Gamelan orchestra, 24
Gardens, 6, 39
GDP. *See* Gross domestic product

General Agreement on Tariffs and Trade, 147
Generalized System of Preferences, 171
"Girl or boy, two is enough" slogan, 29
GNP. See Gross national product
Goh Chok Tong, 11, 12, 13, 28, 29, 68, 69, 71, 73, 74, 75, 76, 89, 90, 100, 111, 116, 117–118(& photo), 119, 121, 122, 123, 124, 125, 126, 128, 129, 178
  Lee Kuan Yew's endorsement of, 118–120
Goh Keng Swee, 19, 55, 57, 61, 79, 86, 103, 105, 126, 129, 143, 172
"Goh Report" (1978), 19–20. See also Education
Gold, 137
Goode, William, 49
Gorbachev, Mikhail, 173
Gossip, 102
Government of Singapore Investment Corporation, 84, 139
Graduate mother scheme. See Women, education and marriage
Grass-roots associations, 53, 55, 57, 74, 84, 85, 89, 100–102, 152, 178
GRCs. See Group Representation Constituencies
Great Britain, 1, 2, 3, 174, 197(n2)
  Labour government, 46
  See also under Singapore
Green paper, 114
Gross domestic product (GDP), 135, 137, 148, 149, 159
Gross national product (GNP), 4, 64, 131, 133, 138, 141
Group Representation Constituencies (GRCs), 69, 70, 71, 72, 74, 96, 122
Guomindang (Chinese Nationalist party), 44, 46

Hadrah, 23
Hainanese, 7
Hakka, 7
Harbour Board Workers' Union, 56
Haw Par Villa, 5
HDB. See Housing and Development Board
Health care, 6, 32, 33–34, 55, 143, 144
Hendrickson affair, 68, 94
Heroin, 8

Hertogh, Maria, riots (1950), 47
High Court, 80
High-tech industries, 134, 136, 137, 141, 150, 151, 152, 154, 180
Hindi (language), 7
Hindus, 7, 14
Hippies, 39
Historic preservation, 38
Hock Lee Riots (1955), 48
Hokkien, 7, 17, 56
Hokkien (dialect), 17, 56
Holding companies, 144
Holland, 1, 42, 43
Home ownership, 31, 33, 35, 36, 142
Hong Kong, 2(fig.), 13, 27, 36, 135, 139, 142, 148, 150, 151, 152, 155, 171, 175
  established (1842), 43
Hong Lim (constituency), 56, 61
Hospitals, 6, 59
  delivery fees, 10, 12
Hotel New World, 158
Housing, 11, 12, 32(illus.), 34, 35–38, 55, 56, 59, 63, 65, 143, 144
  boom (1980s), 136
  estates, 71
Housing and Development Board (HDB), 35, 36(caption), 37, 55, 85, 99, 101, 143
Hu, Richard, 154
Human rights, 127

Imports, 131, 146–147, 170
Import-substitution, 133
Income, 11, 12, 31
  distribution, 31, 150
  per capita, 31, 131
India, 2(fig.), 7, 141
Indians, 7, 12, 13, 43, 46, 82
  education, 23
  fertility rate, 12
  in government, 78
  and housing, 37
  and Parliament, 71
Indonesia, 2(fig.), 3, 5, 7, 10, 13, 28, 43, 132, 135, 141, 147, 153, 156, 165, 168, 172, 175, 176
  and ASEAN, 163
  and Malaysia, 60, 64, 172
Industrial estates, 34, 132
Industrialization, 38, 55, 63, 64, 132, 133, 134–135, 150, 153

capital-intensive, 134, 154
labor-intensive, 134
Industrial Relations Act amendment, 133, 143
Infant mortality rates, 33
Inflation, 56, 134
Information technology, 148, 150
Institute of East Asian Philosophies, 112
Institute of Molecular and Cell Biology, 154
Institute of Policy Studies, 114, 124
Insurance companies, 136
Intellectuals, 100
Interest groups, 84, 96–100, 102
Internal Security Act (ISA), 68, 73, 94, 128
Internal security council, 50
International Labor Organization, 174
Investment, 4, 32, 133, 139, 143, 145, 149, 151
    foreign, 144, 149–151, 162, 173, 175
Iran, 146
ISA. See Internal Security Act
Islamic fundamentalism, 7, 14, 159, 169
Israel, 28, 64, 157, 168, 180

Jade collection, 24
Japan, 1, 2, 44, 109, 112, 137, 140, 150, 164, 165, 167, 170, 172
    foreign financial reserves, 4
    GNP, 4
    import quotas, 148
    income, per capita, 131
    savings, 138
    yen, 147
    See also under Singapore
"Japanese Occupation of Singapore, 1942– 1945" (oral history), 24
Java, 168
Javanese, 1, 23–24
Jayakumar, S., 116
Jek Yeun Thong, 56
Jeyaretnam, J. B., 25, 65, 67, 69, 91, 92, 93–94, 95, 101, 111
Johor, 43, 151, 194(n55)
Joint ventures, 151, 165
Judiciary, 77, 78, 80
Jurong Bird Park, 1, 39
Jurong industrial estates, 132

KAHs. See Key appointment holders

Kallang Park riot (1956), 48
Kampuchea. See Cambodia/Kampuchea
Keep Singapore Clean Campaign, 54
Key appointment holders (KAHs), 158
Khmer Rouge, 166, 167
Kidney transplants, 14
Kipling, Rudyard, 6
Koh, Tommy, 167
Kompang, 23
Korea, 2(fig.), 27. See also South Korea
Kuala Lumpur (Malaysia), 51
Kuo Peo Kun, 25
Kuwait, 146, 153

Labor, 4, 11, 22, 63, 98, 132
    costs, 135, 139
    foreign, 141–142
    shortages, 134, 140
    skilled, 154
    See also Salaries; Trade unions; Wages
Labour Front (LF), 47–48, 49, 50
Land use, 34
Languages, 7, 13, 16–17, 40, 176
    national, 55
    official, 16, 25, 62
    See also specific languages
Laos, 163, 166
"Lateral thinking," 179
Law Society, 68, 81, 99
Lee Hsien Loong (B. G.), 11, 28, 74, 89, 114, 116–117, 118(photo), 119, 125– 126, 129, 130, 135, 142, 144, 145, 150, 152, 154, 162
Lee Kuan Yew, 2, 4, 8, 47, 48, 51, 52, 54(photo), 55, 57, 65, 66, 68, 70, 72, 73, 74, 75, 76, 79, 86, 88, 93, 103– 104, 105, 108, 109, 114, 123, 126, 127, 129, 161, 169, 178
    and Communists, 80–81
    and Confucianism, 112
    on economy, 146
    and education, 19, 20, 22, 30
    as elitist, 110, 111, 112
    and ethnicity, 27
    and eugenics, 11, 12
    on foreign policy, 110
    ideology, 110
    leadership style, 107
    and Malaysia, 60, 61
    and mass media, 26
    and modernization, 39

National Day speeches, 71, 100, 118, 120
nepotism charge, 56
and PAP, 85, 125, 126
political future, 120–122
on protectionism, 170–171
sons, 160. *See also* Lee Hsien Loong
and succession, 115, 116, 117, 118–120
and unions, 97
Lee Siew Choh, 72, 74, 94, 95
Legislative Assembly, 51, 54, 57
LF. *See* Labour Front
Liberal Socialist Party, 48, 51
Life expectancy, 33
Light, Francis, 185(n3)
Lim Chee Onn, 99, 108
Lim Chin Siong, 86
Lim Kim San, 61
Lim Yew Hock, 47, 49, 50, 51, 87
Literacy rate, 30
Littering, 8, 39
"Little India," 5, 37, 38
Long Bar (Raffles Hotel), 6
Long hair, 8, 39
"Love boat" scheme, 12

MacDonald's (restaurant chain), 39, 169
Machinery, 146, 147, 148
Macroeconomic policies, 138
Malacca, 2, 43, 45, 185(n3)
Malacca, Straits of, 1, 42, 156, 168, 172
Malay (language), 16
as national language, 55, 62
newspaper, 26
Malaya, 2(fig.), 16, 45, 46, 47, 86
"Emergency" (1948), 46, 186(n7)
Federation of (1948), 45, 57
independence (1957), 2
See also Malaysia; *under* Singapore
Malay Affairs Committee, 28
Malayalam (language), 7
Malayalees, 37
Malayan Communist Party, 46, 47, 51, 52
as CPM, 46
proscribed, 63
Malayan Democratic Union, 46
Malay Annuals, 42
Malayan Union (1946–1948), 45, 46
Malay Peninsula, 44
Malay/Malays, 7, 10, 12, 13, 16, 28–29, 43, 47, 61, 62, 82, 175

education, 23, 28, 29, 31, 62
fertility rate, 12
in government, 78
housing, 37, 184(n29)
income, 31
in military, 28–29, 156, 157, 158
music, 23
and Parliament, 70, 71
in SAF, 28–29
voting, 74
women, 31
Malaysia, 2(fig.), 7, 10, 13, 28, 29, 57, 134, 136, 164, 172, 174, 175, 197(n2)
and ASEAN, 163
federation (1963), 3, 59–60
income, per capita, 131
internal security, 159
pro-Palestinian, 168
See also under Indonesia; Singapore
Malaysian Chinese Association (MCA), 60, 61, 108
Malaysian Solidarity Committee, 61
Malay States, Federated and Unfederated, 45
Mama (Grandma) Looking for Her Cat (drama), 25
Management and business consultancy, 148
Management skills, 135, 141, 153
Mandarin (language), 7, 17, 25, 27, 65–66, 112, 129, 172
Mandarin oranges, 147
Manufacturing, 132, 133, 135, 136, 137, 147, 149, 153
Mao Zedong, 46, 115
Market socialism, 109
Marriage, 11, 12
Marshall, David, 47, 48, 49, 50, 51, 56–57, 92
Marxists, 14, 81, 128
Mass media, 25–27, 54, 176
foreign, 26–27, 68, 177
Mass rapid transit (MRT), 35
Mattar, Ahmad, 116
Maugham, Somerset, 6
MCA. *See* Malaysian Chinese Association
MCP. *See* Malayan Communist Party
Medisave, 32, 33, 67
"Meet the People" (weekly sessions), 54
Memorial Hall, 5
MENDAKI. *See* Council of Education for Muslim Children

Mental disturbances, 40
Meritocracy, 85, 106, 108, 110
Middle class, 31, 73, 75, 100, 127
Middle Road group, 49, 51
Military, 62, 63, 77, 156
  recruits, 11, 17, 28
  See also Singapore Armed Forces
MINDEF. See Defence, Ministry of
Mineral oil, 136
Minority rights, 114
MNCs. See Multinational corporations
Modernization, 6, 8, 13, 29, 39, 62, 103,
  111, 112, 180
  effects of, 40, 41, 112
Monetary Authority of Singapore, 83, 138
Money brokers, 136
"Moneytheism," 24
Monsoons, 1
Mosque. See Ali-Abrar Mosque
Movies, 24
MRT. See Mass rapid transit
Multinational corporations (MNCs), 63,
  147, 148, 151–153
Municipal Commission, 46
Museums, 6, 24
Music, 23, 24, 169
Muslim Religious Council of Singapore,
  14
Muslims, 7, 10, 12, 13, 16, 23, 28, 47, 61

Nair, C.V. Devan, 78, 97, 107, 108
Nanyang Siang Pau (newspaper), 26
Nanyang University (Nantah), 19, 107
Napoleonic Wars, 42
National Agenda for Action (PAP), 90,
  124, 176
National Day celebrations, 157(illus.), 178
National holidays, 63
National identity, 22, 27, 63
National ideology, 114
Nationalization, 51, 109
National service, compulsory (1967), 64,
  158, 160
National Trades Union Congress (NTUC),
  55, 97, 98–99, 144, 145
National unity, 8, 14, 16, 28
National University of Singapore (NUS),
  19, 118
National Wages Council (NWC) (1972),
  98, 133, 135, 139, 140, 143
Natural resources, 4, 62, 131

Nature reserves, 1, 6
Navy, 156, 159
NCMPs. See Nonconstituency members of
  Parliament
Nehru, Jawaharlal, 115
NEMPs. See Nonelected members of
  Parliament
Nepotism, 108
Neutralization, 164
New Education System, 22. See also
  Education
Ne Win, 161
Newspapers, 26, 54, 102
New towns, 34, 35, 36, 39
New Zealand, 2(fig.), 157, 164, 165, 174,
  197(n2)
NIC. See Singapore, as newly
  industrializing country
Nikkei index (Tokyo stockmarket), 137
Nixon, Richard, 164
Nonalignment, 162, 174
Nonconstituency members of Parliament
  (NCMPs), 68, 74, 93, 94
Nonelected members of Parliament
  (NEMPs), 93, 124
North Borneo, 3
NTUC. See National Trades Union
  Congress
Nuclear-free zone, 173
NUS. See National University of
  Singapore
NWC. See National Wages Council

Oil, 150, 174
  exploration boom (1970s), 132
  prices, 134, 135
  refining and petrochemical industries,
    135, 136, 146, 153
  supply, 131, 146
Ong Eng Guan, 50, 53, 56, 59, 61, 105,
  125
Ong Teng Cheong, 98, 116
Open United Front. See Middle Road
  group
Operation Cold Store (1963), 58–59
Opium, 43
Oral history, 24
Orang Laut, 43
Orchard Road, 5, 74, 178
Overseas Union Bank Centre, 5

PA. See People's Association

Pacific Basin community idea, 164
Padang, 3(illus.), 5
Painting, 24
Palembang (royal family), 42
PAP. *See* People's Action Party
Papua New Guinea, 174
Parks, 39
Parliament, 30, 33, 62, 65, 68, 69–71, 72,
    77–78, 79–80, 84, 90, 93, 94, 95–96,
    100, 114, 120, 121, 124, 161
  committees, 70, 80, 124, 176
  televised debates, 68–69
Parliamentary Select Committee, 70
Parliament House, 5
Paternalism, 8, 108–109, 110, 112
Pearl Harbor (Hawaii) bombing (1941), 45
Penang, 2, 43, 45, 185(n3)
People's Action Party (PAP) (1954), 2, 16,
    19, 47, 48, 50–51, 65, 71, 85–91, 96,
    100, 110, 175, 180
  attitudes toward, 75
  and bureaucracy, 82–83, 84
  Cabinet, 53, 68, 77, 79, 82, 84, 88,
    104–105, 121, 122, 125, 126
  cadre system, 87, 89
  Central Executive Committee (CEC)
    (formerly Executive Committee), 49,
    87, 88, 89, 90, 116, 126
  and change, 124–125, 127, 176, 177,
    178
  Communist wing, 4, 47, 49, 53, 55, 56,
    57, 87. *See also* Communists, pro-
  conferences, 88, 116
  continuity, 123
  defections, 57, 87
  and economy, 132, 138–139, 149
  and education, 18, 19–23, 40, 178–179
  and ethnicity, 27, 28
  and foreign policy, 161
  founder generation, 103–107, 127. *See
    also individual names*
  goals, 62–63, 106–109, 178
  and housing, 35, 37
  ideology, 86, 109, 113, 114
  and mass media, 25, 26–27, 177
  and MCP, 51, 52
  and merger referendum (1962), 58, 59,
    87
  moderate wing, 4, 49, 53, 55, 56, 80,
    86–87, 97
  and NTUC, 97, 98

and opposition parties, 31–32, 58–59,
    67, 68, 69, 70, 74, 87, 91–95, 114,
    123, 128, 132
  power transfer, 8, 67, 69, 75, 76, 88,
    116–123, 125, 128–130, 176, 180. *See
    also* Political succession
  radicals, 55, 56, 57, 87
  reforms, 54–55, 57, 178
  secretary-general, 121
  as socialist, 133. *See also* Democratic
    socialism
  support of, 179
  style, 55, 106–107, 123
  values, 110–114
  Women's Charter (1961), 29
  Women's Wing, 88, 90
  Youth Wing, 88, 89–90
  See also Elections; Grass-roots
    organizations; National Agenda for
    Action; *Petir*
People's Association (PA), 55, 100
Pepper, 43
Percival, Arthur, 45
Petir (PAP journal), 89
Philippines, 1, 2(fig.), 3, 6, 45, 141, 170
  and ASEAN, 163
Photography, 24
Pillai, J. Y., 83
Plato, 180
PMO. *See* Prime Minister's Office
Political demonstrations, 65
"Political Developments in Singapore,
    1945–1965" (oral history), 24
Political participation, 123, 124, 127, 176,
    178
Political parties, 47–48, 50, 59, 65, 67,
    84–95
  first, 46
  See also Barisan Sosialis; People's Action
    Party
Political prisoners, 80, 82
Political socialization, 21
Political stability, 62, 63, 84–85, 106, 123,
    137, 150, 175
Political study center, 82
Political succession, 114–116, 118
Political system, 77–78
Pollution control, 38–39
Pol Pot, 166
Polygamy, 29
Population control, 8, 10–11, 12, 40, 110

Port of Singapore Authority, 65, 145
Post Office Savings Bank, 143, 144, 145
Potong Pasir (constituency), 67, 71, 74, 95
PP. *See* Progressive Party
Pragmatism, 110, 112–114, 170, 177
Precincts, 37
President, 71–72, 77, 78–79, 121, 177
    first, 78
Press, freedom of, 4, 99
Prime Minister, 77, 79, 84, 88. *See also*
    Lee Kuan Yew
Prime Minister's Office (PMO), 83, 101,
    121
Private sector, 133, 134, 138, 140, 143,
    144–145
Privatization, 144–145
Privy Council (Great Britain), 94
    Judicial Committee, 80
Professional groups, 97, 99–100
Professionals, 85, 127, 142
Progressive Party (PP), 46–47, 48, 186(n8)
Protectionism, 147, 148, 150, 155, 170–171
Protestants, 14
Public debt, 54
Public enterprises, 133, 138, 143, 144
Public forums, 113
Public opinion, 114, 123
Public Sector Divestment Committee, 145
Public service bonuses, 72
Public Service Commission, 82
Public Utilities Board, 145
Punjabi (language), 7

Quarrying, 136

Radio, 25, 143
Raffles, Thomas Stamford, 1, 8, 37, 42–43
Raffles College, 86
Raffles Hotel, 5–6
Raffles Institution, 21
Rainfall, 1
Rajaratnam, S., 24, 75, 79, 86, 103, 105,
    109, 113, 116, 156, 164
R and D. *See* Research and development
Rationality, 114
RCs. *See* Residents' Committees
Recession (1985–1986), 35, 56, 122, 134,
    135, 136, 138, 139, 140, 142–143,
    145, 147, 153, 154, 180
Recreation, 39
Regional headquarters, 148–149

Religion, 7, 13, 14, 112
Religious groups, 14, 81, 100. *See also*
    individual interest groups
Rendel, George, 47
Rendel Commission (1953), 47
Rendel Constitution (1955), 47, 48
"Report of the Ministry of Education,
    1978." *See* "Goh Report"
Research and development (R and D),
    141, 154
Reservists, 158, 159, 160
Residents' Committees (RCs), 37, 100, 101
Retirement age, 34, 140
Riau-Johor, 43
Ring concept, 34
Roads, 34
Robotics, 148, 150

Sabah (Malaysia), 62
SAF. *See* Singapore Armed Forces
St. Andrews Cathedral, 5
St. Joseph's Church, 5
Salaries, 31, 83, 108, 135, 142
Sarawak, 3
Saudi Arabia, 146, 153
Savings, 32, 33, 72, 138–139, 142
SCDF. *See* Singapore Civil Defence Force
Schools, 18, 55, 59
Science and technology, 16, 22, 106, 112,
    131
Sculpture, 24
SDP. *See* Singapore Democratic Party
Sea traffic, 1, 136, 168
Secret societies, 44
Security, 62, 64, 68, 159, 162
Self-reliance, 62, 86
Sentosa (island), 5, 6, 82
Seong, Patrick, 81
Seow, Francis, 68, 72, 74, 81, 92, 94, 99
Serangoon Road, 37
Sheares, Benjamin, 78
Shipbuilding and repair, 135, 137, 144,
    147, 153
Shopping center. *See* Orchard Road
Sihanouk, Norodom (Cambodian prince),
    161, 166, 167
Sikhs, 7
Sikorski, Douglas, 109
Singapore, 2(fig.), 3(illus.), 4–5, 6,
    50(illus.), 109
    and ASEAN, 3, 92, 95, 151, 162, 163–
    164, 165, 168, 169, 171, 174

and Borneo, 60
and China, People's Republic of, 169, 171–172
climate, 1
constitution (1955), 47, 48
constitution (1958), 50, 51, 53
constitution (1965), 62, 71, 77, 84, 108, 121
as Crown Colony (1867), 44
early, 42–45
economy, 4, 5, 27, 29, 41, 51, 56, 62, 63–64, 72, 98, 109, 122, 128, 131–139, 143–155, 173, 179
government, 4, 8–9, 13, 25, 27, 40–41, 55, 80–84, 105–106, 126–127, 175, 176–180. See also People's Action Party
and Great Britain, 2, 6, 18, 42–51, 62, 63–64, 77, 80, 86, 132, 133, 156, 157, 161–162, 174, 177
independence (1965), 2, 7, 42, 62, 156
and Japan, 2, 6, 45, 146–147, 148, 150, 169, 173
location, 1, 2(fig.), 131, 132, 156
and Malaya, merger (1963–1965), 51, 55, 57–58, 176
and Malaysia, 3, 59–61, 62, 63, 64, 92, 131, 132, 135, 137, 139, 141, 146, 147, 151, 156, 161, 165, 168–169, 170, 177, 180
name, meaning of, 42
as newly industrializing country (NIC), 131, 154–155, 175
occupations of, 1, 2, 6, 45
population, 1, 8, 10–11, 34, 40, 132. See also Census; Ethnic groups
as port, 4, 43
self-government (1959), 2, 16, 50, 51, 132
size, 1, 131, 161
and Soviet Union, 169, 172–173
as trading center, 1–2, 3, 6, 131, 136, 175
and U.S., 68, 81, 134, 135, 146, 147–148, 150, 162, 169–171
Singapore, Strait of, 172
Singapore Airlines, 84, 143, 144, 153, 180
Singaporean, 7
Singapore Armed Forces (SAF), 28, 64, 157, 159–161
  ethnic composition, 158
  and politics, 126, 176
  scholar-officer program, 159
  size, 159
  technology, 158–159
Singapore Association of Bankers, 99
Singapore Association of Trade Unions, 97
Singapore Broadcasting Corporation, 25
Singapore Civil Defence Force (SCDF), 158
Singapore Cricket Club, 3(illus.), 5
Singapore Democratic Party (SDP), 67, 72, 73, 91, 92
Singapore dollars, 137, 138, 142
Singapore gin sling, 6
Singapore Herald, 26
Singapore Infantry Regiment, 156
Singapore Legislative Council, 44, 46. See also Legislative Assembly
Singapore Malay National Association, 28
Singapore Manufacturers Association, 99
Singapore Order in Council (1958), 50
Singapore People's Alliance (SPA), 50, 51
Singapore Police Force, 159
Singapore River, 34, 43
Singapura, 42
Singlish (Singapore English), 7, 169
Smoking, 8, 39
Smuggling, 168
Social Development Unit, 30
Social engineering, 8, 10, 12
Socialists, 109
Social services, 32–34, 55, 66–67, 109
Social transformation, 40, 109
South Korea, 2(fig.), 135, 139, 140, 148, 150, 151, 155, 164, 171, 175
South Sulawesi, 43
Soviet Union, 2(fig.), 161, 164, 166, 167, 170, 172. See also under Singapore
SPA. See Singapore People's Alliance
Speak Mandarin campaign, 65–66
Special Assistance Plan, 21. See also Education
Spitting, 8
Sri Lanka, 2(fig.), 141, 164, 174
Sri Mariamman Temple, 5, 15(illus.)
Sri Tri Buana (king of Singapura), 42
State capitalism, 109
Statues, 5
Status, 13, 18
Statutory boards, 83–84, 135, 139, 140, 142, 143, 144, 145

Steamship, 44
Sterilization, 10, 11, 12
Stock exchange, 136–137
Straits Settlements, 2, 43–44, 45
Straits Times, 31, 73
Streets, 4, 5
Strikes, 46, 48, 63, 97, 132
Students, 22, 63, 80, 81
  abroad, 86, 169
  protests and riots, 19, 48, 63
  See also under Chinese
Subsidies, 11, 33, 35, 36, 143
Subversives. *See* Operation Cold Store
Suez Canal (1869), 49
Sumatra, 168
Supreme Court, 80
  building, 3(illus.), 5
"Swing Singapore" celebration (1988), 74,
  178
Switzerland, 157
Syah, Hussein (sultan of Johor), 43
Symphony orchestra, 24
Syonan (light of the South), 45

Taiwan, 2(fig.), 27, 135, 139, 140, 148,
  150, 151, 155, 171, 175
Talent pool, 11
Tamil (language), 7, 16
  newspaper, 26
Tamils, 37
Tan, Tony, 22, 116, 118, 126, 129
Tang dynasty (China), 24
Tanjong Pagar container terminal, 4
Tan Koon Swan, 108, 177
Tan Wah Pow, 81
Taoists, 7
Tariffs, 133, 143, 165, 174
Taxes, 54, 56, 138, 142
  corporate income, 138
  disincentives, 10, 12
  incentives, 11, 12
  payroll, 138
Taxis, 4, 35, 113
Teachers, 54
  training program, 18, 21
Technocrats, 98, 99, 105, 115, 128, 129
Technology transfer, 152, 153
Teh Cheang Wan, 94, 108
Telecommunications, 136
Telecommunications Authority, 145
Telegu (language), 7

Telegus, 37
Telephones, 6
Television, 24, 25–26, 68, 73, 143
Temasek Holdings, 144, 151
Temples, 5, 14, 15(illus.)
Teochew, 7
Teo Soh Lung, 82
Thailand, 2(fig.), 3, 141, 168, 172
  and ASEAN, 163
Thian Hock Keng Temple, 5
Third World, 95, 96, 109, 124, 149, 151
"Three is better" slogan, 11
Tiger Balm, 5
Time, 26
Tin, 44
"Today in Parliament" (television
  program), 25
Toh Chin Chye, 67, 86, 103, 105
Tolerance, 114
Tourism, 4, 5, 6, 39, 147, 149, 169, 180
"Towards Excellence in Schools," 21
Town councillors, 69, 92, 101, 102
Town councils, 71, 72, 95, 101, 122, 176
Trade. *See* Exports; Imports; Singapore, as
  trading center
Trade Development Board, 144
Trade unionists, 33, 47, 49, 59, 63, 80, 86
Trade unions, 46, 47, 53, 54, 55, 59, 63,
  97–99, 140
Trade Unions (Amendment) Act (1959),
  55
Traffic, 4, 35
Transportation, 34–35, 136
  equipment, 147
Treaty of Amity and Cooperation (1976),
  163
Trees, 39
Triad, 49
Trial by jury abolished (1970), 80
Tumasik, 42
Tunku Abdul Rahman, 57, 58, 60, 61
Tun Razak, 164
Tun Tan Siew Sin, 60
"Two is enough" slogan, 10, 11
Typhoons, 36

Ulcers, 40
Ultras. *See* United Malays National
  Organization
UMNO. *See* United Malays National
  Organization

Unemployment, 55, 59, 132, 133, 134, 135, 140
United Arab Emirates, 146
United Malays National Organization (UMNO), 60, 61, 64
United Nations, 30, 166, 167, 174
industrial survey mission, 132
United Nations Educational, Scientific, and Cultural Organization, 174
United People's Party, 59
United States, 137, 138, 140, 164, 165, 172, 173. See also under Singapore
University of Singapore, 19
Urban resettlement, 40, 65, 92. See also New towns
U.S. dollar, 138
U.S. Treasury bonds, 137

Value added, 136
Values, 8, 20, 22, 39, 40, 109, 112, 114, 132, 176, 180
Vasil, Raj, 87, 107
Veto, 78, 79, 123
Vice-president, 78, 79
Victoria Theater, 5
Vietnam, 2(fig.), 163, 166, 167, 168, 171, 172, 173
Vietnamese boat people, 174
Vietnam War, 134, 170
"Vision '99" (1984 election theme), 90
Vocational training, 20, 21, 22
Voluntary associations, 37
Voter registration, 47, 50, 51, 66, 96
Voting, compulsory, 51, 96

Wages, 97, 98, 113, 122, 133, 134, 135, 139–140, 142, 149, 152, 180
flexible, 140
and productivity, 139

Washington Naval Treaties (1922), 44
Water supply, 62, 131, 168
Wax museum, 6
Wee Kim Wee, 78, 121
Wee Toon Boon, 108
Welfare, 6, 33, 127. See also Social services
West Asia, 146
Westernization, 8, 20, 39, 40, 75, 109, 111, 114, 162, 169, 180
Western technology, 39, 112
West Germany, 147
Westminster democracy, 106
White paper (1988), 78–79
"White supremacy" myth, 45
Women, 90
and culture, 24
and education, 30, 31
education and marriage, 11, 30, 83, 122, 140
in government, 30
in military, 158
status, 29, 114
wages, 30
in work force, 11, 29, 30, 31, 140
Wong, Aline, 90
Wong Kan Seng, 126
Workers' Party (WP), 50, 51, 56, 65, 72, 73, 74, 91, 92, 94
World War I, 44
World War II, 2, 45, 161, 173
WP. See Workers' Party

Yeo Hiep Seng Ltd., 151
Yeo Ning Hong, 116

Zero population growth, 11
Zone of peace, freedom, and neutrality, 164, 170
Zoo, 1